Global Modernity and Social Contestation

**SAGE STUDIES IN
INTERNATIONAL SOCIOLOGY**

Series Editor (2010–ongoing)
Sujata Patel, Professor of Sociology at University of Hyderabad, India

Global Modernity and Social Contestation

Edited by **Breno M. Bringel** and
José Maurício Domingues

SSIS SERIES   SAGE STUDIES IN INTERNATIONAL SOCIOLOGY:63

Los Angeles | London | New Delhi
Singapore | Washington DC

Los Angeles | London | New Delhi
Singapore | Washington DC

SAGE Publications Ltd
1 Oliver's Yard
55 City Road
London EC1Y 1SP

SAGE Publications Inc.
2455 Teller Road
Thousand Oaks, California 91320

SAGE Publications India Pvt Ltd
B 1/I 1 Mohan Cooperative Industrial Area
Mathura Road
New Delhi 110 044

SAGE Publications Asia-Pacific Pte Ltd
3 Church Street
#10-04 Samsung Hub
Singapore 049483

Editor: Robert Rojek
Editorial assistant: Gemma Sheilds
Production editor: Sushant Nailwal
Copyeditor: Neena Ganjoo
Proofreader: Nand Kumar Jha
Indexer: Value Data Management Systems
Marketing manager: Michael Ainsley
Cover design: Wendy Scott
Typeset by Zaza Eunice, Hosur, Tamilnadu, India
Printed in India at Replika Press Pvt Ltd

Library of Congress Control Number:
2014939877

British Library Cataloguing in Publication data

A catalogue record for this book is available from
the British Library

ISBN 978-1-4462-9574-8
ISBN 978-1-4462-9575-5 (pbk)

Contents

About the Editors and Contributors

The Editors

Breno M. Bringel holds a PhD from the Faculty of Political Science and Sociology at the Complutense University of Madrid (Spain), where he has also taught. He was also a visiting scholar in several universities in Argentina, Brazil, Uruguay, France, Spain, Portugal, Switzerland and the UK. He teaches now at the Institute of Social and Political Studies at the Rio de Janeiro State University (IESP-UERJ), Brazil. He is a member of the Board of the International Sociological Association Research Committee on Social Classes and Social Movements (RC-47) and the Editor-in-chief of *Dados – Revista de Ciências Sociais*. Bringel is the author of several works in Portuguese, Spanish, French and English on social movements, internationalism and Latin American politics and society. His latest books are: *Movimentos sociais na era global* (edited with Maria da Glória Gohn, 2012) and *O MST e o internacionalismo contemporâneo* (2015).

José Maurício Domingues has received a PhD degree in Sociology from the London School of Economics and Political Science. He was a visiting scholar in several universities in Argentina, Britain, Chile, Colombia, Germany, Israel, Mexico and Spain. He teaches at the Institute of Social and Political Studies at the Rio de Janeiro State University (IESP-UERJ), Brazil. Domingues was a member of the board of ISA RC16 (Sociological Theory) and ISA WG02 (Historical and Comparative Sociology). He is also the author of several books on sociological theory and modernity, including: *Global Modernity, Development, and Contemporary Civilization: Towards a Renewal of Critical Theory* (2012); *Latin American and Contemporary Modernity: A Sociological Interpretation* (2008); *Modernity Reconstructed* (2006); *Social Creativity, Collective Subjectivity and Contemporary Modernity* (2000) and *Sociological Theory and Collective Subjectivity* (1995).

The Contributors

Craig Browne has received a PhD in Sociology from the University of New South Wales and teaches at the University of Sydney, Australia. He was editor of *Theory* – Newsletter of the International Sociological Association Research Committee on Sociological Theory (RC16) and was Vice President of ISA RC-35. His research interests include social change, processes of global transformation, subjectivity, intersubjectivity and sociological perspectives on democracy. He recently edited *Violence in France and Australia: Disorder in the Post-Colonial Welfare State* (2010) and has two forthcoming books: *Critical Social Theory* and *Habermas and Giddens on Modernity: A Constructive Comparison*.

Elísio Macamo is an Assistant Professor of African Studies at the University of Basel since 2009. Previously, he taught Development Sociology at the University of Bayreuth, where he was a founding member of the Bayreuth International Graduate School of African Studies. He holds a PhD and 'Habilitation' in General Sociology by the University of Bayreuth and regularly offers methodological workshops to Portuguese-speaking African doctoral students on behalf of the Council for the Development of Social Science Research in Africa (CODESRIA). He is the author of *The Taming of Fate: Approaches to Risk from a Social Action Perspective* (forthcoming) and *Negotiating Modernity: Africa's Ambivalent Experience* (2005).

Gabriela Delamata teaches at the School of Politics and Government at the National University of San Martín, Argentina. She is also a researcher of the Consejo Nacional de Investigaciones Científicas y Técnicas (CONICET). She holds a doctorate in Political Science and Sociology from the Complutense University of Madrid, and was a visiting researcher at the University of California (Berkeley), the Gino Gernami Institute in Buenos Aires and the Institute for Advanced Social Studies in Madrid. She is the author of *Los barrios desbordados: Las organizaciones de desocupados del Gran Buenos Aires* (2004) and has edited *Movilizaciones sociales: ¿nuevas ciudadanías? Reclamos, derechos, Estado en Argentina, Bolivia y Brasil* (2009) and *Ciudadanía y territorio: Las relaciones políticas de las nuevas identidades sociales* (2005).

Geoffrey Pleyers is an FNRS Research Fellow (permanent position) at the Université Catholique de Louvain, Belgium, and a researcher at the Ecole des Hautes Etudes en Sciences Sociales, Paris. He is President of the

Research Committee on Social Classes and Social Movements (RC47), International Sociological Association and the coordinator of the Research Group on Social Movements at the French Sociological Association. His latest books are *Alter-Globalization: Becoming Actors in the Global Age* (2010) and *Forum Sociaux Mondiaux et defies de l'altermondialisme* (2007). He has also edited *La consommation critique. Mouvements pour une alimentation responsable et solidaire* (2011) and *Los movimientos sociales: De lo local a lo global* (2009, with Francis Mestries and Sergio Zermeño).

G Aloysius is an independent Indian activist, researcher and writer. He worked on organizational and educational activities among the tribals and scheduled castes of Jharkhand between 1977 and 1988. After that he worked as a researcher and visiting professor at several Indian centres and universities. He is the author of books such as *Kandhamal: An Interpretative Reading of the District's Recent History of Violence* (2010), *Swami Dharmatheertha's No Freedom with Caste: The Menace of Hindu Imperialism* (2004), *Religion as Emancipatory Identity* (1998) and *Nationalism without a Nation in India* (1997, 10th reprint in 2009).

Heriberto Cairo Carou is full Professor and Dean of the Faculty of Political Science and Sociology at the Complutense University of Madrid, Spain. His research area lies in political geography with a focus on the study of the geopolitics of war and peace, political identities and territorial ideologies and borders. His recent books include: *Descolonizar Europa, descolonizar la modernidad: diálogos Europa-América Latina* (with Ramón Grosfoguel, 2010); *América Latina, una y diversa: teorías y métodos para su análisis* (with Geronimo de Sierra, 2008); *Vertientes americanas del pensamiento y el proyecto descolonial* (with Walter Mignolo, 2008); *La construcción de una región. México y la geopolítica del Plan Puebla-Panamá* (with Jaime Preciado Coronado and Alberto Rocha Valencia, 2007); *Geopolítica, guerras y resistencias* (with Jaime Pastor Verdu, 2006).

Keina Espiñeira is a Researcher at the Department of Geography at the Universitat Autònoma de Barcelona (UAB). She was a visiting scholar at the Ethnic Studies Department, University of Berkeley (California), at the Nijmegen Centre for Border Research, Radboud University (the Netherlands) and at the Department of Geography, Université Abdelmalek Essaâdi (Morocco). She works in two European Commission Seventh Framework Programme (FP7) projects: EUBORDERREGIONS – *European Regions,*

EU External Borders and the Immediate Neighbours. Analysing Regional Development Options through Policies and Practices of Cross-Border Co-operation (www.euborderregions.eu) and EUBORDERSCAPES – *Bordering, Political Landscapes and Social Arenas: Potentials and Challenges of Evolving Border Concepts in a Post-Cold War World* (www. euborderscapes.eu). Research interests include: cultural geography, border studies, postcolonial theories, documentary cinema and Mediterranean area.

Lin Chun has a doctoral degree from Cambridge University and teaches at the London School of Economics. She is the author of *The British New Left* (1993), *The Transformation of Chinese Socialism* (2006), and *China and Global Capitalism* (2013). She is also the editor of *China I, II and III* (2000) and co-editor of *Is Mao Really a Monster?* (2009). Her Chinese language books include *Reflections on China's Reform Trajectory* (2008) and (coedited) *Women: The Longest Revolution* (1997).

Luis Tapia teaches at the Programme of Development Studies at the Universidad Mayor de San Andrés (UMSA), Bolivia. Tapia is the coordinator of the Doctoral Programme in Development Studies at the UMSA since 2002 and also the coordinator of the Master in Philosophy and Political Science at the same university. He holds a PhD from Instituto Universitário de Pesquisas do Rio de Janeiro (IUPERJ) in Brazil and was a visiting professor in several universities in the US, Mexico, Argentina and Uruguay. Among his recent books feature: *La coyuntura de la autonomía relativa del Estado* (2009); *Pensando la democracia geopolíticamente* (2009); *Política salvaje* (2008); *La igualdad es cogobierno, Autodeterminación* (2007) and *La invención del núcleo común. Ciudadanía y gobierno multisocietal* (2006).

Marcelle C. Dawson began her academic career in 1998 at the Rand Afrikaans University lecturing at the Department of Sociology. She is now Senior Lecturer at the Department of Sociology, Gender and Social Work at the University of Otago (New Zealand) and Senior Research Associate at the South African Research Chair in Social Change at the University of Johannesburg (South Africa). In 2008 she completed a doctorate in Politics at the University of Oxford focusing on the mobilisation efforts of the Anti-Privatisation Forum. She is Vice-President of Research Committee 47 (Social Classes and Social Movements) of the International Sociological Association. She is a member of the South African Sociological Association (SASA) and of the Sociological Association of Aotearoa New Zealand (SAANZ). She co-edited *Popular Politics and Resistance Movements in*

South Africa (2010) and *Contesting Transformation: Popular Resistance in Twenty-First-Century South Africa* (2012).

Sarah Ben Néfissa has received a PhD in Public Law from Paris 1 (Panthéon-Sorbonne) in 1986. She is a Researcher at the Research Institute for Development, Egypt. She is a political scientist and judicial anthropologist, specialized in Egypt and the Arab world. Her research works include civil society, social movements, protests in the Arab World, political parties, elections and, more recently, Egyptian transition. She has coordinated several research works on these issues and is author of *Vote et Démocratie dans l'Égypte contemporaine* (2005, with A. Arafat) and *The Associations in Egypt* (1995, published in Arab), besides several articles on academic journals.

Sujata Patel teaches Sociology at the University of Hyderabad, India. She obtained a doctorate from the School of Social Sciences of the Jawaharlal Nehru University in 1984. During this period, she was a fellow at the Nehru Memorial Museum and Library and University Grants Commissions' Research Scientist. In January 1992, she joined the Department of Sociology at the Shreemati Nathibai Damodar Thackersey Women's University (SNDT) as a Professor. Since then she has moved to two other Universities. In October 1996, she joined the University of Pune and in June 2009, University of Hyderabad. In her capacity as the International Sociological Association's first Vice President for National Associations she edited *The ISA Handbook of Diverse Sociological Traditions* (2010), as well as co-editing three books on Bombay as a city, *Thinking Social Science in India* (2002) and *Urban Studies* (2006).

Peter Wagner is an ICREA Research Professor at the University of Barcelona (UB). Before joining the UB, he was a Professor of Sociology at the University of Warwick and at the University of Trento and Professor of Social and Political Theory at the European University Institute, Florence. Currently, he is the Principal Investigator of the European Research Council Advanced Grant project 'Trajectories of Modernity'. Wagner is author of several books on social theory and comparative-historical sociology, such as *Modernity: Understanding the Present* (2012), *Modernity as Experience and Interpretation* (2008) and *A Sociology of Modernity* (1994) as well as editor or co-editor of the volumes *African, American and European Trajectories of Modernity: Past Oppression, Future Justice?* (2015); *The Greek Polis and the Invention of Democracy* (with Johann Arnason and Kurt Raaflaub, 2013), and *Varieties of World-Making: Beyond Globalization* (with Nathalie Karagiannis, 2007).

Introduction

Breno M. Bringel and José Maurício Domingues

Background and Goals

The main objective of this book is the attempt to link the idea of global modernity to social contestation. In other words, to link a general view of contemporary social processes – which in sociology, in particular, have been theorized by the concept of modernity – with contemporary social movements, conflicts and mobilizations, which aim at social change. Although at different times some authors and debates tried to relate capitalism, labour movement or post-industrial society and the emergence of new social movements, current interpretations that try to relate modernity and the dynamics of social contestation, at a global level, seem insufficient. This book tries to fill this gap by bringing together contributions from distinguished scholars working in these fields of studies (sociological theory and modernity, as well as social movement studies and contentious politics) and in the interaction between both the tensions and possibilities of an integrated understanding of global modernity and social contestation. The chapters presented here develop a much needed effort to frame sociology as a global dialogue, rather than leaving it within predefined national and regional traditions.

Thus, we have brought together a group of scholars from different parts of the world, with many perspectives and expertise, to enact this sort of dialogue. Although the chapters address different scales, from distinct theoretical and empirical starting points, they articulate the two main topics that are present in the title of the book: global modernity and social contestation. The book is partly derived from the International Conference 'Global Modernity and Social Contestation', held in Rio de Janeiro 24–26 May 2012. Scholars from several countries and regions attended the conference and discussed many perspectives with a wide geographical reach and dealing with many different subjects. Some of them could not attend, but sent their papers for the book; some could not remain within the fold of the project, while others joined in and strengthened the overall debate and seriously contributed to the outcome presented here to the reader.

Thanks are due to many people who from the beginning have supported the project and especially the elaboration and publication of this book. We cannot mention them all, but a few people must be named. Throughout Sujata Patel was enthusiastic and extremely supportive of this book project. We wholeheartedly thank her for that and would like to acknowledge her concrete commitment to see through a global sociological dialogue in which the voices of the 'south' feature prominently. But a global dialogue always involves a problem of language and speech. Thiago Gomide Nasser was more than efficient, translating some chapters, originally written in other languages, into English. We are also grateful to João Marcelo Maia, Frederic Vandenberghe, Maria da Glória Gohn, Ingrid Sarti and Carlos Milani, who acted as discussants at the seminar, that is, at the origin of this book. The practical support of Beatriz Filgueiras was crucial and we are grateful to her. We would also like to thank our colleagues and especially our students, particularly those who are members of the Research Group on Social Theory and Latin America (NETSAL) coordinated by us at the Institute for Social and Political Studies of Rio de Janeiro State University (IESP-UERJ), whose support and inspiration have also been key for the (thus far partial) completion of this project. For financial support to organize the original seminar we could count on the Brazilian scientific agencies Capes, CNPq, Faperj and Finep, which were crucial in putting together such a challenging endeavour. Finally, we are also grateful to all International Sociological Association (ISA) Research Committees (RC) involved in this project and particularly to the new Board of RC-47 (2014-2018), committed to global sociology and to frame social movements within general sociology.

In what follows, we perform a number of tasks. Firstly, we situate the general horizon that has presided over our debates since May 2012, in theoretical and methodological terms. This involves initially a scalar methodological standpoint. Secondly, two sets of conceptual issues are tackled: the theories of modernity, in particular in what regards what may be called its third phase, and social movement theories within the current phase of modernity. We proceed then to outline the contributions to the book and trace the connections between them.

Theory and Methodology: Spatial and Temporal Axes

To some extent, the main common methodological axes that orient the chapters are spatial and temporal. They are, of course, closely related to one another. The first one can, analytically, be addressed mainly through the topic of scales, in which the local and the global levels stand out, although the national and the regional feature too. To which extent processes initiated directly at the top levels influence bottom ones and vice versa? The very definition of processes unleashed at the global level must be addressed in this connection. Some of them can be fairly abstract and depend on former processes which assume a more globally disembodied character (just take, for instance, the theme of 'human rights', conceptual frameworks or commodity forms), while others stem more explicitly from trends set in other dimensions, which, however, impact other spatial coordinates from the outside (take, for instance, the processes of capital accumulation or the strategies of social movements which can diffuse from one place to the other, as demonstrations from the Middle East have impacted Europe and the US). Nevertheless, the reverse movement must also be analysed, because although local dynamics, social practices and actors are highly localized, there is an increasing global sense of place (Massey, 2005), processes of internationalization and a much more complex relationship between the spatiality of territories and the spatiality of flows. In other words, grassroots social movements or local institutions and imaginaries are not only shaped by processes launched on a global scale, but they also shape these processes.

A useful way to rethink these tensions within the book has been by looking at the interactions between scales, dynamics and processes, avoiding teleological scale shifts and rigid separations between them (although, in analytical terms, some differentiation can be performed) and trying to reveal the social construction of scales. This was carried out in the different chapters sometimes at a more theoretically oriented level, sometimes in more concrete terms. However, space also matters for other reasons: (a) as a locus of experiences and a field of dispute and social conflicts; (b) as a public scene for collective actions and performances; (c) as a place where material and symbolic alternatives and responses to the modern imaginary and institutions are generated, constantly reframing identities, senses of belonging and both the understanding of modernity and the views of social change itself; (d) as a territorial expression of frontiers, borders and bordering processes that affect and are affected by modernity and social conflicts; (e) as socio-spatial practices (lived spaces) and representations of spaces (conceived spaces); and (f) due to the mediation of flows and networks that allows us to glimpse how territories are transformed and shaped by different actors and forces.

Concretely, space is connected to a temporal horizon, which can, nevertheless, also be isolated analytically (Domingues, 1995; Elden, 2001). This horizon mobilizes the past towards the future, either ascertaining social change or striving to keep things as they are. We can think of long- and short-term processes which have been shaping the global landscape and giving specific contours to global modernity. Thus, the contributors in this book discuss how social movements and other collective subjectivities construct their memories in the short, medium and long terms, looking for historical and cognitive references (that are located, for instance, in colonialism, revolutions and transitions to democracy) for present and future struggles. While Koselleck ([1979] 2004) stressed the spatial dimension of the present as a precipitate of experiences and the temporal dimension of the future as a horizon of expectations, we can think also of space–time as a differentiated articulation of processes in specific geographical coordinates, which bind the past, the present and the future. How does global modernity and social contestation feature in this regard? How does each unfold in space and time? How is scale connected to these entangled but more or less densely interconnected space–time configurations? This is especially important insofar as we are dealing with a global contemporary predicament, a general process, which, however, does not exist abstractly, beyond experiences and specific histories, but only through these, in which social contestation is a key element, in both general and specific terms. In this sense, how expressions of social contestation are projecting, in different places, states and regions, their horizon of expectations facing the current global crisis of capitalism? What are the changing meanings acquired not only by notions such as capitalism, democracy, justice, emancipation and revolution, but also those of global modernity and social movements or social contestation?

The contributions of the book propose different perspectives to these questions, that brings us to a third dimension, the general theoretical, that must answer to this set of problems in two respects: in normative–evaluative and in cognitive terms. Unavoidably, we face here the problem of the relation between the universal and the particular. In a sense, we meet here, in a theoretical and epistemological dimension, the problems already touched upon above. Specific scales and space–time coordinates call for distinct strategies of understanding as much as for normative–evaluative views. Whether we start from specific processes or from general issues matters, of course, for the result of an investigation, but we do not necessarily have to oppose such different ways of tackling modernity and contestation. They may be complementary, although perhaps a tension between results stemming from distinct strategies is inevitable. Values must be seen in the same problematic articulation: Are there values that characterize modernity overall and appear in most if not all processes of social contestation or should we look more directly and exclusively to particular valences that emerge in singular processes of social conflict and social change? How to define reflexively and dialectically the tenuous border between what is inside and outside (but somehow related) modernity? In fact, whether we start from a general, bird's eye-like view or from more specific, contextual analysis, inevitably affects the way each researcher deals with such issues. All along the authors and chapters gathered here have precisely looked for narrative forms and concepts capable of mediating between these two possible starting points, without giving up their own strategy.

A productive way to frame such issues and strategies may be offered by the idea of translation: specific contexts relate in a less than straightforward way to other contexts. They may share more or less intensively elements that circulate globally. In any case, even when such elements are clearly 'imported', a process of translation is unleashed which is necessary for their productivity in specific scales or space–time coordinates, either cognitively or normatively – as well as expressively. Thus, the translation has a normative, epistemic and political potential, which may allow for the intelligibility between social struggles and different scales and framings of contestation. We must, however, be aware of how this process occurs, what is translated and what remains outside the translation and who are the actors involved, particularly the translator (Cairo and Bringel, 2010). In this regard, we would like to address some main issues related to the role of the general theory of modernity and the uses of social movement studies.

In the first case, we depart from a view of global modernity as undergoing an advanced phase, which we define as its third one, characterized by increasing heterogeneity and flexibility. Many mutations have impacted modernity, however, with changes spanning all dimensions of social life. In particular, the state and social life have moved in the last decades, in most cases, though not all – notably in Latin America – further apart. This has to do with changes in the patterns of capital accumulation as well as in the roles of the state, forms of construction of subjectivity, individual and collective, and social movements, as well as with a radicalization of modern institutions and the intensification of long-term globalization. Many authors, especially within sociology, have tried to theorize these processes. These include Jürgen Habermas, Anthony Giddens, Shmuel Eisenstadt, Immanuel Wallerstein, Manuel Castells, David Harvey, Göran Therborn, Peter Wagner and José Maurício Domingues, as well as those connected to post/de-colonialism, represented, among others, by Partha Chatterjee and Dipesh Chakrabarty, Aníbal Quijano and Walter Mignolo (see Therborn, 2009; Domingues, 2012; Kerner, 2012; Wagner, 2012).

While we do not intend to provide a full revision of this literature here, a number of basic issues need to be raised. More contingent or more deterministic (often evolutionary) views of social development underpin the theories of modernity. Giddens, Eisenstadt, Wagner and Domingues feature in the first case, to some extent on Weber's footsteps, stressing a discontinuist view of history and/or the episodic development of modernity. Habermas and Wallerstein stand out in the second, in some measure, paying tribute to the Marxist and the Durkheimian–Parsonian heritage, the former, in fact, espousing a strong evolutionary standpoint. The view that modernity is originally a European–Western phenomenon is by and large shared by most of these authors, although to some extent Wallerstein, with world-systems theory, and especially some post/de-colonial authors (in an axiological ambiguous way) have tried to argue for the idea that modernity has been global from its very inception onwards (an even that it was emerging elsewhere, upon which colonial domination and, thus, the frustration of such autonomous modern development was superimposed). At this stage of social theory, despite some more traditional Marxist approaches and a renewed idealistic perspective based on an overvaluation of culture in a number of theoretical strands, most authors in social theory and research have adopted a multidimensional bias, which has been also fundamental for most theories of modernity. Finally, we need to mention here that whether modernity still has an emancipatory potential is an open question, to some at least. While a few, especially post-modernist and post/de-colonial authors, such as Santos (1995, for instance), would deny that, and most theoreticians bring out the institutions connected to domination and exploitation (through the state, capitalism, governmentality, racism, patriarchy, etc.), most still also point, in a way or another, to the remaining emancipatory potential contained in the modern imaginary or by the social forces unleashed modernity.

At a global level, the heterogeneity of modernity – or modernities, as some might prefer – has also proceeded apace, with movements from above and from below implying what we have formerly called space–time scales and two-way translations, if we want to properly grasp the multifarious dynamics of global modernity. In the first case, we have our attention directed to how modernity is concretely weaved by those moves, which include social movements, the state, families, business firms and virtually all collectivities we can think of; in the second, methodologically, it is to the interplay between general concepts and specific realities that we point. This summons, of course, the specific civilizational elements and heritages with which modernity has been confronted in its expansion; hence, the 'hybrid' derivations of such encounters as well as how specifically collective subjectivities 'experience' and 'interpret' the unfolding of such processes and respond to them. The concept of a third phase of modernity has also a periodization at its core. First, it includes a limited liberal phase in the West, more limitedly in Latin America, as well as the beginning of the Western colonial expansion beyond the Americas; second, a state-organized phase, which implies decolonization in the former colonial world and the achievement of autonomy in the periphery and now the semi-periphery as well as, more generally, the effort by the state to increase order and incorporate thus far excluded masses. The third phase, due to its complexity, has made more often recourse to network as a principle of organization in several spheres of social life, while it has become, in each country and globally, increasingly heterogeneous. This directly affects social movements too (Wagner, 1994; Domingues, 2012).

Moreover, a working hypothesis suggested here is that the core emancipatory issues of the modern imaginary – especially 'equal freedom' and new forms of solidarity (see Domingues, 2006) – remain crucial for the development of social life, social movements and the effort to grasp them, although spaces of exteriority are always stressed by social actors (see Bringel, 2011). In this sense, social movements appear as central collective subjectivities that draw upon as well as contest modern imaginaries, and the norms and values embedded in societies, including oftentimes a new relationship of human social formations with nature. In other words, social movements are immanent expressions of society shaped by the internal and external dimensions. While the former includes social practices, organization, internal articulations, discussions and deliberations, the latter refers to outsourcing to society conflicts and grievances through mobilizations and a diverse repertoire of collective action, the relationship with other social and political agents, political culture and the structure of political opportunities. Both dimensions are fed by and construct collective identities and subjectivities and the framing perspective of social movements. Of course, although such elements with a Western origin still have a key global impact on emancipatory movements, they are often entwined with elements stemming from other civilizational sources.

We may suggest that not only do we live a third phase of modernity, but also through a third stage of modern social movements, globally understood (see Bringel and Domingues, 2012). The first stage coincides with the interpretations of 'classical' sociology and, in particular, with the path initiated by Marx. In that first moment, which has its maximum expression in the mid-nineteenth century, interpretations about social movements were marked by the importance attributed to labour conflicts. Labour movements were the privileged actors in emerging national societies, and classic internationalism was the main form of connection and diffusion of social struggles, repertoires and ideologies in the global scenario. Although we can already speak of a global pattern of resistance and offensives, there is during this first phase of global social contestation a profoundly Eurocentric bias in both structural considerations about capitalism, industrialization, urbanization and those more action-oriented reflections that localize the labour movement as a privileged collective subject, somewhat problematic in the periphery of the world in the nineteenth century and the first half of the twentieth century. Perhaps the most problematic issue here is what is meant by 'global' and how certain actions and actors become universal, starting from a particularistic logic.

University expertise, the expansion of social sciences and a wide range of social struggles developed from the mid-twentieth-century onwards led to an academic institutionalization of social movements as a subject of study, especially in the United States and Europe in the 1960s (see Tarrow, 2012). In addition to the broader concerns of the previous debate, a new one emerged – which marks the second phase of modern social movements – over issues related to meso-sociological and internal dimensions of social movements, the characteristics of the 'new' social actors of the conflict, the meanings of their actions and so on. In fact, since the 1960s several theories (such as resource mobilization theory, political process theory and new social movements theory) and perspectives (frame analysis, network analysis, pragmatist, constructive and, also here, post/de-colonial perspectives) have been developed, mainly in the Western countries, to explain questions such as why people participate in social movements, how to explain moments of a higher level of mobilization in some instances than in others, how social movements are organized and how they are related to public policies and other social and political actors. This discussion has helped to consolidate a field of study dedicated to collective action and social movements by addressing – albeit sometimes dichotomously and in a problematic manner – core tensions between disciplines, individual and collective, micro and macro, object and subject, structure and action (Melucci, 1989; Klandermans and Roggeband, 2010).

The fact is that global transformations of the last two decades brought out new questions and significant silences of these theories, which have been criticized. The construction of more complex and relational analyses articulating different levels of study, dimensions of collective action and elements of contemporary modernity appears as a major challenge in order to capture new tensions between local and global, territories and networks, identities and frames as well as to approach old tensions in a renewed way (Bringel, 2014). The proper sense of what activism is seems to be changing now.

We, thus, enter the third stage of modern social movements in a world of greater complexity, marked by new patterns of the global market and financial and cognitive capitalism, the use of new information and communication technologies, contradictory social practices and a democratic hegemony that seem so paradoxical, with processes of democratization and de-democratization at the centre and in the (semi)peripheries (Tilly, 2007). There is still a lack of systematic theorizing about this third phase of social movements in the world, which cannot only be understood as a reactive face of globalization, although the anti-globalization movement and other global actors and transnational networks and struggles, as well as more locally and nationally oriented movements, have been and continue to be pivotal to the renewal of 'global lens' and 'global frames' (McDonald, 2006). They all tackle a plurality of issues, stem from and contribute to the increasing complexity of the contemporary world.

The contentious politics research programme, initially led by Charles Tilly (see McAdam et al., 2001), is one of the main references of the current third phase of social movement debate and has greatly contributed to progress on two issues of interest in this book: firstly, criticizing the compartmentalization of social movement studies that had inhibited the association between social movements and other fields of study (nationalism, revolution and so on) and forms of political struggle and social contestation that are related to, but remain different from, movements; secondly, decentring somehow the excessively *Occidentocentric* research agenda on collective action by including case studies from different regions and countries of the world.

However, this important research agenda has some limitations (some of them highlighted by its own members – see Aminzade et al., 2001), which, conversely, appear as original and distinctive elements of this book. Firstly, the extension of the comparison to non-Western areas has not always meant paying attention to the experiences and social practices of social actors of non-Western countries. Thus, several chapters of the book address non-Western realities seeking to focus on collective subjectivities and the local intelligibility of contestation. Secondly, despite the inclusion of non-Western realities, the contentious politics research agenda barely dialogues with the sociological production in these countries. Similarly, most general discussions on social theory (such as global modernity ones) have not been covered by this programme, since its main concern has been to seek meso-sociological explanations to the episodic, public and collective interaction among makers of claims and their objects, emphasizing the mechanisms, processes and episodes involved therein. In another pole, authors such as Alain Touraine, who had a major contribution during the 1960s and 1970s linking social movements with more comprehensive interpretations of society (Touraine, 1965, 1971), have not provided substantial insights about his relationship in the latest years. Finally, McAdam, Tarrow, Tilly and their colleagues use the term 'contentious politics' because they are worried about the interaction between governments and claimants. Our larger focus on society, rather than on political processes per se (although we do not separate the social and the political as usual in social movement studies), has led us to discuss and explore the notion of social contestation instead of social movement as such so as to include those practices and contemporary forms of social contestation that do not fit into the classical 'movement form'.

Several issues presented in the book can, more concretely, help to embody such discussions. The changing relation between state and social movements, as well as their specific roles in translating issues, which have appeared in different contexts, has been very important. Intellectuals, brokers and experts have played similar roles, often connected to the state, institutions and/or social movements. On the other hand, as recent works have highlighted, if 'modern social movements' have been always analyzed in relation to states, a key political reference of modernity, this has usually led to methodological nationalism and a teleological view of protests, as well as to the invisibility of (trans)local logics, forms and configurations of contestation, the reach of which we submit has to be discerned according to more empirical studies, in any case. The chapters of the book address, one way or another, these tensions, trying and tackling both global protests and localized contestation affected by global processes. The specific dynamics of capitalism have featured in this as well. And, surely, what role and which characteristics a critical theory of contemporary modernity can assume is also a central issue that permeates the debate about global modernity and social contestation. In the same way, the diversity and complexity of contemporary collective action, mediated by new information and communication technologies and cultural meanings, ask for renewed approaches and for sociological imagination to reconnect, once again, the micro/macro, the individual/collective and the local/global dimensions. In sum, the book as a whole presents a series of inquiries, challenges and paths to rethink in a creative worldwide oriented way the debate on global modernity and social contestation.

The connecting thread of the chapters across the book will be offered, therefore, by the connection of social changes and the actualization of the modern imaginary, on the one hand, and the emergence and development of social contestation, at present, in their connection with other elements, imaginary and institutional, of social life, on the other (non-Western values, cognitive frames and conceptions, state functioning, as a form of domination and a site of citizenship and rights, economic processes, with the global polarized and flexible pattern of accumulation of capital, etc.).

The Chapters: Linking Global Modernity and Social Contestation

Although there is some overlapping, due to such common methodological and theoretical threads, between chapters and sections, the first part of this book is mainly concerned with theoretical issues, starting from the more general level, that is, modernity and related debates and arriving at discussions of social contestation, while the second part will deal with such questions by taking the opposite direction, beginning with social contestation and from there moving towards more general theoretical issues of contemporary global civilization. More empirically oriented analyses, in the third part of the book, will more concretely aim at connecting both threads as a meeting point to work issues suggested in more general contemporary discussions, as well as pointing to others which were not encompassed by the frameworks suggested. In this regard, although we have aimed at a very broad reach in geographical–cultural terms, the issue is not so much to cover all countries and regions in the world, but rather to use such a diversity to raise and tackle issues of more general significance, through both those two clusters of conceptual discussions, methodological distinctions and empirically oriented issues.

The first part of the book, titled 'Rethinking Modernity through Social Contestation' has five chapters. In the first one, Peter Wagner examines the repositioning of critique of modernity in contemporary times. The chapter argues that a new understanding of critique is connected to a rethinking of modernity that has been underway since the 1970s and related to the social transformations of the recent past. On the one hand, Wagner establishes some conceptual connections between modernity, critique and world. On the other hand, he suggests that this connection can take highly different forms and meanings in different historical constellations. Four episodes in the history of modernity are analysed by confronting them with the consensus view of around 1970 that is gradually being dismantled. Thereby, this chapter contributes to understand how contemporary modernity differs fundamentally from the preceding organized modernity and is characterized by operating globally on comprehensive and formally equal terms, and by a commitment to equal individual freedom and to collective self-determination. At the same time, it opens new research possibilities on how protests and social movements of the past two decades have started to address these issues.

Also, concerned with the historical and conceptual dimension of modernity, the second chapter takes, however, a different direction. Its author, Sujata Patel, argues that if one of the sociologist's main tasks today is to engage with and reformulate the substantive theories of modernity, then it becomes equally important to confront and contest the universalizing 'episteme' that has organized these theories since the late nineteenth and early twentieth centuries and which relate to the global unequal division of knowledge production in that period. Patel dialogues, thus, with those works seeking to overcome Eurocentrism in social theory, inquiring into their possibilities and limitations and examining the contemporary interventions from scholars in the South as a way to move forward in the reformulations of this critique. Her contribution enables us not only to criticize the epistemic hierarchy that continues to structure disciplines and knowledge systems today, but also suggests possibilities to a new global social science dialogue sensitive to the transformations of the world and capable of generating explanations that are relevant for different contexts.

The third chapter of the book, also framed within a global transition in social sciences and social processes, discusses the contradictions and the violence of market transition in China's minority regions. The argument of Lin Chun is threefold: growing ethnic tensions and conflicts are symptomatic and part of a general crisis of Chinese socialism created by national submission to capitalist globalization; developmentalist accumulation threatens to destroy not only diverse cultural heritages and ethnic peace but also the founding promises of the People's Republic of China on people's power and welfare across ethno-religious cleavages; and that modernization must be decoupled from capitalism and pursued with self-determination. Such a decoupling, political as much as conceptual, is where movements of social contestation for equality and justice can begin to integrate in a transformative politics for a viable alternative.

Moving from minority regions to minority social groups and keeping alive the criticism of incomplete realization of the promises of modernity, stressing its egalitarian principles and contextual analyses, G Aloysius challenges interpretations that frame modernity either in negative terms or as plural, alternative and unique formations. As against these, following a thin but persistent positive reading of the phenomenon, he proposes a singular and normative formulation. Arguing from different vantage points, Aloysius suggests that the core of modernity is more usefully read as the social-egalitarian principle or comprehensive process of democratization, becoming both normative and hegemonic. Secondly, as normative egalitarianism is essentially about power reconfiguration, the resultant multi-faceted contestation within society is read as the source of distortion as well as distorted readings of modernity. Finally, following recent developments in social sciences, he further argues that as culture itself is constituted in dynamic contestation, modernity as formulated here could be read as a process internal to all cultures. In this sense, modernity as normative egalitarianism could well be the axis along which the major contemporary, global contestations and mobilizations could be plotted and grasped.

Finally, José Maurício Domingues closes the first part of the book, addressing critical theory as a strand of questioning of modernity that supports not only its values, against present institutions, but also endeavours to find in it, as well as in the agents that move within it, the potential, the elements and possible subjects of the emancipation promised by modernity. From this understanding, Domingues's chapter sketches new directions for critical theory today and its relations in particular with sociology, with concrete reference to the contemporary world. For the author, it is not a matter of restricting critical theory to the tradition of the so-called Frankfurt School and its offspring, nor of circumscribing it to what has been named 'Western Marxism'. Alternatively, he proposes to frame critical theory in a more 'ecumenical' way, supposing that other authors and currents are included in it more broadly, sharing, however, some common presuppositions. In this sense, the main contribution of this chapter is the attempt to generate some paths that allow us to walk in the direction of a renewal of this theoretical field.

As already mentioned, if the first part of the book deals mainly with theoretical issues, looking at social movements and contestations from more comprehensive discussions, the second part, entitled 'Rethinking Social Contestation through Modernity', makes the reverse operation. In this case, social movement scholars and social theorists from Belgium, Brazil, Mozambique, Egypt and Bolivia examine, combining theoretical reflections and empirical work, some dynamics, challenges and dilemmas of social contestation and movements, the local/global dialectics and its relationship with contemporary modernity.

Geoffrey Pleyers opens the second part of the book, addressing a core question for our argument: Is there a new generation of social movements that correspond to a new phase of modernity? He explores this question in two directions. First, analyzing the social agency and the social change in the global age, Pleyers defines social movement as an heuristic tool and the global age as a social configuration in which life and society are deeply shaped by an increasing reality and consciousness of the interdependence at the scale of humanity and the finitude of the planet. Second, drawing on an agency-centered approach, he examines different social actors and progressive movements towards the global age: indigenous people and small farmers, critical consumption and convivial movements, climate justice non-governmental organizations (NGOs) and global environmentalists. From these cases, Pleyers addresses two central questions of the book: Who are the social actors who challenge the normative orientation at the core of modernization and promote alternative values and practices that may contribute to the rise of a global age or may embody glimpses of a global age society? Can we grasp some dimensions of life and society by studying current social movements?

In a complementary chapter, Breno Bringel aims to differentiate and analyse the main patterns of the contentious collective action of social actors who act globally in the current phase of modernity. The importance of this analysis is twofold: on one hand, it allows us to distinguish, analytically and politically, the diversity of ways of acting, its geographic scope, the variety of actors and their projects; on the other hand, it opens up possibilities for understanding their conceptions of social change and critical views on modernity. The chapter suggests that, from the fall of the Berlin Wall to the present, there is a coexistence of five main patterns of contentious global collective action: the persistence of a more 'classical' pattern of internationalism; the internationalization of territorialized social movements; the transnational advocacy networks; the anti-globalization movement; and, finally, a more recent path which Bringel defines as the 'geopolitics of global outrage'. All these paths are analysed and differences and similarities highlighted.

If Bringel's chapter asks how global are global movements, the next one, written by Elísio Macamo, poses another key question, namely the local intelligibility of global modernity and contestation. The chapter addresses the tension underlying the use of concepts and theoretical frameworks developed in a given setting to a different context. This should not be read as a claim of incommensurability. Rather, it should be read as a word of caution on the scope and reference of concepts. To illustrate this, Macamo discusses the notion of 'social movement' and critically examines its study as a research programme. Doubts are raised concerning the usefulness of this notion to the study of protest in the African context and a discussion on morality is used to offer points of anchorage for the grounding of the study of protest in society and its constitutive processes. The main contribution behind this chapter, illustrated with an empirical case from Mozambique, is the concern to find within global modernity a vocabulary that is sensitive to local settings.

Travelling from Sub-Saharan Africa to North Africa, the next chapter analyses the popular uprisings in several Arab countries across 2011. Sarah Ben Néfissa focuses, particularly, on the upheavals in Tunisia and Egypt, placing them in a broader context, both regional (within the so-called 'Arab Spring') and global (in what Bringel calls in his chapter the 'geopolitics of global outrage'). The chapter tries to answer such questions as: Why did the popular uprisings in the region caught off guard part of the academic community? What were the impacts of the process of demonopolization undergone in the field of media on the protests and uprisings in Egypt and Tunisia? How did the externalization of protests partially modify the action and also the language of social contestation?

How can the hypothesis of the hybridization of political expression in the world enrich the current debate on the 'nature' or the 'qualification' of the Arab uprisings? Can the 'Arab Spring' be fitted into the framework of global modernity?

The diversity of experiences, the complexity of social configuration and the ambivalent meanings of the diffusion of modernity, theory and protests analyzed in theses chapters require a more substantive discussion on cultural diversity itself and its relationship with modernity and social contestation. This is precisely the aim of the last chapter of the second part of the book. In this sense, Luis Tapia defines modernity as a time and a way of transformation of the quality of social relationships, of the structures that organize social life that has being developing for several centuries and spread at world level. Drawing from the Andean region reality, he distinguishes a diversity of forms of cultural movements, sketches a distinction of types and phases of political and social conflicts and contestation in modernity and, finally, characterizes the complexity underlying the protest movements in the Latin American periphery. An important contribution from Tapia's analyzes is the possibility and implications for the main aim of this book of his distinction between social movements and societal movements.

Finally, we enter the third and last part of the book, Borders of Modernity and Frontiers of Exclusion: Rights, Citizenship and Contestation in Comparative Perspective, which merges modernity and social contestation in a more incisive and empirical way. Craig Browne initiates this discussion trying to clarify how structural changes are generating experiences of social subordination and marginality. He revises Habermas's conception of system integration and social integration in order to explain the emergence of new forms of injustice and social conflict. These ensue, he argues, from the fracturing of the capitalist welfare state's channels of integration and the creation of a significant category of individuals occupying 'half-positions'. Browne's contribution suggests that half-positions exemplify the misalignments and contradictions that have developed between the state and the market under the conditions of globalization. Yet, half-positions are experienced by the agents occupying them as a type of exclusionary integration, because race and ethnicity are regularly salient to half-positions. On the other hand, he also argues that tendencies towards social disintegration condition the ways in which half-positions are mobilized in acts of resistance, and that these conflicts often manifest themselves at a level below that of the discursive format of the public sphere. Specifically, these discontents reflect the uncertainty that has developed amongst those in half-positions concerning whether their legitimate expectations to equal treatment and respect will be met. In order to demonstrate these claims, the 2005 French riots are analysed as an example of the conflicts emanating from half-positions.

From the frontiers of integration to the borders of modernity, the next chapter, co-authored by Heriberto Cairo and Keina Espiñeira, explores the importance of borders both as a modern dispositive and as a contentious issue that led to strong social contestation during the latest decades. Particularly, the authors aimed at providing a de-colonial reading of the cleavages separating intra-European borders and colonial borders. They explore, after analyzing the delimitation and demarcation of Spanish boundaries with Portugal, France and Morocco, two different types of border inception: one between European or 'civilized' neighbours and another with 'uncivilized' people. Two legal models function, to some extent, as abyssal lines that differentiate and select who is on each side, or who is inside and who is outside. Dealing with the colonial difference, which underlies the construction of modern Europe, the chapter focuses on the colonial side of the Spanish (European Union) outer perimeter and the ordering/governance of human mobility. By looking at the contestations of modern state borders, and particularly of colonial borders, it comes up with new political devices and new imaginaries about spaces and the sense of community within and between them.

Proceeding with the discussion on legal frontiers and multiscalar dynamics, Gabriela Delamata proposes in the next chapter that Argentina represents a case of exceptional dynamism of the language of human rights. This was incorporated by the human rights movement so as to back local claims during the 1970s–1980s dictatorship. From that founding experience to contemporary social movements, human rights international law has been supplying collective struggles with an instituting dimension. The chapter discusses the local interplay of that global modernity core figure, underlying its historical productivity in the field of social struggles. In order to develop this argument, Delamata presents a summary reconstruction of rights mobilizations from the transition to democracy to the process of constitutional reform, which took place in 1994. She then traces some main features of contemporary 'post-constitutional' rights struggles and illustrates their development with some particular cases. At this point, the chapter offers an alternative perspective to current sociological trends that emphasize the autonomy of social movements from the institutional ground as a distinctive dimension of the present experiences.

At last, a key concept that relates modernity to social movements is critically discussed: citizenship. In this last chapter, Marcelle C. Dawson explores the interconnections between social contestation, citizenship and modernity. Drawing on empirical research in South Africa as well as on insights into popular mobilization elsewhere in the African continent, she argues that citizenship in the contemporary South African context is flimsy, owing largely to the liberal, capitalist underpinnings of its relatively young democracy. The discussion highlights, from a specific case, a more general tendency of contemporary social movements: the need for citizenship education for an anti-capitalist society as a progressive step towards the attainment of social equality. At the same time, it illustrates how making demands on the state without challenging its legitimacy hampers the potential of social contestation to fundamentally change the 'rules' of citizenship.

We hope this book will provide researchers in the two theoretical fields connected here – global modernity and social contestation – to advance in an agenda that is becoming everyday more urgent and far-reaching. Much has remained the same since the beginnings of modernity, but lots of novelty has been thrown up by more recent developments, characterizing a more plural and complex phase in its worldwide development. Social movements have changed their ways of action and expression, but emancipation lingers as a project and task yet to be accomplished, whatever strides we have made thus far, among victories and defeats. A more subtle and full understanding of contemporary processes can surely help us in furthering it in the context of our increasingly concrete global humanity.

References

Aminzade, R., Goldstone J.A., McAdam, D., Perry, E.J., Sewell, W.H. Jr., Tarrow, S. and Tilly, C. (2001). *Silence and Voice in the Study of Contentious Politics*. Cambridge: Cambridge University Press.

Bringel, B. and Domingues, J.M. (2012). Teoria crítica e contestações sociais. In B. Bringel and M.G. Gohn (Eds.), *Movimentos sociais na era global*. Rio de Janeiro: Vozes.

Bringel, B. (2011). El estudio de los movimientos sociales en América Latina: Reflexiones sobre el debate postcolonial y las nuevas geografías del activismo transnacional. In Y. Acosta et al. (Eds.), *Pensamiento crítico y sujetos colectivos en América Latina: perspectivas interdisciplinarias*. Montevideo: Ediciones Trilce.

Bringel, B. (2014). MST's Agenda of Emancipation: Interfaces of National Politics and Global Contestation. In J.N. Pieterse and A. Cardoso (Eds.). *Brazil Emerging: Inequality and Emancipation*. New York and London: Routledge.

Cairo, H. and Bringel, B. (2010). Articulaciones del Sur global: afinidad cultural, internacionalismo solidario e Iberoamérica en la globalización contra-hegemónica. *Geopolitica(s)*, *1*(1), 41–63.

Domingues, J.M. (1995). The Space-Time Dimension of Social Systems. *Time & Society*, *4*(2), 233–250.

Domingues, J.M. (2006). *Modernity Reconstructed*. Cardiff: University of Wales Press.

Domingues, J.M. (2012). *Global Modernity, Development, and Contemporary Civilization: Towards a Renewal of Critical Theory*. New York and London: Routledge.

Elden, S. (2001). *Mapping the Present: Heidegger, Foucault and the Project of a Spatial History*. London: Continuum.

Kerner, I. (2012). *Postkoloniale Theorien. Zur Einführung*. Hamburg: Junios.

Klandermans, B. and Roggeband, C. (Eds.). (2010). *Handbook of Social Movements across Disciplines*. New York: Springer.

Koselleck, R. ([1979] 2004). 'Space of Experience' and 'Horizon of Expectation': Two Historical Categories. In *Futures Past: On the Semantics of Historical Time*. New York: Columbia University Press.

Massey, D. (2005). *For Space*. London: Sage Publications.

McAdam, D., Tarrow, S. and and Tilly, C. (2001). *Dynamics of Contention*. Cambridge: Cambridge University Press.

McDonald, K. (2006). *Global Movements: Action and Culture*. Oxford: Blackwell.

Melucci, A. (1989). *Nomads of the Present: Social Movements and Individual Needs in Contemporary Society*. Philadelphia, PA: Temple University Press.

Santos, B.S. (1995). *Toward a New Common Sense: Law, Science, and Politics in the Paradigmatic Transition*. New York and London: Routledge.

Tarrow, S. (2012). *Stranges at the Gates: Movements and States in Contentious Politics*. Cambridge: Cambridge University Press.

Therborn, G. (2009). *From Marxism to post-Marxism*. New York and London: Verso.

Tilly, C. (2007). *Democracy*. Cambridge: Cambridge University Press.

Touraine, A. (1965). *Sociologie de l'action*. Paris: Seuil.

Touraine, A. (1971). *The Post-Industrial Society. Tomorrow's Social History: Classes, Conflicts and Culture in the Programmed Society*. New York: Random House.

Wagner, P. (1994). *A Sociology of Modernity: Liberty and Discipline*. New York and London: Routledge.

Wagner, P. (2012). *Modernity: Understanding the Present*. Cambridge: Polity.

Part I

Rethinking Modernity through Social Contestation

1

Modernity and Critique: Elements of a World Sociology[1]

Peter Wagner

Introduction

After the parallel demise of modernization theory and its critical opponent, the neo-Marxist theory of late capitalism, which together dominated the sociological analysis of contemporary societies up to the 1970s, no new convincing approach to understanding current socio-political configurations has emerged. Neither neo-modernization theory nor the 'multiple modernities' approach, which stand in loose relation to modernization theory and its critics, respectively, have the same coherence and comprehensiveness of their predecessors, and, indeed, they suffer from considerable weaknesses. I have discussed the changing conceptual constellations in the analysis of modernity elsewhere (most recently, Wagner, 2012: Chapters 1 and 2) and will not return to this matter in any detail here.

For current purposes, I want to suggest that one of the fatal problems of the sociology of modernity up to the 1970s was its peculiar division of normative labour. In neo-Hegelian fashion, considering the real as rational, modernization theory assumed that 'modern societies' were superior to other societies and that modernization, indeed, was a process leading to normative progress. Critique could only ever be the critique of incomplete, delayed or distorted modernization, never of modernization as such. In contrast, the neo-Marxist analysis of late capitalism – as objectivist as its opponent – claimed critical insight as its specificity, the exclusive capacity namely of unveiling forms of domination and exploitation hidden behind the facade of modernity, unrecognizable for both ordinary people and mainstream scholarship.

If we are currently living in a new constellation of modernity, a theme taken up by the editors in their introduction to this volume, one of its features is certainly the repositioning of critique. Rather than either making reality immune from critique or monopolizing critique for the critical analyst, the emphasis is now placed on the critical capacity of human beings themselves, aiming to identify the appropriate action as well as the adequacy, or not, of institutional arrangements in the light of a plurality of registers of justification (Boltanski and Thévenot, 1991; Boltanski, 2009). In historical perspective, social change is no longer seen as steered by an actorless and predetermined dynamics of progress, either smooth or conflictive, but crucially as driven by the critical engagement of actors with their situations and with the institutional arrangements that they inhabit, emphasizing the contingency of outcomes (Wagner, 1994: Chapter 4; 2008: Chapter 13; 2012: Chapter 4; Boltanski and Chiapello, 1999).

World-Making or Worldlessness: The Stakes of Global Modernity

This repositioning of critique is certainly related to the social transformations of the recent past, an issue that I shall try to address towards the end of this chapter, as a point of arrival. To get to this point, however, I want to first suggest that the new understanding of critique is also connected – maybe somewhat obliquely – to a rethinking of modernity that has been underway since the 1970s. Until that moment, modernity was analysed as an institutional arrangement, characterized in different ways but always including bureaucratic politico-administrative institutions, a capitalist market economy and other institutions that were seen either as having functional specificity or as being hierarchically determined by the most basic institutions. More recently, however, the emphasis has been placed on the ways in which human beings conceive of their living together, on the institution of society through imaginary significations (Castoriadis, 1987 [1975]). The specificity of the imaginary signification of modernity, in Castoriadis's language, was the centrality of the human commitment to autonomy (Castoriadis, 1990).

In its most straightforward sense, the commitment to autonomy means that human beings do not rely on external resources to determine their ways of life, but (have to) find themselves the solutions to the problems they are facing. The absence of external resources entails that every solution that has been arrived at in a given moment – the instituted moment, in Castoriadis's terminology – can be contested, and a process of re-instituting can set in. It is in this sense, in general, that modernity is closely related to contestation and critique. If there is no external measure, no institutionalization of modernity is ever entirely stable, in contrast to the view held by modernization theory. The commitment to autonomy associated with the power of political imagination, furthermore, entails that the target and direction of critique are not determined either, in contrast to Marxist thinking.

For Castoriadis, human beings collectively institute 'world' by creating significations. Any such instituted world is always 'social' because it is a creation of society, of 'instituting society'. And societies create 'world' in the sense that 'it can and must enclose everything [...]. The institution of the common world is necessarily the institution of that which is and is not' (Castoriadis, 1987 [1975]: 370–1; see Karagiannis and Wagner, 2012a). Castoriadis's use of the term 'world' is similar to that of Hannah Arendt (1958), who explicitly added a distinction between 'world' and 'earth'. Earth is the planet on which we live, the ground of our existence; world, in turn, is the social space that human beings create between each other. There is only one earth, but the political imagination of human beings can institute different worlds – worlds that can coexist with each other, and worlds that can be the imaginary point of reference for action (Karagiannis and Wagner, 2007, 2012b).

Significantly, Arendt's reflections on 'world' were driven by her concern about the loss of the human capacity for world-making. The modern commitment to autonomy certainly involves mastery: to give oneself one's own law (*auto-nomos*) means both freedom and giving laws, creating an orderly world. However, giving laws does not necessarily entail considering others, nature or oneself as an object to be used for a purpose – instrumentality is a possible form of mastery, understanding another. From the moment onwards, symbolically, that human beings can look at the earth from the outside, due to space travel, Arendt thought, the planet might cease to be recognized as the ground for existence and become an object to be instrumentally treated. This instrumental attitude is mirrored in the ways human action is considered in the behaviorist and quantitative social sciences. When human action merely follows signals and society is nothing but the statistical aggregate of many of those actions, then world disappears and 'worldlessness' reigns.

These reflections – both Castoriadis's and Arendt's – on world, world-making and worldlessness gain particular significance in a time of the so-called globalization. This latter term suggests that something becomes global, in the sense of extending across the round planet earth, that had not been so before, but most of the debate fails to specify what this is that becomes global. It can neither be the globe itself, which has always been global, nor our human lives, which have always been and will always be local. Regardless of all communication and transportation technology that is and may become available, if I am at one place I cannot be at another. If it has any sense at all, the term globalization, thus, must refer to the extension of relations between human beings, the possibility of effectively connecting to others over long, global distances in very short time – be it stock brokers, Chinese traders or activists of contestation.

This is a reasonable view, but it begs further questions, at least two. First, such relations do not exist as such, as 'social facts', they need to be created and sustained through the action of living human beings (following what I take to be one outcome of the agency-structure debate of the 1970s and 1980s). Thus, 'globality' – if this is a term that describes the consequence of 'globalization' – is never just there, or at best latently so. It needs to be manifested through persistent action. Second, if such globality is seen as the unintended outcome of numerous human actions, then the process leading towards it, called globalization, is not one of world-making, but one leading to worldlessness.[2] These are questions that cannot be answered by further conceptual exploration; they require engagement with the socio-historical transformations that created the current global constellation as well with the forms of interaction across long extensions of social relations that we witness today, sometimes referred to as 'globalization from below'. This short chapter can at best indicate ways of doing so, but it will try.

Historical Constellations of Modernity

The preceding reflections have suggested some conceptual connections between modernity, critique and world. The following observations, in turn, are meant to suggest that this connection can take highly different forms and meanings in different historical constellations. Given the limitations of space, I will need to confine myself to characterize four episodes in the history of modernity, and I will tie them together by confronting them with the consensus view of around 1970 that is gradually being dismantled, as discussed earlier.

The established view held that the period around 1800 brought the onset of modernity *tout court*. Prepared by the Enlightenment elaborations on freedom and reason, the very epitome of modern thinking, the French Revolution created the conditions for political modernity in the combination of individual freedom and collective self-determination, and the market–industrial revolution provided the foundations for the modern economy in which the sum of individual actions guided by the market would maximize the benefit for all. The history of modernity after 1800 is the history of the gradual realization of the promises made up to that moment, the completion of the project of modernity, to paraphrase Jürgen Habermas. By now, many will say that this brief description is a caricature, in which no one believes any more. A caricature deviates from the truth by exaggerating essential features; this picture, however, is grossly misleading. Thus, a more fundamental rethinking of modernity needs to occur, for which I hope to provide a few elements.

1. If modernity is understood as the human commitment to autonomy, we find in known history the first, and in some respects most radical, expression of *modernity in ancient Greece*, more precisely in the era of the democratic city-state exemplified by Athens. The Athenians were fundamentally convinced by the idea that they have to determine their fate themselves – that no gods or other external resource will do this for them – and that they can only do so in collective self-determination based on the freedom of the person – given that the human being is a political animal, as Aristotle put it (Arnason et al., 2013). As a collective phenomenon, such radical interpretation of modernity should not re-occur before the late eighteenth century, to the best of our knowledge.[3] In particular, we should note that the phenomenon that is often referred to as the birth of philosophy in ancient Greece is better characterized as the commitment to the questioning of everything that exists, as opening the way for radical critique, including importantly the critique of democracy itself, of collective self-determination.[4]

   At the same time, the world that was created by the modern ancient Greeks had very particular features. First, it was a world (*cosmos*) that through human law-giving (*nomos*) was created from the chaos that preceded world-making and had no revealed or intelligible laws of its own, in contrast to later Christian and scientific-philosophical thinking. And for that very reason, second, it was a spatially limited world, limited by the reach of conscious human intervention, outside of which beings were living whom one could not understand, barbarians. There was no globe that was known of. Thirdly, the commitment to self-determination was not inclusive (as we would say today). It was assumed that the satisfaction of material human needs was determined by necessities and, therefore, limited freedom. These tasks were to be performed by women and slaves to allow the male citizens the possibility to act politically with full freedom, not constrained by needs.

2. As a consequence of the so-called voyages of discovery, the period around 1500 witnessed the emergence of global consciousness, of the insight into the nature of the planet earth and the limits of its space. This is the most significant deviation from preceding periods: from now on there is no radical outside any longer about which nothing at all is known. 'Globalization' starts at this moment. In common Eurocentric accounts, which see here the beginning of 'early modernity' on the arduous three-century long path to the onset of true modernity at around 1800, two important features are often overlooked: Rather than being a triumphant moment of European man conquering the earth, first, this was a moment of crisis in European history triggered by the fall of the Byzantine Empire and the concomitant endangering of the terrestrial trade routes to Asia. The Portuguese and Spaniards set to sea out of necessity rather than will to mastery (Darwin, 2009). Long-distance maritime trade, second, was not an invention of this period. It had been practiced across the Indian Ocean between Asia and East Africa for a long time. The effect of the European voyages rather was to open the Atlantic to create a similar maritime trade area with particular features, most importantly the slave trade and an emerging new division of economic

tasks, that should bear full consequences only three centuries after the first voyages.

Notwithstanding these moderations of the dominant image, the period stands out as providing a particular interpretation of modernity in two main respects. First, an insight into the spatial limits of the earth was accompanied by attempts at claiming complete territorial mastery. The key example for such ambition is the Treaty of Tordesillas signed between Spain and Portugal in 1494. The actual line of demarcation remained far from being trampled by colonizers for a long time, and the complete division of the earth between the existing powers was much more clearly at issue in the so-called scramble for Africa during the second half of the nineteenth century, the Berlin conference of 1884–1885 being a major attempt at settling the claims. In this sense, Carl Schmitt's *Nomos of the Earth* (1997 [1950]) misreads politico-legal history from a twentieth-century vantage point. However, Schmitt is right in suggesting that global law-making as world-making is on the horizon from this period onwards. Significantly, it is not world-making under the sign of equal autonomy, but by European powers dividing the earth among themselves and setting up different criteria for dealing with each other than with the subjected others.

The question of the recognition of the other is the second issue at stake in this period. With entering the 'New World', the seafarers also encountered human beings whom they did not expect, whom they had not been aware of. In distinction from members of other 'Old World' civilizations, who were different in many respects but to some extent knowable and known, the Native Americans were the radical other. In the first discussion, at the core of which was the Las Casas-Sepúlveda controversy in 1550, their common humanity needed to be determined, and Christian thought helped towards that end, even though it could also be used for denying equal status (Pagden, 2000). Subsequently, the otherness of contemporaneous Native Americans served to construct a dichotomous perception of world-history, distinguishing a state of nature, in which the Native Americans lived, from the civil society, which Europeans had reached. As much as it was of a conceptual nature in social contract theories, this distinction opened the path for later evolutionary thinking about modernity and modernization.

3. This observation brings us to the period around 1800, the one in which social contract theories were being mobilized, and underpinned the Declaration of Independence of the emerging United States of America, the French Revolution, the Haitian Revolution and other political events. Against the background of the Enlightenment thinking of the preceding century, a radical political imaginary was at work, aiming at the instituting of a new world on significantly different foundations. From the angle of intellectual history, this period marked an important transformation in the conceptualization of political modernity. This is not the same, however, as saying that it marked the onset of political modernity *tout court*, for two main reasons.

In *conceptual* terms, first, it is erroneous to consider the late-eighteenth century debates as providing a model for modernity; they rather elaborate a novel, very particular interpretation of political modernity. On the one hand, they concentrate on the individual as rights-holder, thus importantly underpinning individual liberties, but at the same time weakening or underemphasizing other components of a viable social ontology. The concomitant idea of liberation as the dissolution of all social ties, prevalent in the French Revolution and endorsed as a step forward in Marx and Engels's *Communist Manifesto*, was already criticized by romanticist and idealist counter-currents to atomistic individualism (see Karagiannis and Wagner, 2013, on conceptions of liberty). On the other hand, the question of the relation between individual autonomy and collective self-determination was clearly central to the revolutionary political imaginary of the period, but it was never adequately answered. Social contract theory waivered on the question as to how to get from the will of all to the general will, to use Rouseau's terms, and the liberalism of the nineteenth century basically jettisoned democracy in favour of individual liberties, as even a resolute liberal as Isaiah Berlin recognized (Berlin, 1971).

This latter move looks less surprising when, second, one regards the *political* aftermath of the revolutionary period. To put it briefly, the radical political imaginary of the years around 1800 was defeated in Europe in the internal and international battles of the early nineteenth century. Instead of being dominated by the rising bourgeoisie of liberal-capitalist modernity, the old aristocratic elites gradually changed outlook and started building new alliances, containing any radical new visions as created in the French Revolution and in political economy and imposing their power in the novel constellation through violence at home and abroad. The period between the Vienna Congress of 1815 and the Versailles Peace Treaty of 1919 in Europe was neither as peaceful nor as revolutionary as has often been suggested. True, it witnessed the rise of industry, and with it of wealth and power, both highly asymmetrically distributed. But the socio-political transformation that has often been seen to accompany the techno-economic transformation remained very limited (Mayer, 1981; Halperin, 2004; Stråth, forthcoming). In the Americas, the political imaginary remained partially alive, supporting the calls for independence from Europe and for the building of republics. At the same time, however, the more radical components of the imaginary calling for equal rights for all and democracy were disregarded by the oligarchy of settler elites.

As a consequence, the interpretation of political modernity proposed by 1800 was very far from being put onto a straight evolutionary path towards 'completion'. The nineteenth century experience is best captured by the term *restricted liberal modernity* (Wagner, 1994). By 1900, European societies, supposedly instantiating high modernity, could hardly deviate more from the imagery of a century before: many of them were not nation-states but colonial empires; they were not inclusive democracies but oligarchies that operated with restricted suffrage; there was capitalism but market self-regulation had been found deficient and economic exchange was highly regulated; the Christian churches mostly operated in close institutionalized alliance with the state; the idea of the autonomous individual was largely limited to bourgeois and 'bohémien', entrepreneurial and artistic models of self-realization, thus to small groups in society. With the partial exception of the US, despite the racial domination that continued after the juridical abolition of slavery, self-determination was embraced in the so-called settler societies in very restricted forms. If there was an empirical situation that approached the ideal-type of socio-political organization in settler societies, it was the one of the 'Boer republics' in Southern Africa, the Orange Free State and the Transvaal Republic, during the second half of the nineteenth century. These were self-governing polities inspired by Enlightenment republicanism. At the same time, its citizens had no qualms with subjecting the native population, excluding them from participation, all the while employing them as domestic and farm labourers.

4. In Europe, this restricted interpretation of modernity could no longer be sustained after the First World War. Between 1919 and the 1960s, through civil wars, authoritarian and totalitarian regimes, an inclusivist reinterpretation was created, entailing full and equal political participation, recognition of the workers as producers through the trade unions and as consumers who would buy the products they themselves had produced. The new accumulation regime of mass production coupled with mass consumption (Aglietta, 1979) was the precondition for the inward turn of European societies – one also spoke of 'internal colonization' – that meant the elaboration of a societal self-understanding in which the collectivity became a community of mutual responsibility, overcoming the class divides of earlier eras (Wagner and Zimmermann, 2003). This internally *organized modernity* (Wagner, 1994) required a political centre, the state apparatus, which was capable of organizing political forces through mass organizations and the media, monitoring and steering the economy, and sustaining boundary control towards other societies. Although inclusivist, it was not necessarily democratic – the experiences of Franco Spain and Salazar Portugal can also be described in these terms. Furthermore, this conception of a second phase of modernity, after the restricted liberal one of the nineteenth century, has by and large been found plausible also for Latin America, including the Vargas and Peron regimes first and military dictatorships later in the twentieth century (Larrain, 2000; Domingues, 2008).

The Specificity of the Current Constellation of Modernity

The current constellation of modernity, gradually emerging since the 1960s, differs fundamentally from the preceding organized modernity. We shall start our characterization of the present by distinguishing it – somewhat schematically for reasons of brevity – from all the constellations of modernity described earlier.

Currently, since decolonization, we witness for the first time a constellation of modernity that operates *globally* on comprehensive and formally equal terms. In this respect, it differs from ancient modernity when there was no globality; from the modern constellations of 1500 and 1800 because the global linkages then, while existing, were still weak and left many people but little affected; and from the constellation of 1900, which was marked by European domination over, and subjugation of, the colonies and ex-colonies.

The current constellation of modernity, furthermore, is based on a commitment to *equal individual freedom*. In this respect, it differs radically not only from ancient modernity, but also from the periods of 'early' modernity in which personal liberty was at best on the normative horizon, and restricted liberal modernity in which it was largely limited to the male, property-owning elites. The organized modernity after 1900 was often committed to equality, but its notion of inclusion was strictly confined within given polities and, furthermore, it was framed in such a way that individual freedom was curtailed – sometimes formally as in authoritarian periods, sometimes more socio-culturally with entrenched expectations of conformism and loyalty, otherwise called normative integration.

Finally, the current constellation of modernity is marked by the commitment to collective self-determination, as not least reflected in the excessive use of the term 'democratization' in current political science. At the face of it, it shares this commitment with ancient modernity and organized modernity. In between, around 1500, the term democracy was barely in use; and around 1800 its proponents were defeated (Wagner, 2013). But in contrast to antiquity, the idea of collective self-determination is now extended to all members of a polity and all over the globe. And in distinction from organized modernity, it is not exclusively located in the institutional containers of the existing states. Democratization is supposed to have become a global trend as well as a global concern that reaches beyond the boundaries of one's own polity.

It is understandable that the current constellation of modernity is occasionally confounded with the ultimate breakthrough of modernity, with the completion of modernity. Modernity is now truly global, as it appears, and it is committed to both equal individual freedom and to collective self-determination, as indicated by the discourse that holds that our era is the one of the global realization of human rights and democracy. This view, however, is erroneous, as I want to show in two concluding steps.

The Emergence of Current Modernity through Contestation

Let me first underline that the current constellation of modernity did not evolve smoothly from the preceding organized modernity; its emergence was not driven by any logic of capital nor by linear progress towards greater individualization and inclusion. Rather, the organized modernity of the 1960s – to which some authors today look nostalgically back (for two

very different forms of nostalgia see Dlamini, 2009; Offe, 2010) – was
actively contested and exposed to critique, on a number of fronts and often
in radical ways 'from below'. In the then so-called Third World, movements for national liberation called for decolonization and collective
self-determination, these struggles reaching a high point around 1960. In
the then so-called First World, the year 1968 marked a climax of workers'
and students' contestation, often seen as the combination of a political and
cultural revolution of which the latter aspect should become dominant. In
the wake of 1968, time-honoured issues were returned to the political
agenda, with greater force and urgency, by the feminist movement and the
ecological movement. During the later twentieth century, new movements
of the poor and excluded emerged in response to the consequences of
global economic-financial restructuring. There, where democracy had
been abolished by military regimes, they merged with movements for the
restoration of liberty and democracy. And there, where exclusion and
oppression had a marked ethnic/racial component, contestations centred
on political and cultural claims for self-determination.

These contestations, in their sum, had a considerable share in what we
now recognize as the dismantling of organized modernity. Decolonization
dismantled (most of) what had remained of the empires. The women's
movement achieved – in many, though not all societies – the abolition of
remainders of patriarchal law. Restrictions to information and expression
were lifted, partly enabled by new technologies. The party structures, of
which political scientists thought that they mirrored lasting social divides,
crumbled partly because of the formation of movement parties, partly
because of a blurring of those social divides. In other words, and again in
very sweeping terms, the contestations proved highly successful, to the
degree of bringing about a pronounced social transformation.

Many of these occurrences can be described in terms of normative
achievements, of progress: of recognition, of freedom, of equality. This,
precisely, is where the success of contestations can be located. There are
two qualifications to be added, however. First, other components of organized modernity were dismantled in parallel, but the normative assessment of these processes is much more ambivalent, to say the least: The
capacity of states to direct national economies diminished; commercial
and financial flows are increasingly beyond control; the institutional
frames for collective self-determination have been weakened, partly deliberately in favour of supranational or global cooperation, partly because of
an escape of socio-political phenomena from the view and grasp of political institutions.

In more general terms, secondly, one can probably say that any socio-
political transformation entails the dismantling of existing institutions,

but that this dismantling is often accompanied by building new institutions, or by giving new purpose and meaning to existing institutional containers. The transformation from restricted liberal to organized modernity is a strong example for the building of collective institutions to address problems that restricted liberal modernity had created. The contestations of organized modernity, however, have often had the oppressive, exploiting or excluding nature of existing institutions as their target, and have therefore been aiming at de-institutionalization in the first place. As an unintended side-effect, this orientation has tended to incapacitate collective action: on the one hand, because specific existing institutions are weakened, and on the other, because institutional rebuilding in general is delegitimized in the name of some generic concept of equal individual freedom.

Towards a Sustainable Reinterpretation of Modernity

The combination of globality, equal freedom and collective self-determination, which we have identified as the characteristic for the current constellation of modernity above, has effectively guided the dismantling of organized modernity, but the components of this constellation are insufficiently articulated to provide for a sustainable reinterpretation of modernity yet. Re-instituting, however, requires a new imaginary signification, a deliberate construction of an interpretation of modernity that better satisfies normative requirements than the dismantled organized modernity. To grasp some of the issues at stake, I return to the brief discussions of the earlier interpretations of modernity.

1. Ancient modernity worked with a distinction of freedom and necessity that assigned different social roles to categories of persons. This is unjustifiable under conditions of equal freedom. The socio-political consequences of detaching the freedom-necessity distinction from categories of persons, however, have never been adequately addressed (see Casassas, 2010, for an attempt to detect this issue in Adam Smith's writings). Through the transformations of modernity, those categories have kept changing – women, serfs, slaves, inferior races, proletarians, illegal immigrants, people of poorer societies across the borders – but current modernity is far from acknowledging that, in global practice today, many people lastingly take care of the needs of others and enable those others to live lives of greater freedom, without being able to exercise similar freedom themselves.

2. In the colonial encounter of the New World, early modernity took a step towards the recognition of otherness. If it was not through annihilation, however, otherness kept being dealt with through assimilation, integration, inclusion, thus doing away with what was the characteristic of the other (Peiró and

Rosich, 2014). From the nineteenth century onwards, otherness was supposed to be addressed through the features of nations, which in sovereignty could equally contribute their specificity to humankind. The nation-states, however, were integral parts of the organization of modernity. The flaws of their interpretation of otherness have been identified and criticized, without any other approach having strongly emerged.

3. Similarly, the individualist conception of freedom, which emerged in parts of the Enlightenment, left human beings without strong attachment, ignoring the significance of their being of a time and a place. While such de-attaching can certainly be liberating, it can also produce loss of meaning, in particular when individualistic freedom becomes the guiding principle and when de-attaching of ties is enforced rather than chosen, as it is for ever more people today for reasons of survival.

4. Finally, the broad commitment to collective self-determination has lost out of sight the need for frameworks for collective self-determination. Political thought is still caught in the idea that there are 'natural' collectivities, held together by culture or language, so that the question of the 'self' that determines its collective life does not pose itself – or if there are not, that global, cosmopolitan self-determination is on the horizon. Today, however, it is clear both that political collectivities need to form themselves, that they are not just there, and that the conditions for the forming of a global polity do not exist, even though global political communication is necessary (Rosich, 2015).

Let me conclude by taking a topical turn. One can recognize that protest movements of the past two decades have started to address these issues, maybe most notably in the South. A turn away from dismantling unwanted institutions towards rebuilding better institutions is under way, and it has had some success. In Brazil and South Africa, for instance, the struggle against military dictatorship and apartheid, respectively, has brought forth rather stable political majorities with the declared aim of transforming these societies. I will not address here the record of the current governments, often enough ridden with tensions, but will just suggest that the above-mentioned issues are centrally at stake.

Brazil and South Africa are highly unequal societies in which the majority of the population has taken care of the necessities of the ruling minority for a long time. They are also highly diverse societies, with different languages, ways of living, and these differences overlap with – past and present – socio-economic positions, but are not reducible to the latter. Furthermore, they witnessed a past of oppression and injustice which marks the lives until today, making it impossible to argue politically under a 'veil of ignorance' (Mills, 2015). And finally, they are strongly committed to collective self-determination, having been deprived of it in the past, but face the problems of defining the collectivity, in South Africa, and balancing institutional politics with intensity of participation, more pro-nouncedly in Brazil. All these issues are recognized, and the intention is to address them forcefully and convincingly. In both societies, the commit-ment to transformative collective action is pronounced, much more so than in most societies of the North. However, Brazilians and South Africans do not only face social situations that are much more dramatic than currently in most of the North. The 'local' commitment to self-determination is both difficult and insufficient in current global modernity, simultaneously char-acterized by the weakening of collective capacity of action and the need for enhanced collective coordination at a global scale.

The view that our current modernity embraces a global commitment to individual human rights and democracy, partially correct as it is, conceals urgent questions and makes it more difficult to address them: individual rights are not an answer to questions of material deprivation and absence of meaning; and democracy becomes an empty term when there is little of significance a limited collectivity can truly decide upon. What is required is not only the elaboration of a novel interpretation of modernity, which is globally oriented and committed to equal freedom and democracy, but also addresses the inescapable issues explored above with a view to re-instituting modernity in a way that is adequate for our time. Given the existing forms of domination, both internationally and domestically, this is a struggle whose outcome is uncertain. It may well end with the common ruin of the contending classes, as Marx and Engels once suspected. But if it is not led, the novel planetary constellation of modernity, which contains enormous promises, runs the risk of ending in worldlessness.

Notes

1   Work on this chapter has benefitted from support by the European Research Council for the project 'Trajectories of modernity: comparing non-European and European variet-ies', funded as Advanced Grant no. 249438.

2   In French debates, a distinction between *globalization* and *mondialization* was for some time proposed, the former capturing the processes and tendencies without guiding intention, the latter being close to our 'world-making' (Nancy, 2002; see Karagiannis and Wagner, 2007). Kostas Axelos spoke early on of 'the planetary age' as the epoch in which technique reigns and which, thus, demands a novel way of questioning the world (Axelos, 1964; see Karagiannis and Wagner, 2012a).

3   I use expressions such as 'known history' and 'our best knowledge' to indicate that it is well possible, probable even, that similar commitments to self-determination prevailed in societies about which we have much less record than those of near Eastern antiquity (see Detienne, 2009).

4   Aiming to avoid what he calls 'Hellenocentrism' and in line with the interpretation on which the theology of liberation is based, Enrique Dussel (2007) locates the emergence of liberty and critique in early Christianity, which is at odds with the character of Christianity

as a religion of revelation. It seems more convincing to credit early Christianity with the commitment to (what we would now call) an inclusive egalitarian humanism. A further exploration of this issue would require a look at the debate about the politico-cultural transformations during the so-called axial age (Arnason et al., 2005).

References

Aglietta, M. (1979). *A Theory of Capitalist Regulation*. London: New Left Books.

Arendt, H. (1958). *The Human Condition*. Chicago, IL: University of Chicago Press.

Arnason, J.P., Eisenstadt S. and Wittrock, B. (Eds.) (2005). *Axial Civilizations and World History*. Leiden: Brill.

Arnason, J.P., Raaflaub, K. and Wagner, P. (Eds.). (2013). *The Greek Polis and the Invention of Democracy*. Oxford: Blackwell.

Axelos, K. (1964). *Vers la pensée planétaire*. Paris: Minuit.

Berlin, I. (1971). Two Concepts of Liberty. *Four Essays on Liberty*. Oxford: Oxford University Press.

Boltanski, L. (2009). *De la critique*. Paris: Gallimard.

Boltanski, L. and Chiapello E. (1999). *Le nouvel esprit du capitalisme*. Paris: Gallimard.

Boltanski, L. and Thévenot L. (1991). *De la justification*. Paris: Gallimard.

Casassas, D. (2010). *La ciudad en llamas. La vigencia del republicanismo comercial de Adam Smith*. Barcelona: Montesinos.

Castoriadis, C. (1987 [1975]). *The Imaginary Institution of Society*. Cambridge, MA: MIT Press.

Castoriadis, C. (1990). Pouvoir, politique, autonomie. *Le monde morcelé. Les carrefours du labyrinthe III*. Paris: Seuil, pp. 113–39.

Detienne, M. (2009). *Les Grecs et nous*. Paris: Perrin.

Dlamini, J. (2009). *Native Nostalgia*. Johannesburg: Jacana.

Darwin, J. (2009). *After Tamerlane: The Rise and Fall of Global Empires, 1400–2000*. London: Bloomsbury.

Domingues, J.M. (2008). *Latin America and Contemporary Modernity*. London: Routledge.

Dussel, E. (2007). *Política de la liberación: historia mundial y crítica*. Madrid: Trotta.

Halperin, S. (2004). *War and Social Change in Modern Europe*. Cambridge: Cambridge University Press.

Karagiannis, N. and Wagner P. (Eds.) (2007). *Varieties of World-Making: Beyond Globalization*. Liverpool: Liverpool University Press.

Karagiannis, N. and Wagner P. (2012a). What is to be Thought? What is to be Done? The Polyscopic Thought of Kostas Axelos and Cornelius Castoriadis. *European Journal of Social Theory*, *15*(3), 403–17.

Karagiannis, N. and Wagner, P. (2012b). Imagination and Tragic Democracy. *Critical Horizons*, *13*(1), 12–28.

Karagiannis, N. and Wagner, P. (2013). The Liberty of the Moderns Compared to the Liberty of the Ancients. In J.P. Arnason, K. Raaflaub and P. Wagner (Eds.). *The Greek Polis and the Invention of Democracy*. Oxford: Blackwell, pp. 371–88.

Larrain, J. (2000). *Identity and Modernity in Latin America*. Cambridge: Polity.

Mayer, A. (1981). *The Persistence of the Old Regime*. New York: Pantheon.

Mills, C. (2015). Decolonizing Western Political Philosophy. In G. Rosich and P. Wagner (Eds.). *Political Modernity in the 21st Century*.

Nancy, J.L. (2002). *La création du monde ou la mondialisation*. Paris: Galilée.

Offe, C. (2010). Was (falls überhaupt etwas) können wir uns heute unter politischem Fortschritt' vorstellen? *Westend. Neue Zeitschrift für Sozialforschung*, 7(2), 3–14.

Pagden, A. (Ed.) (2000). *Facing Each Other* (Vol. 2). Farnham: Ashgate.

Peiró Fuster, A.L. and Rosich G. (2014). The Limits of Recognition: History, Otherness and Autonomy. In P. Wagner (Ed.), *African, American and European Trajectories of Modernity, Annual of European and Global Studies* (Vol. 2). Edinburgh: Edinburgh University Press.

Rosich, G. (2015). Autonomy in and Between Polities. In G. Rosich and P. Wagner (Eds.). *Political Modernity in the 21st Century.*

Schmitt, C. (1997 [1950]). *Der Nomos der Erde im Völkerrecht des Jus Publicum Europaeum.* Berlin: Duncker & Humbolt.

Stråth, B. (Forthcoming). *Three Utopias of Peace and the Search for a Political Economy.*

Wagner, P. (1994). *A Sociology of Modernity.* London: Routledge.

Wagner, P. (2008). *Modernity as Experience and Interpretation.* Cambridge: Polity.

Wagner, P. (2012). *Modernity: Understanding the Present.* Cambridge: Polity.

Wagner, P. (2013). Transformations of Democracy. In J.P. Arnason, K. Raaflaub and P. Wagner (Eds.), *The Greek Polis and the Invention of Democracy.* Oxford: Blackwell, pp. 47–68.

Wagner, P. and Zimmermann, B. (2003). Nation – Die Konstitution einer politischen Ordnung als Verantwortungsgemeinschaft. In S. Lessenich (Ed.), *Wohlfahrtsstaatliche Grundbegriffe.* Frankfurt: Campus, pp. 243–266.

2

The Global Transition and the Challenge to Social Sciences

Sujata Patel

Introduction

Five concerns direct the arguments presented in this chapter. First, if we agree that the main task of sociologists is to engage with and reformulate the substantive theories of modernity, then, second, it becomes equally important to confront and contest the universalizing 'episteme' that has organized these theories since the late 19th and early 20th centuries and which relate to the global unequal division of knowledge production in that period. This is known in social theory as Eurocentric methodology (Wallerstein, 1997, 2006) or coloniality of power (Quijano, 1993, 2000, 2007). Third, a critique of this episteme emerged in various parts of the world and particularly in India from the decade of the forties to sixties; the chapter discusses this critique and its limitations. Fourth, the chapter deliberates on the present interventions from scholars in the South on this theme (in terms of provincialism Chakrabarty, 2008), endogeneity (Hountondji, 1995, 1997) and the trans-modern perspective (Dussel, 1993, 2000, 2002; Mignolo, 2002), and argues that these resources provide a possible way to move forward in the reformulations of this critique. Fifth, I suggest that the present moment provides an opportunity to move beyond the trappings of the received episteme and the chapter spells out possible strategies for the same.

These concerns direct me to make an historical assessment of the framing of social science theory in the world and particularly in India; the focus is on the disciplines of sociology and anthropology. I argue that 19th century social science structured the disciplines in terms of a hierarchy based on an epistemic difference, of modern and pre-modern/traditional and reduced this episteme to spatial distinctions: the west and east. I suggest that this epistemic hierarchy continues to structure disciplines and knowledge systems today and are a hindrance to the growth of global social science interdisciplinarity.[1]

Colonial Modernity and the Formation of Anthropology

Anthropology was the first discipline or knowledge system to be established in India, and I start my discussion with an assessment of its Eurocentric epistemic moorings located in 18th century discussions of European modernity. Lévi-Strauss famously stated: anthropology was a handmaiden of colonialism and it is to this issue I now turn my attention.

Samir Amin (2008) is the first theorist who presents a historical argument regarding the growth of the Eurocentric episteme in the 18th century, when he argues that this episteme is entwined in the twin processes of crystallization of the European society and Europe's conquest of the world. Eurocentrism, Amin argues, clothes these twin processes by emphasizing the first and disregarding the significance of the latter in the formation of the first.

Amin's argument is presented at three levels: First, he contends that Europe was the periphery of the Mediterranean tributary states (the other being that of the Afro-Asiatic region) whose centre was at its eastern edge. Scholastic and metaphysical culture of these tributary systems created four systems of scholastic metaphysics: Hellenistic, Eastern Christian, Islamic and Western Christian. While all of these contributed to the formation of culture and consciousness of Europe, it was the contribution of Egypt and later of medieval Islamic scholastics which was decisive in changing Europe's culture from being metaphysical to scientific. (Amin, 2008: 38). Second, he shows how since the period of Renaissance, this history of Europe has been distilled and diluted to be replaced with another history that narrated its growth as being the sole consequence of its birth within the Hellenic-Roman civilization. Third, through the means of what the Latin American philosopher Enrique Dussel (2000: 465) has called 'semantic slippages', Amin argues that the European narrative made Europe the centre of the world and of modern 'civilization', the distinctive characteristic of which was science and 'universal reason'. The rest of the world was constructed to be its peripheries, which, it was argued could not or did not have the means to become modern.

Immanuel Wallerstein (1997, 2006) has extended this perspective to suggest that Eurocentrism is also a theory of social science. As latter, it is able to 'naturalize' the distinctions between 'scientific universalism against essential particulars' as it develops a discourse in the 19th century through the mode of historiography, the analysis of (Western) civilization, through Orientalism, and its attempts to impose a theory of progress (Wallerstein, 1997: 94). These trends crystallized an 'original epistemology' (Wallerstein, 2006: 48), which becomes 'a key element' in maintaining the reproduction of modernity.

This argument is further extended by Enrique Dussel and Anibal Quijano when they assert what Amin had said earlier – that Eurocentrism was a theory of constructing a self-defined ethnocentric theory of history, that of 'I'. They also affirm, in a manner similar to Amin, that the European narrative and thus its theory of history simultaneously makes invisible and silences events, processes and actions of violence against the rest of the world, without which Europe could not have become modern. They extend this thesis to suggest that Eurocentrism is not only a theory of history but also an episteme, a theory of power/knowledge. If this episteme theorized the 'I', it also theorized the 'other', the 'periphery'. Thus, Dussel argues:

> …modernity is, in fact, an European phenomena, but one constituted in a dia-
> lectical relation with a non-modern alterity that is its ultimate content. Modernity
> appears when Europe appears itself as the 'centre' of *World* history that it inau-
> gurates; the periphery that surrounds this centre is consequently part of its
> self-definition. The occlusion of this periphery … leads the major thinkers of
> the centre into a Eurocentric fallacy in their understanding of modernity.
> (Dussel, 1993: 65)

Second, this episteme now termed 'categorical imperative', simultane-
ously creates the knowledge of the 'I' (Europe, the moderns, the West) against the 'other' (as the peripheral, non-modern and the East). This per-
spective legitimizes a theory of the separate and divided nature of the knowledge of the West and the East. It divides the attributes of the West and the East by giving value to the two divisions; while one is universal, superior and 'emancipatory', the other is particular and non-emancipatory and thus inferior. Dussel quotes Immanuel Kant who argued that while European 'Enlightenment is the exodus of humanity by its own efforts from the state of guilty immaturity'…'laziness and cowardice are the reasons why the great part of humanity remains pleasurably in the state of immaturity' (Dussel, 1993: 68). This inferiority, a condition of its not becoming modern, in turn further legitimates the need to emulate the 'moderns' and to accept the colonizing process as a 'civilizing' process. This was the myth of modernity and led, according to Dussel, to the management of the world system's 'centrality':

> If one understands Europe's modernity – a long process of five centuries – as
> the unfolding of new possibilities derived from its centrality in world history
> and the corollary constitution of all other cultures as its periphery, it becomes
> clear that, even though all cultures are ethnocentric, modern European ethno-
> centrism is the only one that might pretend to claim universality for itself.
> Modernity's Eurocentrism lies in the confusion between abstract universality

and the concrete world hegemony derived from Europe's position as center. (Dussel, 2002: 222)

Third, as mentioned above, Eurocentric knowledge is based on the construction of multiple and repeated divisions or oppositions which gets constructed as hierarchies. These oppositions, Anibal Quijano (2000) argues are based on a racial classification of the world population. This principle becomes the assumption to further divide the peoples of the world into geo-cultural terms, with which are attached further oppositions, such as reason and body, science and religion, subject and object, culture and nature, masculine and feminine, modern and traditional. While European modernity conceptualized its growth in terms of linear time, it sequestered the (various) East(s) divided between two cultural groups, the 'primitives'/ barbarians and the civilized as being enclosed in their (own) spaces. No wonder this episteme could not provide the resources to elaborate a theory of space, affirming David Harvey's insightful statement of 'annihilation of space by time'.

The consolidation of these attributes across the West–East axis and its subsequent hierarchization across spatial regions in the world allow for social science to discover the 'nature' of the various peoples, nations and ethnic groups in the world in terms of the attributes of the binaries. This structure of power, control and hegemony termed by Quijano as 'coloniality of power' is founded on two myths:

> …first, the idea of the history of human civilization as a trajectory that departed from a state of nature and culminated in Europe; second, a view of the differences between Europe and non-Europe as natural (racial) differences and not consequences of a history of power. Both myths can be unequivocally recognized in the foundations of evolutionism and dualism, two of the nuclear elements of Eurocentrism. (Quijano, 2000: 542)

These seminal assumptions were embodied in the framing of the disciplines of sociology and anthropology in late 19th century. Sociology became the study of modern (European – later to be extended to western) society, while anthropology was the study of (non-European and non-Western) traditional societies. Thus, sociologists studied how the new societies evolved from the deadwood of the old; a notion of time and history was embedded in its discourse. Contrary anthropologists studied how space/place organized 'static' culture that could not transcend its internal structures to become modern.

These frames also constructed the academic knowledge of India as elaborated by colonial anthropologists and administrators, who further divided the East that they were studying in separate geo-spatial territories with each territory given an overarching cultural value. In the case of India, it was religion: Hinduism. The discourse of coloniality collapsed India and Hinduism into each other (Patel, 2006, 2007). Later those living in the subcontinent were further classified geographically in spatial cultural zones and 'regionally' subdivided by its relationship with Hinduism. Those that were directly related to Hinduism, such as castes and tribes were termed the 'majority' and organized in terms of distinct hierarchies (castes were considered more superior than tribes who were thought to be 'primitive'), while those that were not were conceived as 'minorities', these being mainly groups who practiced Islam, Sikhism and Christianity (Patel, 2006).

Fourth, this classificatory schema, that of the use of the attribute of race to divide the peoples of the world, found its own 'local' legitimation, its own articulation and a 'voice', once colonial authorities had imposed these to divide the 'natives'. Thus, this project found an expression (ironically and paradoxically) in the work of indigenous intellectuals in the subcontinent searching to find an identity against colonialism. For them, the immediate necessity was to locate 'our modernities'. Thus, unlike the Europeans for whom, 'the present was the site of one's escape from the past', for the indigenous Indian intellectuals 'it is precisely the present [given the colonial experience] from which we feel we must escape'. As a result the desire to be creative and search for a new modernity is transposed to the past of India, a past ironically constructed by orientalist colonial modernity. Thus, Chatterjee argues, 'we construct a picture of "those days" when there was beauty, prosperity and healthy sociability. This makes the very modality of our coping with modernity radically different from the historically evolved modes of Western modernity' (Chatterjee, 1997: 19). This past was now rarefied to understand the present and the future; an orientalist imagination came to define the so-called indigenous expression.

In a different way, the historian Sumit Sarkar makes a similar argument when he suggests that while modern Western history writing has generally been state oriented (with an understanding of nation as a reflection of the nation-state), the historical consciousness of the Indian intelligentsia, in the late 19th and early 20th centuries, was oriented to the valorization of culture against the state. He states:

In this period *samaj* (society, community) came to be counterposed to *rashtra* or *rajshakti* (state, the political domain). The real history of India, it was repeatedly asserted, was located in the first, not the second, for *samaj* embodied the distinctive qualities peculiar to the genius, culture and religion of the Indian people. (Sarkar, 1997: 21) and

> .... *samaj* was simultaneously all too often conceptualised in Hindu, high caste gentry, and paternalistic terms.... (Sarkar, 1997: 23).

Obviously, racial constructions of 'difference' found a new legitimacy within a Brahminical casteist ideology as these two overlapped each other to organize the study of social sciences through new reconstructed major-itarian and or/casteist positions or through rationalist and 'secular' silences of this process that, in turn, allowed its legitimation.

'Eurocentric episteme' thus became part of the 'background under-standings' and 'beliefs' and have obfuscated a critical look at knowledge production of social sciences in India. In the case of India, this knowledge (a) was produced as part of colonial politics of rule, (b) was expressed and organized in terms of values that were in opposition to modernity, (c) used disciplinary practices such as Indology and ethnography to elaborate these positions, (d) was codified with the help of native intelligentsia, especially the Brahmins, and (e) thus reflected the social order as represented by this group both in its expressed articulations (in anthropology and later social anthropology) and in its silences (in economics) and (g) lastly, mitigated an examination of the way classification systems of the state organized new forms of inequalities in the colonial territory.

Endogenous Critique of Colonial Social Sciences

The legacy of Eurocentrism was thus not only in creating a global hierar-chy of knowledge divisions in terms of universal and particular but also to ensure that this episteme is diffused across the colonial space and through this process obfuscate an analysis of the principles organizing the transi-tion process across the colonized globe.

Partha Chatterjee (1997: 19) has reminded us that '... [T]here is no promised land of modernity outside the network of power' and one may add, outside its discourse. Modernity brought together for the once colo-nized two promises: the struggle for 'dreams of freedom' and, at the same time, the experience of being 'victims of modernity'; its episteme orga-nized both the 'desire for power' and the 'resistance of power'. No wonder the discussion on modernity in India has been steeped in ambiguity given colonialism's framing of modernity, as a discourse simultaneously of free-dom and of subjugation. Nationalism structured an understanding of being both unfree and free to change the world. In doing so, it now reconstructed the colonial binary in a new context, that of the nation-state. How did this ambiguity play itself out in context with the faming nationalist social sciences?

As in the case of many countries, and so was it in India, social science disciplines were moored in the project of nationalism. And because nationalism in India evolved into three different currents, we find similar trends also within social sciences. These were the modernists, the traditionalists and modern-traditionalists. (Parekh, 1995). There was little disagreement between the three on the causes of the nation's degeneration and decadence. All three agreed that these were related to colonialism, domination by the British, the extraction and control for imperialist purposes of India's rich material resources and the destruction of its vitality and ideas by the colonial elite. However, there were differences regarding the possible solutions.

The 'modernists' wanted India to identify with the future and with progress. They argued that the problem was with the past, with Indian culture which had made the 'Indian' people passive, lifeless and non-productive. They advocated the path set by Europe earlier and wanted India to have a new industrial economy, free from agrarian dependencies. It is no coincidence that these ideas became the source for building a new discipline of economics and helped to chart the knowledge regarding planning and developmental in independent India. This knowledge, we know, has rarely engaged with and most often been silent regarding the issues of pollution and purity as they structure and organize inequities in the country. It is in this silence that it continues to accept the 'colonial episteme'.

The modernist perspective was countered by the 'real traditionalists'. They argued for a need to draw out concepts and theories from the past – from that of India's rich histories and its civilization. Though this civilization had suffered a decline, it was essentially and fundamentally sound and was embodied with much strength. These strengths had kept the 'Indian' people together over centuries and these ideas will continue to bind them together in the future. The Indian society had a distinct character and history and had evolved in interaction with its people and its agencies. Indians and its social sciences needed to mobilize their society's creative resources for its regeneration without losing its coherence and inner balance. They also cautioned Indians not to imitate the West, take its language and its values. India has to work out its own salvation in its own terms – its temperaments, traditions and circumstances. This set of ideas framed sociological language in India and can be best seen in the work of G.S. Ghurye (1893–1983), the 'father' of Indian sociology, who was the Head of the Department of Sociology at the University of Bombay, for 35 long years and trained most of the next generation of sociologists in India.[2]

He used an Orientalist methodology to discuss indigenous concepts that organized Indian traditions: such as caste, tribe and family system and Hinduism3 (Patel, 2013a, 2013b). Even today, his theories are considered to have foundational implications for the study of Indian society. How did he understand civilization and how did this affect the sociological study of India?

For Ghurye, culture and civilization were understood as being the same: as a complex of ideas, beliefs, values and social practices (Upadhya, 2002: 44). His work rarely mentions any material practices. He eschews any discussion on livelihoods, control over resources or classes. Briefly, Ghurye argued that India was a civilization. He suggested that Indian civilization drew its unity from Hinduism and that Brahminism, and its ideas and values provided the core values of this Hindu civilization. Brahmins were considered 'natural' leaders, the torch bearers of this civilization and its 'moral guides'. As a result, sociology in India was initiated with the Orientalist idea that the territory of the nation state is equivalent with its culture.

Ghurye reproduced a design of Indian society as it was represented in Orientalist language.[4] Thus for him, Hindu civilization was structured around the caste system wherein if Brahmins were the most civilized, the tribals were the most backward. Other religious groups, such as Muslims, Zorastrians and Christians were deviants from this norm and needed to be assimilated into the Hindu fourfold system. The most difficult to assimilate would be the Muslims who were perceived to be separate from Hindus, in culture, ideas and values and who were responsible for the current social evils of India. Indian society was seen as a set of rules which all Hindus followed and Ghurye's understanding of law was based on a compendium of Hindu laws. No wonder Upadhya can state that

> Ghurye's sociology adopted almost wholesale the Orientalist vision of Indian society as a Vedic civilization and ultimately of the 'Aryan invasion'. And of Indian civilization as Hindu.... (Upadhya, 2002: 47)

The third trend, the 'modern-traditionalists' framed the ideas of syncretism. The goal of modern-traditionalists was to understand the present and construct a social science language best suited to bring in transformation of the specific culture that they were studying: India. Unlike the traditionalists, they did not advocate the necessity to go back to the golden age; some of them even suggested that democracy has indigenous moorings.

A focused critique to the traditionalist argument emerged in the work of the historian D.D. Kosambi,[5] who critiqued the Indological[6] assumption that India did not have a continuous history, that its history was a series of episodes, that the sources of this history can be located within the written texts rather than non-written sources and that culture and religion organize the unity of India's territory, rather than its diverse material and ecological experiences. He inaugurated a paradigm shift from colonial and nationalist frameworks and the centrality of dynastic history to a new framework integrating social and economic history that related the cultural dimensions of the past to these investigations. Kosambi's theories displaced the episteme of colonial modernity which coupled place/territory with cultural identity (India as civilization). This position together with his assertion that India had a long history allowed contemporary Marxists (henceforth) to wholly disregard the 'culturist' language that structured colonial and nationalist discourse.

For Kosambi, the history of ancient India cannot be extracted from texts written by 'Brahmins' and reconstructed during the colonial period as part of its project to codify 'ancient Indian civilization'. Rather what was needed was the use of combined methods inputting linguistics, archaeology, anthropology and sociology together in the perspective of the materialistic social theory of history (Thapar, 2008). Third, Marxism was thus seen as a tool to assess and understand the material and environmental history. It was not perceived as an all pervasive ideology or a positivist theory that structured the debates of historical sociology. Given the phenomenal diversity of India, Kosambi completely rejected any unilinear sequence of 'modes of production' and argued for the simultaneous presence of several modes of production at any given time in India's long history (Thapar, 2008).

Kosambi argues that this 'diversity' is part of a collective memory of the people of India. Oftentimes this is legitimized by using scriptures that elaborate theories of this 'diversity' and thereby allowed certain classes and the elite to relive these precepts as values and ideals. Instead, as a Marxist historian, he would argue that material conditions organizing ancient Indian civilization stagnated and died out, leaving only its 'culturist' memories in place. A society, according to Kosambi, is held together by bonds of production. The philosophic individual cannot reshape a mechanized world nearer to heart's desire by the 'eternal' ideologies developed over two thousand years ago in a bullock-cart country (Kosambi, 1956: xiii).

Following him historians of ancient India have tried to demystify the ways in which the past was constructed by Indologists and then used as political ideologies. Thapar (1989) argues that contemporary manifestation of Hinduism has not emphasized, first, the different premises that structured various religions in pre-colonial India. This implies that the Semitic model cannot be applied to India. Second, in the codification of religion, texts received preference over other sources of understanding the religious expressions. Third, these expressions can be seen in the diversity of rituals that expressed religion rather than in its manifestation as theological texts. Fourth, the variety of non-textual sources attest to the fact that these diverse rituals were part of the groups who practiced popular religion called Sramanism rather than Brahminism. And lastly, both these religious expressions changed over space and time as state consolidation took place differentially across the sub-continent, this unevenness and thus practices that became institutionalized as being diverse characterized the experience of religion within pre-colonial India.

The Politics of Travelling Theory

Till now, the paper has suggested that Eurocentrism was a 'episteme' that needed to be contested and indicated how one historian in India was able to displace its coloniality. However, Eurocentrism is not only an 'episteme', it is also a way to organize the production, distribution, consumption and reproduction of knowledge unequally across the different parts of the world. The Malaysian thinker Syed Hussein Alatas (1972) and the African philosopher, Paulin Hountondji (1997), have discussed these as the 'captive mind' and 'extraversion' (or externally oriented knowledge), respectively. They argue that the syndrome of 'captive mind' and 'extraversion' can be seen in the teaching and learning processes, in the way the curriculum and syllabi is framed; in the processes of research: the designing of research questions and in the methods and methodologies being used; in the formulation of criteria adopted for accepting articles for journals and books, and ultimately in defining what and where one publishes and what is academic excellence. The argument here is that the trenches of this 'episteme' are deep and layered. Thus, this 'episteme' cannot be merely replaced through cognitive supplants of concepts, theories and methods, which was what the best of nationalist social science attempted to do.

The consequence of this dependence has been the 'infantilization' of scientific practices within the Global South regions.[7] Not only are these at an incipient stage of growth but this very condition also encourages brain drain and further intellectual dependencies. Additionally, an intellectual culture defined by northern social science is held out as a model for the rest of the world. It is backed by the sheer size of its intellectual, human, physical, and capital resources together with the infrastructure that is necessary for its reproduction. This includes not only equipment, but also archives, libraries, publishing houses and journals; an evolution of a professional culture of intellectual commitment and engagement which connects the producers and consumers of knowledge; institutions such as universities and students having links with others based in northern nation-states and global knowledge production agencies. Farid Alatas has called this academic dependency.[8]

This is also the history of many newly independent countries such as Nigeria, Brazil or South Africa. Scholars have noted some positive outcomes of this strategy, e.g. the growth of a nationally oriented intellectual infrastructure which include not only universities, research institutes and laboratories, but also journals, publishing houses, together with professional norms and ethics. However, it has also promoted varied but uneven intellectual traditions within different nation states and its professional orientation is very limited. More importantly this strategy has not been able to question that Eurocentrism is an episteme. Institutionalization under the aegis of the elite nationalist orientation has reproduced practices in place across the Global North.

The question that we need to address is how do we confront it?

Present Challenges

Since the late 1970s and particularly after the 1990s, the dynamics of the world have changed. At one level, the world has contracted. It has opened up the possibilities of diverse kinds of trans-border flows and movements, of capital and labour and of signs and symbols, organized oftentimes in intersecting spatial circuits. It is no longer north to south, and space no longer encapsulates culture at all points of time. While in some contexts and moments these attributes cooperate, at other times, these are in conflict and contest each other. Thus, even though we all live in one global capitalist world with a dominant form of modernity, inequalities and hierarchies are increasing and so are fragmented identities. Lack of access to livelihoods, infrastructure, and political citizenship now blends with exclusions relating to cultural and group identity and are organized in varied spatial and temporal zones. Fluidity of identities and their continuous expression in unstable social manifestations and in new geographical regions demand a fresh perspective to assess and examine them. Not only do contemporary social processes, sociabilities and structures need to be perceived through new and novel spaces, prisms and perspectives but also it is increasingly clear that these need to be seen through new methodological protocols. As a consequence, should we not be in search of a new framework that moves beyond the 19th and early 20th century social science language and addresses the new challenges posed by contemporary processes?

Some social scientists have argued that the best way out of this epistemic and methodological difficulty is to particularize the universals of European thought. Dipesh Chakrabarty, the historian of subaltern studies, has made a similar argument. He coined a new methodology called, 'provincialization', and suggested that its quest was the following:

> To "provincialize" Europe was precisely to find out how and in what sense European ideas that were universal were also, at one and the same time, drawn from the very particular intellectual and historical traditions that could not claim universal validity. (Chakrabarty, 2008: xiii)

I would argue that we have to evolve a twofold strategy. On one hand, there is a need to deconstruct and provincialize Eurocentrism and make discrete its entanglements with casteist and patriarchal ideologies, imageries and dispositions in social science theories and practices. This is what Hountondji (1997) means when he advocates the need for endogenizing social science. Suggesting that all nationalist knowledge remain particularistic (he calls it 'ethnoscience') and thus part of the colonial and neo-colonial binaries of the universal-particular and the global-national, he presents a new alternative which he calls endogeneity. The latter appropriates and assimilates through a critical mind all international heritage available including the very process of scientific and technological innovation and then interfaces it with a critical assessment and re-appropriation of one's heritage recognizing its adaptability and creativity. 'This is not traditionalism, but the exact opposite' (Hountondji, 1995: 9).

Much the same is suggested by Enrique Dussel through his conception of 'transmodernity'. Dussel suggests a need for a new theory of modernity that simultaneously comprehends the dialectic of exploitation together with the epistemic subjugation and which excavates and builds new versions as these manifest themselves through an exterior reading of its history. 'Trans'-modernity affirms 'from without' the essential components of modernity's own excluded cultures in order to develop a new civilization for the 21st century. In the context of India, this perspective implies a necessity to explore not only the pre-modern but also the way colonialism and later nationalism mobilized Brahminical and patriarchal visions together with social science practices which absented an analysis of the same to assess organized inequities and exclusions since the late 19th century.

This implies secondly a need to go beyond the 'content' of the social sciences, that is the explanations they offer and the narratives they construct shaped as they are by a genealogy that is both European and colonial. Rather, we need to analyse their very 'form' that is, the concepts through which explanations become possible, including the very idea of what counts as an explanation. Obviously, it is not possible to suggest that the social sciences are purely and simply European and are, therefore, 'wrong'. Such an argument has little relevance given the fact that we are and remain within one world capitalist system. We cannot dispense with many of these categories, but it is important to recognize that they often provide only partial and oftentimes flawed understandings. We need not reinvent the wheel; however, there is a necessity to generate explanations that are relevant for different contexts.

Notes

1   This chapter is based on earlier published work. See Patel, 2006, 2007, 2010a, 2010b, 2010c, 2011a, 2011b, 2013a, 2013b.

2   Ghurye addresses the question of civilization in his Magnus opus, *Caste and Race in India* (1932).

3   The traditional nationalists suggested that India was a civilization and, thereby, borrowed and reinterpreted Orientalist knowledge to articulate an Indian version. The notion of civilization has a long history in Orientalism. In the late 18th and early 19th century, Orientalists generalized on the basis of the Greek and Egyptian civilizations. Later with the discovery of 'Indian' civilization, the study of India was absorbed into the existing discourse about antique civilizations. Early British Orientalists used Sanskrit texts to study this civilization and to place it within the linear theories of history. Some even argued that the high culture of Hindu civilization emerged from Greek influence. However, the traditional nationalists inverted this argument to suggest that Greek culture has learnt its science from India.

4   The chapter is, of course, not arguing that such discourses are limited to the theories of sociology in India and the integration of Orientalist thought with it. Ghurye's perspective may be resonated in other theories.

5   Kosambi (1907–1966) was a mathematician who was an historian by choice. Contemporary historians have argued that he has reframed Indian historiography (Gurukkal, 2008).

6   In India, Orientalist thought was defined as Indology, a field that laid out the theory and methodology of the study of language, religion and history of India's past through textual sources.

7   See the UNESCO report on the social science production in India, and Chatterjee (2003) on regional and Delhi-centric bias of Indian social science publishing.

8   Farid Alatas (2003) defines academic dependencies as having six attributes: (a) dependence on ideas; (b) dependence on the media of ideas; (c) dependence on the technology of education; (d) dependence on aid for research as well as teaching; (e) dependence on investment in education; and (f) dependence of Third World social scientists on demand in the West for their skills.

References

Amin, Samir (2008). *Eurocentrisism*. London: Zed Books.

Chatterjee, P. (1997). *Our Modernity*. Rotterdam/Dakar: Sephis Codesria Publication, pp. 1–20.

Chatterjee, P. (2003). Institutional Context of Social Science Research in India. *Economic and Political Weekly, 37*(35), 3604–3612.

Chakrabarty, D. (2008). *Provincializing Europe. Post-Colonial Thought and Historical Difference*. Princeton: Princeton University Press.

Dussel, E. (1993). Eurocentrism and Modernity. *Boundary, 2*(3), 65–76.

Dussel, E. (2000). Europe, Modernity and Eurocentrism. *Nepantla: Views from South, 1*(3), 465–478.

Dussel, E. (2002). World-System and 'Trans'-Modernity. *Nepantla: Views from South, 3*(2), 221–244.

Ghurye, G.S. (1932). *Caste and Race in India*. Bombay: Popular Prakashan.

Gurukkal, R. (2008). The Kosambi Effect. The Hermeneutic Turn that Shook Indian Historiography. [Special Issue, D.D. Kosambi. The Man and his Work]. *Economic and Political Weekly, 43*(30), 89–96.

Hountondji, P. (1995). Producing Knowledge in Africa Today. *African Studies Review, 38*(3), 1–10.

Hountondji, P. (1997). Introduction. In P. Hountondji (Ed.), *Endogenous Knowledge. Research Trails*. Dakar: Codesria, pp. 1–39.

Kosambi, D.D. (1956). *An Introduction to the Study of Indian History*. Bombay: Popular Prakashan.

Mignolo, Walter D. (2002). The Geopolitics of Knowledge and the Colonial Difference. *The South Atlantic Quarterly, 101*(1), 57–96.

Patel, S. (2006). Beyond Binaries. A Case for Self Reflexive Sociologies. *Current Sociology, 54*(3), 381–395.

Patel, S. (2007). Sociological Study of Religion: Colonial Modernity and Nineteenth Century Majoritarianism. *Economic and Political Weekly, 42*(13), 1089–1094.

Patel, S. (2010a). The Imperative and the Challenge of Diversity. Reconstructing Sociological Traditions in an Unequal World. In M. Burawoy et al. (Eds.), *Facing an Unequal World, Challenges for a Global Sociology (Vol. 1)*. Taiwan: Academia Sinica, 48–62.

Patel, S. (2010b). Sociology's 'Other'. *The Debate on European Universals in The Encyclopaedia of Life Support Systems* (Social Sciences and Humanities), UNESCO. Retrieved on 12 June 2014, from www.eolss.net/

Patel, S. (2010c). Introduction. Diversities of Sociological Traditions. In Sujata Patel (Ed.), *The ISA Handbook of Diverse Sociological Traditions*. London: SAGE Publications, pp. 1–18.

Patel, S. (2011a). Ruminating on Sociological Traditions in India. In S. Patel (Ed.), *Doing Sociology in India: Genealogies, Locations, and Practices*. New Delhi: Oxford University Press, pp. xi–xxxviii.

Patel, S. (2011b). Sociology in India: Trajectories and Challenges. *Contributions to Indian Sociology, 45*(3), 427–435.

Patel, S. (2013a). Orientalist-Eurocentric Framing of Sociology in India: A discussion on Three Twentieth Century Sociologists. *Political Power and Social Theory: A Research Annual*. Bingley. UK: Emerald Books, *25*, 107–130.

Patel, S. (2013b). Are the Theories of Multiple Modernities Eurocentric? The Problem of Colonialism and Its Knowledge(s). In S. Arjomand and E. Reis (Eds.), *Worlds of Difference*. London: SAGE Studies in International Sociology, pp. 28–45.

Parekh, B. (1995). Jawaharlal Nehru and the Crisis of Modernisation. In U. Baxi and B. Parekh (Eds.), *Crisis and Change in Contemporary India*. New Delhi: Sage Publications.

Quijano, A. (1993). Modernity, Identity, and Utopia in Latin America. *Boundary 2, 20*(3), 140–155.

Quijano, A. (2000). Coloniality of Power, Eurocentricism and Latin America. *Nepantla: Views from South, 1*, 553–800.

Quijano, A. (2007). Coloniality and Modernity/Rationality. *Cultural Studies, 21*(2–3), 168–178.

Sarkar, S. (1997). *The Many Worlds of Indian History in Writing Social History*. Delhi: Oxford University Press, pp. 1–49.

Thapar, R. (1989). Imagined Religious Communities? Ancient History and the Modern Search for a Hindu Identity. *Modern Asian Studies, 23*(2), 209–231.

Thapar, R. (2008). Early Indian History and the Legacy of D.D. Kosambi [Special Issue, D.D. Kosambi. The Man and his Work]. *Economic and Political Weekly, 43*(30), 43–51.

Upadhya, C. (2002). The Hindu Nationalist Sociology of G. S. Ghurye, *Sociological Bulletin*, 51 (1): 27–55.

Upadhya, C. (2007). The Idea of Indian Society: G.S. Ghurye and the Making of Indian Sociology. In P. Uberoi, N. Sundar and S. Deshpande (Eds.), *Anthropology in the East. Founders of Indian Sociology and Anthropology*. Delhi: Permanent Black, pp. 194–255.

Wallerstein, I. (1997). Eurocentrism and Its Avatars: The Dilemmas of Social Science. *New Left Review, 226*, 93–107.

Wallerstein, I. (2006). *European Universalism: The Rhetoric of Power*. London: New Press.

3

Modernity and the Violence of Global Accumulation: The Ethnic Question in China

Lin Chun

Introduction

The modern nation of People's Republic of China (PRC) has more or less inherited the Qing empire's geographic and demographic configurations. It is immensely diverse with 55 officially recognized, autonomous minority nationalities besides the Han majority, which constitute about 9 per cent of a national population of 1.35 billion people.[1] The PRC is, thus, a multiethnic, multicultural and quasi-federal state of 'one country, many worlds'. A conspicuous feature of these multiplicities is the coincidence of ethnic makeup and regional divisions mostly in west China, and of poorer and often naturally more resourceful hinterland being strategically critical by the nation's interior borders. Since such regions are either dominated by one ethno-religious group or shared by a constellation of several minority identities, in over half of the PRC territories 'ethnicity' and 'region' overlap, geographically as much as sociologically. Regional disparities, therefore, easily have an ethnic dimension or appearance, which can be deceptive and manipulated in a contentious identity politics.

There is a large, strong and variously controversial literature in the field. There is also a highly ideological global media oftentimes engaged in a fierce propaganda war not so much with Beijing's policies directly as with their misrepresentations by local actors, outside observers and Chinese officials themselves. The internationalisation of China's ethnic problems in an information age is not only an effect but also a causal factor in understanding the proliferation and explosion of antagonisms in Tibet and Xinjiang, the country's largest minority entities. In the larger background is the neoliberal phase of global integration, in which China has become a willing participant since the early 1990s.

This chapter aims at clarifying a few confusions in the relevant debates by addressing questions concerning the relationship between ethnicity and modernity. What explains the rise of cultural nationalism and worsening ethnic tensions in China in recent years, and the formation of a vicious circle of resistance and oppression? Why have certain institutional arrangements and policy decisions had more positive or negative results than others? How might the impacts of external agitation and domestic catalyses on ethnic relations be properly delineated and compared? Where could necessary repairs begin to redress the most serious and urgent problems? Is the advocacy, claimed to be in the interest of the whole nation of all nationalities, for departing from minority regional autonomy and ethnically based affirmative actions morally and practically sound? Pondering on these questions, the central argument will be threefold: that intensified ethnic strains are only symptomatic and part of China's general crisis of capitalist developmentalism; that relentless accumulation of capital in the name of modernisation threatens to destroy not only minority cultures and ethnic peace but also the entire edifice of socialist fundamentals required for achieving popular power and welfare across ethno-religious divisions; and that an alternative imaginary of modernity against the chimera of global and modern standardisation is both imperative and achievable as a matter of transformative politics.[2]

This analysis is set in its historical and theoretical contexts first. The next section then critically assesses the guidelines of communist revolution and post-revolutionary institutional arrangements and policy initiatives regarding minority rights and protection. The causes of their erosion leading to the present predicament are examined in the third section. The last section depicts missing links in a cul-de-sac framing of contentious politics and explains the focal point of a broad social movement that can unite sites of resistance. The chapter concludes that it is not modernity as such but the horrors of both capitalist polarisation and homogenisation that must be rejected.

Global Modernity and China's Lost Alternative

Is there such a thing as 'global modernity' based on capitalist globalisation and its ideological claim for integration – 'the world is flat'? Concerning its most superficial signification, so called global modernity is illusory in the face of the perpetuation of poverty and inequalities, dispossession and deprivation, wars and conflicts, as well as environmental disasters affecting the economically disadvantaged more severely. Such discrepancies are evident both within and without nations, and continue to spread transnationally. Trade and other privileges of rich countries are guarded to endure the quandary of unachieved 'surplus retention' in the poor ones. Within the poor countries, globalisation has enlarged rather than reduced income and other gaps. While any development seems now to be subordinated to market convergence, the process is one of extraction and profits, not equalising. Instead of integrating the peripheries, the global expansion of capital and its profit-making machines rather marginalise the marginal and deprive the deprived still further, creating new beneficiaries but also many more victims along the way. As capitalism keeps polarising and inflicting calamities upon societies and nature, the lack of minimal levelling reveals the deception of global modernisation.

Meanwhile, market greed does entail certain consumerist integration, which obliterates some indigenous ways of life. The latter could be of a more humane, less wasteful and ecologically better fitting character than those engendered by crude industrialisation and urbanisation. Culturally, while fetishism of money, market and private property together with electoral democracy (which is in a functional crisis the world over of representation and plutocracy) conquer the globe, wiping out non-confirming traditions, what modernity supposed to stand for in its enlightenment origin – freedom, rationality, secularism and progress – have certainly not. The overwhelming temporality of the modern ranks and controls spatially divided communities and localities, with time being 'the principal tool of power and domination' (Bauman, 2000: 9).

In a very different conceptualisation, 'global modernity' captures genuinely globalising tendencies without the arrogance and teleological message of 'globalisation'. It recognises commercial homogeneity as much as social disparities, underscoring the contradictions of modernity and their transnational and cross-regional universalisation (Dirlik, 2003). At issue is then not just Eurocentrism or modernity being generically parochial yet pretending to be universal. Nor is it merely about acknowledging 'the heterogeneity out of which this universalism is produced' (Mitchell, 2000: viii), as non-European sacrifices for and contributions to the constitution of the modern are extensively recorded as commonsense. That is, modernity has to be global from the outset. In the present conjuncture of world history, the most relevant question is rather if there remains any opening for a truly modern alternative to the existing model of 'imperial modernity' characterised by imperialist financial-military monopoly as well as discursive hegemony.

If modernity has become a heterogeneous global civilisation (Domingues, 2012), socialist modernity must still be a creative political ambition rather than a merely modern cultural variant. In other words, socialism is not about pluralising globality. It implies a negation of capitalism, not the west; and construction of a socially more desirable world, not preservation of national specificities – unless in concurrence with socialist preference. There is hardly any unified culture of any nation, certainly nothing of mythical Chineseness, in the first place. After all, the

singular capitalist modernity cannot be effectively countered by any particularistic alternatives; and the global nature of capitalism and its main
contradictions necessitate universality of any genuinely post-capitalist
project. Nothing less, and nothing of an ethnocentric disposition, can beat
a pervasive system of epochal dominance. This is then where the world-his-
torical significance of the communist revolution and socialist experiments
in China can be appreciated. The case of Chinese anti-imperialist and
anti-capitalist struggles is not among capitalism's local modifications or
'multiple modernities'; they instead have broken the ideological equitation
between modernity and capitalism, thereby redefining the modern. Taking
into account such attempts and their normative articulations in the modern
perspective as a move in both history and theory means an intellectual
undoing of not exactly Eurocentrism but capitalist centrism.

In stark contrast to crippled colonial modernity, China's 20th-century
revolutionary transformations enabled the country to rapidly modernise
its human and physical infrastructure through public investment and mass
mobilisation. Despite grave errors and limitations, the People's Republic
took the lead in the third world in meeting basic needs, poverty alleviation, life expectancy surge and educational attainment for both genders.[3]
The revolution's internationalist aspiration and intrinsic sympathy for
oppressed peoples also nurtured a united agency of all ethnicities in
building a new society. The moral commitment to fundamental ethnic
equality was a prerequisite for an institutionalised system of minority
regional autonomy and socialist nationality policies in the 1950s. Retreats
from that system in an age of *jiegui* (global integration) are among the
signs of capitalist triumph in China, where socialism has been tried,
advanced, and then more or less abandoned. The outcomes of this enormous loss are catastrophic, and even more acutely so for the national
minorities.

Minority Rights in Chinese Socialism: Commitment, Institutions and Policies

Traditionally, China's imperial rulers managed ethnic, religious and
regional diversities through a sophisticated mix of methods, from local
autonomy, integrated socialisation, political marriage and mutuality within
a tributary fold to various forms of repression. The governing crisis in late
Qing following the Opium Wars resulted in an increased distrust between
the Han and the Manchu ruling class as well as among other 'racial' communities as perceived at the time. Colonial exploitation and destruction
along with warlords and local bullies at home since the mid-19th century

deepened the crisis and wreaked more collides. Only in view of foreign and domestic imperialism and anti-imperialist movements can the evolving ethnic relations in modern China be adequately understood. The political formation of a modern *zhonghua minzu* or Chinese nation, and that of the Chinese nationals disregarding individual ethnicity as citizens with a common national identity, was a foremost outcome of collective struggles involving all the ethnic groups for national and social liberation. China's oppressed 'class' position in the global power structure has since been reversed,[4] bringing the country into the modern world as an equal with other nations. Consequently, national sovereignty makes every sense in a China baptised by an epic revolution which, in turn, has to be simultaneously nationalist and internationalist. Amalgamating the majority and minorities alike into a cohesive, sovereign 'Chinese people' as a supreme political entity and identity is a classical case of 'we the people' arising as a historical subject from great social revolutions. A core legacy of the Chinese revolution is thus also the unwavering insistence on national integrity and independence.

Concerning the status and rights of minorities, the PRC constitution promotes autonomy but forbids secession. In the earlier stages of the revolution, the communist party faithfully followed Marx to believe that 'no nation can be free if it oppresses other nations'.[5] One of the 'ten great demands' of the party was to 'unify China and recognise… [minority] national self-determination' (1928). The red regime in Jiangxi (1931–1934) emulated the Soviet model to pledge for the non-Han 'tolling masses' to 'have the right to determine for themselves' whether they wish to establish their own state, or join the socialist Chinese union, or form a self-governing unit inside the union (1931). Mao told Edgar Snow in 1939 that after revolutionary victory Tibet, Mongolia, Burma, Indo-China and Korea could become autonomous republics voluntarily attached to a Chinese confederation. The party formally envisioned a democratic 'federal republic based on the free union of all nationalities' in 1945. In power, the communists shifted their position on right to secede (Connor, 1984: 68, 74, 82–83; Yahuda, 2000: 27–30; Harding, 1993: 679).[6] The 1954 constitution makes it clear that the PRC is a unitary state (while utilising semi-federal organisations). Accordingly, 'acts which undermine the unity of the nationalities are prohibited'; and the 'national autonomous areas are inalienable parts of the PRC'. The hostile international and geopolitical conditions imposed on a new regime in need of consolidation and in fear of disunity only reinforced this stance.

One of the first tasks new China assigned to itself was to redress past wrongs of discrimination against minorities. To do so, the central and local governments dispatched to the minority regions hundreds of work teams to carry out a painstaking identification program for personal ethnic identities to be decided or differentiated at the grassroots. This work certainly had nothing to do with the familiar colonial technique of 'divide and rule', since it aimed at a policy framework in which historical injustice would be corrected to enable all the ethnic communities to flourish. The process turned out to be also an effort to rescue disappearing languages, cultures, artistic traditions, and quite a few tinier groups themselves. However artificial or excessive the project might have been with hindsight, it was necessary and instrumental for the socialist formulation of egalitarian policies.

None of the major constitutional amendments since has ever touched Article 4: 'All nationalities in the People's Republic of China are equal. The state protects the lawful rights and interests of the minority nationalities and upholds and develops a relationship of equality, unity and mutual assistance'. Minority rights stipulated in the constitution are ideologically and legally protected by the socialist mandate. A key concept of national cohesion is 'amalgamation' (*ronghe*) or mutual absorption as opposed to majority 'assimilation' (*tonghua*) (Dreyer, 1999: 591). Mao, more than any other leaders, stressed the need of fighting against Han chauvinism as a main danger over that of nationalist sentiments among the minorities (*On Ten Great Relationships,* 1956). Under these guidelines, five provincial level administrations of regional autonomy were established in the 1950s and 1960s – Inner Mongolia, Xinjiang, Hui, Zhuang and Tibet. They were supplemented by dozens of autonomous municipalities and prefectures and over a hundred of autonomous counties. This institutionalisation was pursued with great care, detailed designing and an understanding of administrative autonomy as essentially a regional rather than an ethnic concept. Such an understanding was due to mixed nationalities in affected regions and needed regional cooperation for the economically more underdeveloped ones to catch up.[7] In such multilayered jurisdictions, local governments via local people's congresses 'have the power to enact regulations on the exercise of autonomy and other separate regulations in accordance with the political, economic and cultural characteristics' of their localities (Articles 115 and 116). This innovative configuration of socialist semifederalism was intended to optimize coordinated authorities based on both autonomy and consensus, so as to achieve unity in diversity for common prosperity.

Also putting in place were policies of preferential treatment to enable the hindrances and victimisation of minorities under the old regimes to be overcome. The first test, for example, was that the minority communities should enjoy 'freedom to develop their spoken and written languages, to preserve or reform their traditions, customs and religious beliefs' (the Common Program 1949, Article 53). Indeed, until the 1980s 'great efforts were made to bring education to all the minority areas, and in some cases this meant first of all creating a written language which could serve as the basis for education' (Ferdinand, 1991: 241–242). Other provisions followed, such as easier access to financial assistance, more generous welfare subsidies, lower entry scores for university admission and exemption from the one-child policy implemented stringently among the Han since 1979 (Dreyer, 1976: 262–263; Goldstein and Beall, 1991; Sautman, 1998). These programs were so effective that they had 'encouraged Han people to marry into or otherwise seek to join these nationalities'.[8] To reduce regional disparities, the central government consistently and hugely invested in infrastructural upgrading in the poorer minority heartlands while sustaining a large scale of transfers of funds, technologies and experts from coastal provinces. A paternalistic overtone and unintended side effects notwithstanding, on balance neither 'dependent development' (to borrow a concept from the dependency theory) nor 'internal peripheralisation' was the case. As such, 'ethnic minorities are not only recognised as nationalities, but also are respected by public law and – according to this law – enjoy the same rights as the ethnic majority' (Heberer, 2000: 19). Substantial social gains could then be expected and confirmed by human development and overall inter-group peace (Bulag, 2000; He, 2005).

Remarkably, the socialist mandate on ethnic equality and solidarity is not formally repudiated in the post-socialist rhetoric and politics. However, the unprecedented crisis of ethnic relations in China must be traced to losing commitment on the part of the reform regime to the liberation of 'weak and small nationalities' in the revolutionary tradition that underlined previous successes. The Chinese story is one of capitalist conversion of modernisation that is morally bankrupt and practically responsible for this crisis as a most deplorable regress from egalitarian politics.

The Origins of Crisis: Region, Religion, Ethnicity and Class

'Reform and opening' since the late 1970s have transformed China's economic structure and social relations, as well as its ideological and regime character. The first reform decade lifted 400 million people out of abject poverty and began to raise the country's general living standards. After Tiananmen 1989, instead of addressing the emerging problems of corruption and waning social security which gave rise to the student movement, the second reform decade featured an all-out shift to market liberalisation.

The 'free market' moves were ironically pushed for by an authoritarian 'communist' state in awkward alliance with the neoliberal elites who had since been positioned at top levels of the party, government and legislature. Under popular pressure the third phase of reform into the 21st century saw both corrective social policies and continuation of privatisation. The direction of *jiegui* was not faltered but became bolder to eventually include also privatising the land and liberalising the financial sector. The more enriched the private and bureaucratic-comprador actors, the more politically dependent their vested interests would be. It is perfectly logical that market freedom and state tyranny can be compatible. Many well-connected capitalists are already communist party representatives and branch secretaries or deputies to the national and local people's congresses. The police force has long been deployed to handle not only violent resistance and political challengers but also ordinary petitioners, protestors and demonstrators.

Unable to shed its costly yet entrenched growth pattern, China has allowed 'cheap labour' to remain a symbol of its long departure from a workers' and peasants' state, causing also a profound ideological disorientation and social decay. Predictably, the normative values concerning ethnicity also deteriorate, making ethnic–regional relations ever harder to manage. Accompanying a decentralised economic geography of augmented local power and leverages, pluralism, transparency and responsiveness in governance tend to generally increase, aided by the rise of associational activism, internet and social media. But any trend of devolution, flexibility and bottom-up participation seems to have bypassed large areas of minority and frontier territories, where central control is tightened – the autonomous regions end up enjoying less autonomy. The gulf signified in this breakdown of autonomy is wide and deep between what policy makers consider necessary for interconnected regional and national interests and what is perceived locally. The latter is rather about illegitimate violation or ignorance of constitutionally and legally protected local rights and preferences.

How has China come to where it is? The intensity of its spatial politics today is attributable to a range of intervening variables. The historical and international backgrounds loom large, in which concerns for economic unevenness and national unity intertwine, buttressed by a duality of globalisation and nationalism. In particular, growth-centred marketisation in the minority regions has encouraged private businesses often run by the Han people and promoted exhaustive resource exploitation. The priority given to growth also entails toleration of inequalities as well as corruption; while economic benefits are thought to be compensable for religious restrictions. The joint effects have been inflamed confrontations and deadly riots in recent years. The blending of old socialist paternalism, new capitalist developmentalism and 'striking hard' (at times pre-emptively) campaigns against extremists may have reflected accumulated frustration and paranoia but is not working. The simple truth of 'the more oppression, the more resistance' (which the revolutionary communist generation should know better) is yet to be registered for China's political class. The grim lesson of Xinjiang becoming a hotbed of violence has yet to be learned. Incidents of Tibetan self-immolation or bloody unrests in Xinjiang must end, which however would not be achievable without a thorough going self-critical policy scrutiny. The far-sighted moral and political wisdoms needed for such a scrutiny are nowhere else attainable other than trusting and allowing honest criticisms while tapping into the egalitarian socialist legacies.

Take the external factors first. The colonial making and cold war continuation of the 'Tibet question' have involved direct British invasions and manoeuvre in the Himalayan region before the communist revolution, the CIA training and arming of Tibetan rebels after, and a growing Free Tibet lobby with considerable government backing of several major countries since the 1990s (Grunfeld, 1996: Chapters 5 and 8; Wang, 2011: 165–175; Conboy & Morrison, 2002). The 1951 Agreement for the peaceful liberation of Tibet signed between Beijing and Lhasa was followed by regional transformations before and after cultural revolutionary disruptions. The 'democratic reform' of 1959 targeted manorial land and 'feudal' relations of a theological serfdom; the economic reform since the 1980s like the rest of China, featured market opening and commercialisation (Goldstein, 1997). The gains and losses for the Tibetan people and their proud place in the PRC remain controversial, but none of the changes is explainable without considering outside catalyses. In particular, forces beyond the Chinese borders infuriated in the events of 1959 and propelled the Dalai Lama to flee, of which the lasting impact has turned out to be mainly negative.[9] Not only had his future potential collaboration been missed out, but his unavoidable denouncement was also a head-on contradiction to local mass opinion, which together meant a weighty element of coercion in the subsequent, otherwise valid social reforms in terms of equality and justice. The communist revolution, initially skipped Tibet, now must proceed to abolish large landholdings and replace an anachronistic theocracy. From a socialist point of view, even if class mobilisation was limited among the former serfs, the changes were liberating.[10] Yet the shadows of 1959 as an episode of a wounded history stayed. The economic reform, in contrast, was in many ways socially retreating. The newly generated problems kindled an unrelenting global orchestra played also by the Tibetan exiles and conducted in the west. However disconcerted it may be, the international cry over the Tibetan plight has become a formidable obstacle to the nonnegotiable Chinese position on an 'internally' forged solution as a matter of sovereignty. As the past two precious decades passed by, a generation of radicalised militants grew up to denounce non-violent means of promoting the Tibetan cause.

In Xinjiang, too, the militant separatist organisations cannot be shielded from external ties. They could also draw an array of reinforcements from spreading political Islam and a Central Asian realigning in the Soviet Union's disintegration and vast geopolitical aftermath. Meanwhile, as part of its global and Middle East strategy, the US 'war against terror' with an anti-Muslim overtone managed to get straight into the Chinese framing of security, which has nevertheless proven counterproductive for both countries. It looks as though the globalisation of local conflicts and internalisation of global ones feed each other to amplify effects at both ends.

Among domestic triggers, the first is inflow of Han, Hui and other settlers to Tibet and Xinjiang is first to consider. To be sure, spatial ramification of market transition in China is nowhere more visible than in the massive migration, short and long distances, often back and forth, as an everyday experience. But ethnic-specific population movements can be more disruptive when the redrawing of regional economic–demographic landscape induces resentment from the locals. If there was never a deliberate state policy of undermining Tibetan or Muslim domination and heritages in these regions, then an invasive market is doing the job most ruthlessly and effectively.[11] An immediate result is the ever tighter labour market for local job seekers. As committed government provision with minority quotas has diminished, discrimination against minorities becomes rife not only in the private but also public sector wherever the formal rules are ignored. As told in a news report, in the Kashgar prefecture in Xinjiang, where ethnic Uyghurs make up nearly 90 per cent of the population, for half of the positions recently advertised on the government's civil servant examination information website only native Mandarin speakers would be eligible. In 2011, 80 per cent of the 60,000 jobless graduates in Xinjiang were Uyghurs (Pai, 2012: 286). Important spots in state agencies are regularly filled by people from other regions, and many local workers are frozen out of the gas and oil industry built on the treasured local resources.[12] What initiated in market spontaneity has mutated into institutionalised social exclusion.

Apart from employment hurdles, there is also the fear of losing one's cultural traditions or identities. An inadvertent upshot of the language barrier to job opportunities is that the constitutionally required minority language education is compromised when majority assimilation appears to be practically inescapable. The bilingual education initiated in 2000 intended to help minority groups to cope with the market was quickly deformed into mandatory Mandarin in nearly all the subjects being taught in many regional schools, putting local languages at an utter disadvantage. This is viewed by some as a sign of 'desertification' of once flourishing, officially promoted and legally protected minority cultures, if not the beginning of their extinction.[13] As the state cannot decisively modernise religious societies, market modernisation only signals a horrifying prospect of commercial homogenisation. It is the market that could be the ultimate path towards a 'cultural genocide' if the state fails to step in (Sautman, 2006). Equally alarming is not only a growing antipathy between Uyghur and Han communities but also their physical segregation of residential quarters in the ethnically mixed areas in Xinjiang. Cross-boundary communications are ever more bitter and difficult, making communal tensions prone to outbreaks of violence (Palme, 2013). The collapse of the old socialist rules and codes in extreme cases sees Muslim scarf, clothing and symbols being arbitrarily banned by local governments through such impositions as self-criticism sessions, fining and depriving social benefit entitlement. The return of unchecked Han chauvinism also led to a demonised Uyghur image, permitting discriminative practices at the points from hiring and business licensing to hotel and airport check-ins.[14]

Thirdly, within the broader conditions of widening socioeconomic inequalities, both causal and consequential of decreased participation from ethnic minorities in the urban workforce is their political marginalisation. By law and in the nature of autonomy, 70 per cent of regional and lower level administrators should be from the local ethnic groups. Yet in reality the Han now regularly outnumber non-Han cadres especially in more responsible positions (e.g., the party secretary). Moreover, minority nationalities are seriously under-represented in the national legislative and governmental bodies, and their members take far fewer leading posts than before the economic reform. The army and police are also grossly disproportional in their ethnic compositions. The lack of badly needed, democratically spirited consultation and conversation between the centre (along with its regional appointees) and locally rooted leaders and intellectuals fortifies a dwindling mutual trust. The latter's allegedly diminishing civic loyalty to the Chinese nation then rationalises an overestimation of, and, and excesses in handling, 'separatist' tendencies (Toxti, 2013).

The fourth expression of the present crisis is the spectacular upsurge of religion in a traditionally secular civilisation (aside from Confucianism or

Taoism and other churchless philosophical schools) reinforced also by communist atheism. The movements that have drawn tens of millions followers for Christianity, Catholicism and the more orthodox sects of Buddhism is phenomenal. As commonly noted it is in part a response to the ideological and moral erosion brought about by market transition. The phenomenon has a manifested class dimension: religious fervour grows faster and stronger when conjoined by poverty and despair, as happened in the poorer counties in southern Xinjiang and Tibetan inhabited central-west provincial peripheries.[15] But there is also a direct state contribution, contrary to the common impression of China's formal religious policies (Leung, 2005). In Tibet, Xinjiang and Inner Mongolia, with huge public funds overwhelming private donations, monasteries and temples have been massively and in many cases lavishly built or rebuilt since the 1980s. Monks and priests were recruited in record numbers.[16] Rather than reducing any religious sentiment or resistance on the ground, quite a few of these monasteries serve as safe heavens for political networking and sabotage. If the dynamics of globalization 'allowed temples to become nodes along horizontal networks linking local communities and identities to transnational flows of capital, people, and memory' (Goossaert & Palmer, 2011: 242), the post-socialist Chinese state is doubtlessly its largest agent. In the same vein, the simultaneity of religious resurgence and market secularisation is no paradox, fashioning forms of 'religion for profit' not least in temple and church management and tourism. As market values permeated religious ideas, artefacts and rituals, orientalist – western, Chinese or nativist – productions of religiously identified 'ethnicity', 'locality', and 'culture' abound.[17]

Finally, in the broad socioeconomic arena, single-minded developmentalism is blamable for damaged ethnic relations. On the national stage, allocating budgetary, technological and other resources in the minority regions continues to be firmly the case; and in principle the Chinese economic and administrative structure can accommodate a system of central management embracing decentralised market mechanisms to more or less redeem developmental unevenness. Accordingly, from poverty alleviation and tax breaks to preferential quotas and multi-provincially coordinated training schemes (for cadres, technicians, skilled workers, doctors and teachers), prioritised programs for minority development are still in full swing. At the same time of national largesse being poured into the poorer, multiethnic western regions, however, a superstitious developmentalist impel overpowers spatial-cultural sensibilities. Disregarded are not only the likely social and eco-environmental costs of an unsustainable growth pattern, but also its social injuries and political risks. That participants in the 2008 Lhasa riot included rural migrants without stable jobs is an example in point (Hu & Salazar, 2008: 18–21). So is anger over the massive exploration of Xinjiang's natural resources without substantial local sharing in productive, distributive and investment decisions. Urumqi has meanwhile become one of China's most polluted municipals.

As noted, inequalities in whatever guises are not ethnic specific in China's reforms. But market pathologies do seem to upset more lethally in the minority regions. Researches find that forms of seemingly ethnically related economic imparity are often not actually due to ethnic identities but rather differences in levels of education, residential locations and so on. Ethnicity is by and large not directly correlated with income and life chances in China.[18] The commodification of land, labour, and people themselves; the hardship involved in migration, low-graded and low-paid jobs, or joblessness; regional and sectoral disparities; class polarisation; corruption and other abuses of power; land shortage, urbanisation squeezing and pollution are common factors across the whole country. They could nevertheless all have an ethnic face. Worse still, the repudiation of class politics without a rigorous defence of the communist revolution's most popular achievements has inevitably resulted in demoralisation of non-Han party members and socialism's traditional local supporters. This redrawing of political landscape required by a capitalist modernisation has paved the way for a contentious identity politics that ethnicises or essentialises ethnicity and religion in interpreting social relations.

The Politics of Contestation: Which Modernisation? Whose Choice?

The argument that ethnic and religious problems are rooted in social ills, that they are only part of China's general post-socialist crisis, and that state-sponsored neoliberal globalisation is behind the present impasse of ethnic relations amounts to a depiction of an identity crisis of the People's Republic itself. Having retreated so radically from its founding ideas the regime faces an acute internal challenge to its ruling legitimacy. Restoring trust between the party and people seems a daunting task. The situation, however, should not be beyond repair, given the socialist path dependency in both policy debates and popular contestation traversing nationalities and regions. The point is thus indivisibility of socialism and nationalism in any credible political articulation of China's ethnic question. Presupposing spatial and temporal pluralities, the PRC state must carry with it a sacred duty of securing sovereignty and unity while enhancing social cohesion and ethnic harmony. Its trajectory of revolutionary modernity makes national integrity not only a nationalist but also a socialist mission, as mighty as defending and completing the revolution being ultimately measured by defeating capitalism and imperialism. This conviction obliged the people's liberation army to cross the *Yangzi* and march into all corners of the country then; and still inspires popular obsession with China's sovereign integrity and global equal status now. However, the vanishing ambitions of socialist egalitarianism and proletarian internationalism, and degradation of the Chinese people and labour as the 'master of society', entail neglected or damaged ethnic solidarity. These degenerations make official Chinese nationalist claims unappealing without their historically constituted social substance.

Any remedy can only begin with bringing the people – in its multinational and multicultural makeup – back in, drawing critical lessons from both socialist and post-socialist transformations. Without such a democratic agenda categorically different from a 'political reform' to match and facilitate further capitalist subordination, neither ethnic nor wider social crises would resolve. Indeed, the socialist towering order is not just about managing multiethnicity but its celebration within a greater union of shared social goals and common citizenship. As splendidly demonstrated in new China, minority communities can succeed socioeconomically as much as culturally and politically in beneficial and confident linkages with overall national development. The fact that the notions of equal nationalities and regional autonomy in China have survived an otherwise diluted ideology in contrast with the disintegrated Soviet bloc speaks volumes of the legitimation depth of the Chinese revolution. Only by honouring its modern revolutionary origin and subsequent social contracts would China and its central and local governments be able to correct those policies and approaches which contradict their own objectives.

Lacking this awareness of a missing socialist foundation, the well-intended and high-profile proposal for a 'second generation' of ethnicity policies seems misconceived (Leibold, 2012). It holds that affirmative actions in the market conditions do not actually benefit the needy, and that the established policies, regulations and languages are liable to antagonism by solidifying ethnic differences and consciousness. Partly blamable is the terminology of 'nationality' itself, which is viewed as conceptually inaccurate and politically detrimental while functioning to instigate or strengthen cultural nationalism. De-ethnicisation is therefore called for, believed to be doable through economic regional balancing and a phasing out of existing arrangements since the 1950s. But even if theoretically ethnic divisions can wither away, the requisite of general equality is unfortunately not there. Reversing the socialist convention could then be confusing, offensive, and politically disastrous. A correct diagnosis and prescription should instead respect the historical evidence of the overall efficacy of normative socialist principles, institutions and policies concerning minority rights and protection. Also to be recognised is that the old scars from past wrongs or more recent 'autonomous deficits' are yet to heal. Responsible for today's crisis is not the persistence of socialist management but its corrosion. This is not to deny that there could be a few undue identity-based entitlements, and certain policy vocabularies might be in need of fine tuning. 'Diversity in unity' conditioned on equality, autonomy and solidarity is an unfinished project to be fulfilled. Abandoning it in favour of 'unity over diversity' would end up attaining neither.

Paradoxically, as market transition tears apart organic social tissues while fostering a culture of greed, fear, dissonance and public apathy, contentious politics in the nature of Polanyian social self-defence is bound to ascend. Such a resistant movement in a post-socialist environment could catalyse the formation of a non-sectarian social power in defiance of atomised diversities and inequality induced fragmentation. The dilemma of modernity for ethnic-religious distinctions could be acute but superficial,[19] if modernisation and capitalism can be duly decoupled to undercut a teleological 'world time' ignorant of not only multiple but also alternative temporalities. Two additional observations follow. First, capitalist modernity, even if materially feasible, will still never win over the hearts and souls (as Marx puts it) in its geo-economic and cultural peripheries. Reorienting development is needed functionally to deter local conflicts as much as influence from foreign agitation, but it is also a fundamental requisite. Second, modernisation does not have to be tied to ruthless and endless expansion of capital, and can thus become an intrinsic want of the peoples and communities themselves in their collective subjectivity. The violence of modernity can be transcended.

Challenging capitalism's false universality and true monopoly over global accumulation and standardised industrialism, urbanism, private property and market supremacy, the remaking of the modern is feasible by relinking modernity with socialism. A corresponding epistemological paradigm shift is overdue in a country where capitalist standardisation is incomplete in the first place. In the end, a popularly participatory socialist reconstruction would be the only contour for China's ethnic minorities to modernise; and they certainly have the moral right and institutional means to do so in their own interest, terms, pace and rhythms as a matter of self-determination.

Notes

1   The notion of 'nationality' is considered by some scholars as conceptually confusing and politically unwise: its linguistic affinity with 'nation' encourages nationalist feelings among the minorities (Ma, 2012a). In disagreement, I see the usage as legitimate in its

modern and revolutionary historical context. 'Nationality' and 'ethnicity' in this chapter are mostly interchangeable unless otherwise specified. On the Chinese adaption of the language from the Soviet Union, see Connor (1984) and Ma (2007). For the Euro-genetic notion of 'nation' being itself questionable in the Chinese context see Wang (2011: Chapter 2).

2   Revolutionary and socialist modernity as a political rather than cultural and thus universalist alternative to late capitalism is discussed in Lin (2006: Chapter1; 2013: Chapters 2 and 8). My conception of 'alternative modernity' differs from that of 'multiple modernities' premised on a paradigmatic modernity modifiable only locally as cultural variations.

3   See UNDP's annual Human Development Reports. For long-run index tables 1950–2000; see Crafts (2002). Comparisons between China and India are most telling; see Sen (2011); Dreze and Sen (2002).

4   Ernest Gellner observes that 'only when a nation became a class... did it become politically conscious and activist... [as] a nation-for-itself' (1983: 12).

5   Addressing the Irish question Marx warns that 'the English working class will never accomplish anything until it had got rid of Ireland'. Lenin in 'The right of nations to self-determination' (1914) reconfirms this position. See Chauhan (1976: 101–112).

6   Relevant original documents are collected in Brandt, Schwartz and Fairbank (1967).

7   Zhou Enlai explains these considerations with superb clarity, as quoted in Wang Hui (2011: 179–187). The Xinjiang Autonomous Region, for example, is home to 47 mostly Muslim communities with a Uyghur majority alongside the Han.

8   Between 1982 and 1990, for instance, the Hui population grew by 19 per cent in eight years (Goossaert & Palmer, 2011: 375). Thomas Heberer notes that the proportion of China's minority population grew from 6.1 per cent in 1953 to 9 per cent in 1995: a few groups doubled, tripled or times more in size (2000: 3). By 2005, the population of the Tibetan Autonomous Region (TAR) had grown 15.6 per cent, of which the Tibetans accounted for 11.3 per cent, as compared with the national average of 5.9 per cent (Ma, 2012b: 68).

9   The events also helped Dalai Lama's ascendance from being the spiritual leader of Gelugpa lineage to a supreme status in the hierarchy of whole Tibetan Buddhism. Standing for non-violence and genuine autonomy within the PRC, he confirmed his position in an interview with BBC as recent as on 24 June 2012. Remembering fondly his 'very good relationship' with Mao, like father and son, he recounted his attraction to the Marxist idea of equal distribution. www.ibtimes.com/dalai-lama-says-mao-considered-him-son-recalls-his-attraction-communism-704140

10   The party's inconsistent tactics between an 'untied front' with the Tibetan elites and class struggle from below in the post-1951 decades caused confusions among the former serfs and lower social strata in the new regime's power base. This in turn also limited the separation of religion and politics as a modern marker in the region.

11   According to the 1990 and 2000 Chinese censuses, the Han population in TAR rose from 3.68 per cent to 5.9 per cent in those ten years, which 'do not point to any mass influx of Han' (Mackerras, 2010: 233). The figure rapidly increased afterwards, with the settlers concentrated in Lhasa as temporary or long term residents, making the city's Han/Hui component a much higher proportion.

12   Among many examples, see Andrew Jacobs 'Uighurs in China say bias is growing', *New York Times*, 9 Oct. 2013 and stories reported by Gabriele Battaglia in 'Creaks in western China's door to Asia', *Asia Times*, 24 Oct.

13   Concerning Tibetan culture, Colin Mackerras observes that despite some decline the Tibetan language was 'in absolutely no danger of dying out' (2010: 234). The fear,

however, is real. In urban Xinjiang, the ignorance of Uyghur traditions and literature among the younger generation is an increasing concern.

14   Cf. Hastings (2011). David Tobin points out that the security quandary in Xinjiang might be solvable only if local grievance can be addressed 'beyond relying on lazy essentialisations of Islam' ('The Tiananmen attack and China's insecurity problem,' *Beijing Cream: a dollop of China*, 1 November 2013, http://beijingcream.com/2013/11/the-tiananmen-attack-and-chinas-insecurity-problem/).

15   Marx's critical sympathy is accurately resonant: '*Religious* suffering is, at one and the same time, the *expression* of real suffering and a *protest* against real suffering. Religion is the sigh of the oppressed creature, the heart of a heartless world, and the soul of soulless conditions'. In this sense, it is 'the opium of the people' ('A contribution to the critique of Hegel's philosophy of right,' 1843, www.marxists.org/archive/marx/works/1843/critique-hpr/intro.htm).

16   An economically pressing issue, especially in Tibet, is how a disproportionately large group of unproductive monks might be sustained without government subsidies. Cf. Goossaert and Palmer (2011: 362).

17   For a critique of Orientalism under the rubric of 'depoliticisation', see Wang (2011: 153, 194–209).

18   See Ma (2012b: 286–287). An observer puts it bluntly concerning the case of Tibet: 'There is no systematic discrimination of Tibetans by employers. The labour market operates according to market principles and the most skilled people are getting the jobs regardless of ethnicity' (Ben Hillman, 2008).

19   The secular segments within religious societies are faced with a perplexity between modernisation and Han-assimilation, superficially mirroring the ambiguities of the Chinese reformers at the turn of the 20th century confronted with a modern yet imperialist west. If history is of any guide, the earlier though limited success of revolutionary and socialist modernity in a few multiethnic and (semi-) federal socialist countries indicates the viability of modernisation not sacrificing but boosting autonomy.

References

Bauman, Z. (2000). *Liquid Modernity*. Cambridge: Polity Press.

Brandt, C., Schwartz B. and Fairbank, J.K. (Eds.) (1967). *A Documentary History of Chinese Communism*. New York: Atheneum.

Bulag, U. (2000). Ethnic Resistance with Socialist Characteristics. In E. Perry and M. Selden (Eds.), *Chinese Society: Change, Conflict and Resistance*. London and New York: Routledge.

Chauhan, S. (1976). *Nationalities Question in USA and USSR*. New Delhi: Sterling.

Conboy, K. and Morrison J. (2002), *The CIA's Secret War in Tibet*. Lawrence: Kansas University Press.

Connor, W. (1984). *The National Question in Marxist–Leninist Theory and Strategy*. Princeton: Princeton University Press.

Crafts, N. (2002). The Human Development Index, 1870–1999: Some Revised Estimates. *European Review of Economic History*, 6(3), 395–405.

Dirlik, A. (2003). Global modernity? *European Journal of Social Theory*, 6(3), 275–292.

Domingues, J.M. (2012). *Global Modernity, Development, and Contemporary Civilisation: Towards a Renewal of Critical Theory.* New York: Routledge.

Dreyer, J. (1976). *China's Forty Millions: Minority Nationalities and National Integration in the PRC* (Harvard East Asian Series, 87). Cambridge, MA: Harvard University Press.

Dreyer, J. (1999). China, the Monocultural Paradigm. *Orbis*, *43*(4), 581–597.

Dreze, J. and Sen, A. (2002). India in Comparative Perspective'; 'India and China'. In *India: Development and Participation*. Oxford: Oxford University Press.

Ferdinand, P. (1991). *Communist Regimes in Comparative Perspective: The Evolution of the Soviet, Chinese and Yugoslav Systems*. London: Harvester Wheatsheaf.

Gellner, E. (1983). *Nations and Nationalism*. Oxford: Blackwell.

Goldstein, M. and Cynthia B. (1991). China's Birth Control Policy in the Tibet Autonomous Region: Myths and Realities. *Asian Survey*, *31*(3), 285–303.

Goldstein, M. (1997). *The Snow Lion and the Dragon: China, Tibet, and the Dalai Lama*. Berkeley: University of California Press.

Goossaert, V. and Palmer D. (2011). *The Religious Question in Modern China*. Chicago: University of Chicago Press.

Grunfeld, A.T. (1996). *The Making of Modern Tibet*. Armonk, NY: East Gate Books.

Harding, H. (1993). The Concept of 'Greater China': Themes, Variations and Reservations. *China Quarterly*, *136*, 660–686.

Hastings, J. (2011). Charting the Course of Uyghur Unrest. *China Quarterly*, *208*, 893–912.

He, B. (2005). Minority Rights with Chinese Characteristics. In W. Kymlicka and B. He (Eds.), *Multiculturalism in Asia*. Oxford: Oxford University Press, pp. 56–79.

Heberer, T. (2000). Some Considerations on China's Minorities in the 21st Century: Conflict or Conciliation. Duisburg Working Papers on East Asian Studies 31/2000. Retrieved on 13 June, 2014 from http://ir.minpaku.ac.jp/dspace/bitstream/10502/1755/1/SER50_002.pdf

Hillman, B. (2008). Money Can't Buy Tibetans' Love. *Far Eastern Economic Review*, *171*(3), 10.

Hu, Xiaojiang and Salazar M. (2008). Ethnicity, Rurality and Status: Hukou and the Institutional and Cultural Determinants of Social Status in Tibet. *The China Journal*, *60*(July), 1–21.

Leibold, J. (2012). Toward a Second Generation of Ethnic Policies? *China Brief*, *12*(13).

Leung, B.L. (2005). China's Religious Freedom Policy: The Art of Managing Religious Activity. *China Quarterly*, *184*, 894–913.

Lin, C. (2006). *The Transformation of Chinese Socialism*. Durham, NC: Duke University Press.

Lin, C. (2013). *China and Global Capitalism: Reflections on Marxism, History, and Contemporary Politics*. London and New York: Palgrave Macmillan.

Ma, R. (2007). A New Perspective in Guiding Ethnic Relations in the 21st Century: 'Depoliticisation' of Ethnicity in China. *Discussion Paper 21*, University of Nottingham.

Ma, R. (2012a). How to Understand 'Nation' and 'The Chinese Nation'. *Journal of South-Central University for Nationalities*, *5*, 1–12.

Ma, R. (2012b). *Social Development and Ethnic Relations in Chinese Minority Regions*. Beijing: Social Science Academic Publisher.

Mackerras, C. (2010). Tibetans, Uyghurs, and multinationa 'China'. In P.H. Gries and S. Rosen (Eds.), *Chinese Politics: State, Society and the Market*. London and New York: Routledge.

Mitchell, T. (2000). *Questions of Modernity*. Minneapolis, MN: University of Minnesota Press.

Pai, Hsiao-Hung (2012). *Scattered Sand: The Story of China's Rural Migrants*. London: Verso.

Palme, J. (2013). Blood, Fear and Hip-Hop in Xinjiang. *China Digital Times*, 27 September. Retrieved on 13 June, 2014 from http://chinadigitaltimes.net/2013/09/blood-fear-hip-hop-xinjiang/

Sautman, B. (1998). Preferential Policies for Ethnic Minorities in China: The Case of Xinjiang. In W. Safran (Ed.), *Nationalism and Ethno-Regional Identities in China*. London: Frank Cass.

Sautman, B. (2006). Tibet and The (Mis)Representation of Cultural Genocide. In B. Sautman (Ed.), *Cultural Genocide and Asian State Peripheries*. London: Palgrave.

Sen, A. (2011). Quality of Life: India vs. China. *New York Review of Books*, 12 May.

Toxti, I. (2013). Why Have the Uyghurs Felt Defeated. Interview. Retrieved on 13 June, 2014 from www.chinese.rfi.fr/node/132196

Wang, H. (2007). The Politics of Imagining *Asia*: A Genealogical Analysis. *Inter-Asia Cultural Studies*, 8(1), 1–33.

Wang, H. (2011). *The Politics of Imagining Asia*. Cambridge, MA: Harvard University Press.

Yahuda, M. (2000). The Changing Faces of Chinese Nationalism: The Dimensions of Statehood. In M. Leifer (Ed.), *Asian Nationalism*. London: Routledge, pp. 21–37.

4

Demystifying Modernity: In Defence of a Singular and Normative Ideal

G Aloysius

The Context

If Social Sciences had emerged with and in the course of transition to modernity – a series of massive structural, cultural and discursive changes – the question of modernity itself – its nature, characteristics and implications – has been the main pre-occupation of the social scientists. This has not changed even after the rise of many and varied forms of primordialism everywhere recently and the emergence of post-modernism in Europe. In fact, these two somewhat related tendencies have only intensified and broadened the investigations on modernity. Grasping the nature of modernity not only appears to be interesting and important in itself, but it also seems necessary to understand the whole range of socio-political questions of contemporary times.

If one is to identify a single characteristic common to almost all serious readings of modernity, it is certainly that of 'ambiguity'. Modernity is seen as a double-edged, Janus-like, almost seductive and also tragic combination of the good and bad, not only liberating but also ensnaring. This ambiguity to which the classicists themselves were sensitive, gradually wore off and modernity came to be read increasingly in pejorative terms and in one influential reading resulted in post-modernity. But a parallel reading, while not being insensitive to the negative dimensions of modernity, insisted on seeing in it something indispensable, precious and non-negotiable, and found enough reasons for continuous though tortuous engagement with it.

Elsewhere, the response to modernity has been ranging from a wholesale rejection to equally indiscriminate submission to what was mostly perceived as 'Westernity'. Ideologically, often also academically, modernity was identified as Westernity and accordingly rejected or criticised as an imposition from without. In practice, however, the scenario was, more often than not, the mirror opposite. For, when some form or other of 'modernisation' could not be avoided as the agenda of the new states, the rhetoric of nativism/traditionalism or anti-modernity gave way to a more nuanced argument: Modernity need not be singular *ala* the Western model, each society works out its own model of modernity; one need not therefore be judgemental about other peoples' modernity or apologetic either, of one's own. Accordingly, we have here, alternative, multiple and regional modernities (Gaonkar, 2001). We have even 'our own modernity' apparently pre-empting and foreclosing all critical reflections on it (Chatterjee, 1997).

If the Western reading is caught up in the 'paradox' of modernity and unable to confront the challenges of 'post-modernism', it is largely because of its inability to pinpoint the nature of the core and indispensable minimum of the phenomenon; for, too many things and processes of peripheral, subsidiary, instrumental or consequential nature have been posited as constituting modernity. The same problem, however, could be said to plague, though with different implications, the non-Western responses to modernity. Here, modernity is identified as suggested above, with so many of the socially alien, hence, culturally undesirable. Identifying the core minimum, the unavoidable, precious and non-negotiable, of modernity would hopefully show first of all, the root cause of its apparent paradox, and, secondly, the phenomenon as culturally less specific/alien, and may also remove the self-justificatory tones of the more recent and plural formulations. The search in this tentative attempt then, is unabashedly for a singular, minimal and normative modernity which would not be specifically Western but truly global. While the specific context from which this attempt is made, are the discursive problems of contemporary South Asia, it is hoped it would shed some light on the theme and search for global modernity and also make space for comprehending most forms of social protestation.

Modernity: Singular and Normative

Modernity as the Meaning and Measure of Enlightenment

The philosophical inspiration behind modernity is rightly said to be the Enlightenment – a complex constellation of ideas and practices. However, it is customary to quote the magisterial statement of Immanuel Kant on the issue – 'Man's emergence from his self-imposed tutelage'. Such a reading is truly philosophical, a summary statement of the writings of the encyclopaedists and others of the period. The 'self-imposed tutelage' spoken of here refers to the subject condition of humanity to the belief in and submission to the transcendental reality. However, it is truly said that the tutelage is self-imposed, but only perceived (falsely) as from above. If the emergence is viewed as merely moving out of such falsity, then by implication, must be limited to the metaphysical and epistemological realms, but as such insufficient to explain the enormous changes that have resulted in the existential lives of the masses. Such an explanation further would be an *explanation from above/without* with all its attendant limitations. The true significance as well as substance of the self-imposed nature of the tutelage has to be then sought, not vertically in the sphere of the alleged supernatural, but horizontally in that of the concrete social and societal relations projected as the reflection or consequence of the former. The social and societal relations of the period of self-imposed tutelage had a specific characteristic, and that was *hierarchical*, presumably reflecting and reproducing the heavenly. The realisation that the heavenly has ceased to exist or does not matter anymore was indeed significant for the philosophers, but for the mass of people, the revolution that this realisation brought about in their *social relations* is the most important thing in grasping the nature of modernity. Replacement of the divine with the human, that is, man becoming the centre of the universe is the self-same process by which he also came to be seen and interpreted as a different sort of man.

Much too long and often, the Enlightenment has been interpreted in the terms and categories solely of the philosophers. It is time to come down from the clouds. The Enlightenment, even in the philosopher's interpretation, triggered off a social revolution which cannot be explained within it. Emergence of man in modernity would then mean the emergence of a new philosophy of social–relational man, who could not emerge hitherto because of his self-imposed, but falsely perceived as other-imposed tutelage. The removal of the self-imposed tutelage directly resulted not merely in a new intellectual understanding but a new social being. If this is to be true, a sociological re-formulation of the answer to the question, 'What is enlightenment?' could be summarised thus: Men are born differently under different circumstances of birth, but such ascriptive differences are of no consequence, because the humans are all of the same essence and as such entitled to be treated as of equal worth, respect and dignity. This indeed is the Enlightenment transition from the pre-enlightenment position that if men are born differently under different circumstances and with different characteristics, these differences do matter, they are divinely ordained, they indicate their differential inner worth and, hence, they ought to be differentially positioned and treated in society. Emergence of man from self-imposed tutelage, that is, freedom from the supernatural, the other-centredness or other-determination, etc., sociologically means, the transition from an understanding that religion-legitimated ascriptive differences among men being significant to an understanding that such differences do not matter and that all persons are *free and equal*. This in effect is the sociologically significant core philosophy of Enlightenment, also a normative inspiration behind the project of modernity.

Modernity as Universalist Ethics

The same philosopher, who gave us the most influential reading of Enlightenment, when it came to converting it to a social–ethical principle, gave us a more precise and definitive answer to the problem of modernity. That his various formulations of what he termed as categorical *imperative*, could easily be interpreted as the absolutely minimal and normative essence of modernity, has gone by and large unregistered in critical–social consciousness (Sullivan, 1989). Interpreted for our purpose here, the different formulations seek to unify three abstract notions which have become the conceptual pillars of modernity – Universality, Equality and Rationality. In a philosophical sense, these three abstract notions express one and the same essence of human sociality. Combinations of these notions in differential proportions could be deployed to explain the different aspects of modernity. However, where the issue is the explanation of modern social behaviour, it is the dimension of equality which precedes or better subsumes the other two. Categorical imperative could be said to be the modern version of the Golden Rule of yore. The undercurrent of aspiration, 'ought' and impulse towards, 'even-handedness,' 'fair-mindedness,' and 'egalitarianism' in both cannot be overemphasised. Modernity as a universalistic social ethic is but normative egalitarianism directed both towards cognition and conduct.

Modernity as Rational Sociality

That reason, rationality and rationalisation, in some sense or other, loom large in most explanations of modernity is clear enough. The dominant formulation of Enlightenment itself hovers around some form or other of metaphysical rationalisation of the humans. At a more experiential level, modernity has been read pessimistically as the dominance of either instrumental, bureaucratic or technological rationality. Most such accounts also suggest that such a dominance is a perversion in the sense that what ought to be the means has become an end in itself. If these forms of rationality and rationalisation are but means to an end, how could this end itself be formulated within the multi-level process of rationalisation? Taking off from our earlier interpretation of the core philosophy of Enlightenment, it is suggested that modernity is a normative prescription of social rationality on individual and collective lives of humanity. That is, rational sociality or social rationality as normative modernity suggests that it is irrational and other-worldly ordered and legitimated, that is, of the period of 'man's self-imposed tutelage,' to treat human beings discriminatorily on account of their ascriptive characteristics. Social rationality as modernity on the other hand would demand that despite real ascriptive differences, the humans ought to be treated equally that is non-discriminatorily. As the actualisation of such a norm would theoretically and practically bring forward for the first time in history, the entire society for egalitarian/rational accessing of the desired material and non-material goods, that the other forms of rationalisations are called into play. Instrumental, bureaucratic, technological and even metaphysical rationalisations are but handmaids and means to serve, facilitate and fulfil the foundational rationalisation of social and societal relations (Wallerstein, 1995). If these former are perceived as having overstepped their brief, their mandate to serve social rationality could be grasped without any ambiguity within the critique itself.

Modernity as Social Change

Modernity has been consensually grasped as a process or a cluster of processes of social change (Haferkamp & Smelser, 1992). At one level, this change has been described as a series of parallel but discrete transitional processes as from high rate to low rate of fertility and death, agrarian to industrial way of life, rural to urban, monarchy to democracy, community orientation to individualism, ascriptivity to achievement, etc. At another level, it has also been viewed synthetically within rounded up rubrics – from one mode of production or unity to another – by the founders of sociology. Again, there has also been excessive interest in describing the pre-modern Europe as feudalism and there have been various schools of European Feudalism.

However, in the midst of all these different strands of reading, there runs a not-so-thin and common thread of interpretation which unfortunately has not received sufficient attention in sociological readings of macro and historical social change. The pre-modern Europe has not only been systematically described as one of *orders* or *estates*, based on the circumstances of birth of individuals and groups, relatively separated from one another, but also differentially empowered (Duby, 1980; Blum, 1998). Differential empowerment of groups is but another term to indicate hierarchical social structuring. *Homo hierarchicus* was the philosophical anthropology of pre-modern Europe as much as it has been elsewhere. Transition from this could be grasped within macro-historical framework as towards a discursive-ideological formation of a horizontal man, *homo equalis*. This transition has been interpreted as from caste-like estate to class, rigid to flexible stratification, etc. However, this is a process by which a democratised vision and version of man was imagined and also produced. What several thinkers have described as 'modern social arrangement' consists precisely in the eruption of a process of ideological and actual social egalitarianisation/ democratisation. Transition from pre-modernity to modernity in the context of Europe is the abolition of the *ancien regime*, which has often been interpreted unwarrantedly as referring to only the political sphere. From estates to class, the transition is in fact a comprehensive levelling and equalising as a discursive formation. While this change did not happen all of a sudden, but took fairly a long time and the process may even said to be far from complete, the fact of the ideological change bringing about a newer form of social reality cannot be missed. And the core of this social change could again be formulated as the rise to hegemony of the enlightenment principle of egalitarianism – a new vision of social relations.

Modernity as Nationalism

Modernity seems to come inevitably in nationalist packages. It is said that nation is the cultural contour of modernity. But it could also be said that nation is the political contour of modernity. Modernity is actualised everywhere in putative politico-cultural communities called nation or nation states (Greenfeld, 2006). Within such communities, human beings are perceived as *citizens*. By consensus, the citizens are imagined and also sought to be treated as *free* and *equal* with respect to one another. The Enlightenment insight that human beings differentiated though in their circumstances of birth and birth-derived qualities, they ought to be considered equal, that is of equal value, is concretised only as citizens of different nation states. The modern man is a citizen and he cannot be otherwise; thereby, by definition he is equal and free with respect to all others.

Nationalism not only engenders modernity through the principle of citizenship, it also secures modernity through another principle – the rule of law. The easily identifiable aspect of contemporary, collective life is the ubiquitous (often over-bearing) presence of peculiarly characterised institutions. The logic on which these 'modern' institutions are based and operate from is known as the Rule of Law. The implication of this rule is that ascriptive differentiations among the 'individuals' whom these institutions serve do not matter and that only the rule based on some form of universality does. This could very well be interpreted as the juridical and institutionalised form of the same egalitarian principle imagined to have been discursively inscribed within society as the desired normative. It is not difficult to see that it is the self-same Enlightenment normative principle of non-discrimination among the humans, transforms itself into the prescriptive rule of law within the modern institutions. Nationalism, in this view, seems to be the concrete device, at least in theory to actualise, protect, sustain and carry forward the democratic/egalitarian promise of the Enlightenment.

Modernity Historicised: The French Revolution

Historically, the promise of Enlightenment was actualised most dramatically in the formation of the nation state of France. The core ideological imaginary of the revolution has been simple and clear, though not often sharply or systematically highlighted in complexly written academic texts. It was a discursive transition from a society of orders/estates to that of a homogenised single community, involving a multi-faceted process of democratisation. It signalled the enablement as well as ennoblement of the hitherto relegated majority of the population. Those whose identity was 'serf' came to acquire a new identity of 'French man.' The single most significant event of the Revolution, at least from the point of view of the problem on hand, was the abolition of different and differentially empowered chambers of representatives and their amalgamation into one. This was clearly sensed by Alexis de Tocqueville, (Read, 2003; Guinard, 2001; De Tocqueville, 2011) but more sharply problematised by Abbe Sieyies (1963) in his *What is the third Estate?* The questions he raised therein were: what was the third estate, what is the third estate and what does the third estate hopes to be. The quintessence of the process, pointed out here is that the modernity as it emerged in France was not compatible with the discriminatory ascriptive differentiation but had to inevitably destroy it. The inter-connected processes by which modernity manifested itself there, are radical democratisation, abolition of ascriptive privileges, ennoblement of the hitherto relegated masses, the consequent emergence of public sphere/civil society and thereby the constitution of a differently imagined national–political community of free and equal citizens. This, that is, social democratisation and its political institutionalisation indeed constituted the core sociological logic of that massive and world-significant event.

In addition to the several causes behind the Revolution identified by scholars, one could profitably add the pervasive and persistent 'disturbances' in pre-modern Europe by the lower orders, recognised as 'looting', 'revolts', 'rebellions', 'fituri' and 'jacquarie'. Along with the earlier works of Cohn, Rude and others, the literature on pre-modern social resistance movements in Europe is proliferating (Cohn, 2006; De Moor, 2008). While many of these studies describe in detail the various occurrences and interpret them against abstract paradigms, it may be worthwhile to study their structural implications for the overall transition to modernity. These subaltern restlessness and movements certainly indicate, despite their concrete differences, their common trajectory of bringing down the *ancien regime* of privileges and liabilities and create a unified and modern-egalitarian one.

Modernity as Human Rights

In a world which is increasingly becoming insensitive to ideologies and any form of moral ought, it is the Universal Declaration of Human Rights which keeps alive the flame of minimum socio-political normativity. And this normativity is nothing but once again the enlightenment principle of equality for all or discrimination towards none. Apart from the culturalist counter-arguments of some of the dubious regimes, the idea of Universal Human Rights – basic freedom and equality – has become the new/modern normative, acceptable to almost all political hues and religious beliefs. In addition to this very first clause of the Declaration, the idea of universality and the formation of the singular 'human,' express a near-consensual modernity which could only be formulated as equality and egalitarianism as having become truly hegemonic. Presumably, some sections of people always did enjoy rights and freedom. As against this, this modern formulation asserts the *universality* of Rights and Freedom for all human beings. What is new/modern then, in this formulation, is the fact that a vast number of people, who hitherto had no rights or freedom, not been treated as humans are now to get rights equal to that of others and treated as human beings like the others.

Essence of Modernity

In the above paragraphs, we have tried to review and reformulate the core issue of modernity from several and cumulative vantage points and the main argument all along has been that modernity is grasped better as radical and continuously expanding process of democratisation, normatively set in motion within different cultures and societies. The normative assertion here is that human beings are the same and that this sameness should be the foundation on which socio-political organisations be constructed. All other formulations of modernity proffered in different contexts are better understood either as peripheral, instrumental or consequential, engaged in the service or disservice of this core, or even plainly unnecessary. Egalitarianism/democratisation becoming normative and hegemonic is the essence of modernity. The intellectual–moral insight is that it is right to treat human beings as equal. That is, modernity has introduced a new morality or discipline.

Identifying the core of modernity with the normative principle of egalitarianism achieving hegemony, though does not explain everything, has certainly some advantages over other explanations. *First*, is its parsimony. A lot of things have been projected as essential to modernity, which this explanation avoids. *Second*, this formulation is not so far removed from many major academic articulations on modernity. It already constitutes a strong undercurrent or a substantial component in the writings of important thinkers, both classical and contemporary (Heller, 1999; Taylor, 1992, 1995; Wallerstein, 1995). *Third*, egalitarianism, socio-political democratisation or the aspiration for and the very real possibility of the emergence of autonomous and equal selves seems to be the most precious non-negotiable that makes even the deeply disillusioned writers hesitate before giving up hopes on modernity.

Modernity as a Paradox

Moving Away from Essentialised Modernity

If this minimal–normative formulation of modernity is accepted at least tentatively, then its paradoxical/ambiguous nature becomes easier to grasp. As a preliminary, we need to move away, however, first, from the plastic-like picture of modernity produced within most of the counter/post-modernity discourses in which it is projected as a rounded up whole, leading its own life independent of the working and imagining of people, in other words, essentialised/reified; modernity here is something that happens to us, more often than not, in spite of us. Secondly, most of these pejorative accounts are also quasi-philosophical, that is, far removed from the actual aspirations, struggles, frustrations and successes of living humans. Viewing modernity as normative egalitarianism demanding change in social and structural relations on the other hand, squarely brings down and contextualizes the issue in the midst of the concrete social and societal struggles; for, the imperative here is for the rational and inclusive/universal reconfiguration of social relations.

Taking off from the promise of Enlightenment, we suggest that this normative of modernity has released a pervasive and unceasing conflict within society between what *is* and what *ought* to be. Expressive of actual interests within society, it has opened up the floodgate of power-contestation in material, non-material and representational spheres. The normative principle calls on individuals and groups hitherto considered as higher/privileged on account of their ascriptive characteristics, to shed their extra power, merge with the hitherto considered inferior/relegated, and together become a single common or public. The privileged, however, cannot be expected to meekly accept this imperative, abide by it or, much less, implement it. The relegated on the other hand, having got a glimpse of the new, will not also anymore rest content with their hitherto subservience. Power and privileges are nowhere surrendered voluntarily, but everywhere confronted, contested and appropriated. Ceaseless efforts are made at all levels then, to retain, retrieve and re-establish the threatened and vanishing privileges, with varying degrees of success, in ever newer, subtler and covert forms through methods, ranging from brute force to interpretation of meanings of things, events and processes. On the other hand, efforts are equally ceaseless to change the scenario, relocate power more democratically, read reality differently and stabilize the emerging. Thus, what appears to be a simple normative ideal of modernity indeed has given birth to a plethora of multi-faceted and multi-layered conflicts originating first, from attempts to retain asymmetrical power, two, from attempts to achieve symmetrical power and three, from plural attempts to define and determine the exact content and contour of the symmetry itself?

Between modernity's prescription and practice lie the concrete worlds of multi-layered and multifaceted and contested realities. Sectarian privileges, feelings of superiority and sense of aggrandisement do not easily wear off. Even after centuries, we see the world still grappling with the very elementary aspects of this norm of Enlightenment. Much of the conflicts – material and non-material of the contemporary world, revolve around the persisting notions of ascriptive superiority of one group or another. Racism, communalism, casteism and what has been termed as civilisational clash, all these could be explained substantially as being caused by an unwillingness to relinquish pre-modern/irrational privileges and concede ascriptive equality to all. The holocaust, which recent writers have highlighted so tellingly was in fact carried out on the alleged ascriptive superiority of the so-called Aryan – a direct negation of the Enlightenment principle as formulated here. The same Aryanism in the Indian subcontinent, in the form of Brahminism has consistently been at the root of both communalism and casteism, the two evils plaguing the societies here (Aloysius, 2009). Aryanism of the East or West is directly opposed to the notion that human beings all are of equal worth and as such ought to be treated with such respect and dignity. The sharp critique of Feminism is not also different from the point being made here. The question of gender is increasingly being seen as a discriminatory social construction based on the idea that birth circumstances, matter in the evaluation and treatment of human beings. Today, if the society is seen to be in the grip of all forms of inequality and conflicts ensuing from them, it is also seen to be wrongly so. Such a pervasive critical consciousness of prevailing inequality is better grasped within modernity of our formulation.

If conceptual modernity is about homogenisation of power, its concrete forms are the dynamically negotiated settlements between the two antago- nistically related forces in terms of sharing power. It is empirical evidence that the co-presence of the positive and negative of modernity is not to be found in the same proportion everywhere. This should suggest the upper hand of one tendency either positive or negative at one point in time and place. Means becoming an end, equality being turned mechanical, sectar- ian rationality presented as universal, democratisation twisted into major- ity rule, scientism and technologism substituting social rationality, collapsing the conceptual with the actual and much more are perversions not inherent to 'modernity' but doings and machinations of vested interests resisting modernity as the actualisation and perennial extension of the democratic principle. In fact, the counterrevolution of France, though eventually defeated at least at some levels at that point of time is a clear example of how modernity does not just happen but has to be brought about and maintained against continued, multi-faceted and layered resis- tance. The defeated forces, being expressions of actual power interests of individuals and groups within society, continually tend to come back to have persisting influence of distortion, in material as well as non-material realms. The increasingly ambiguous nature of modernity and the fading away of the Enlightenment promise then need to be viewed in this specific context of changing as well as challenging social power in contestation.

Modernity as Cultural Imperialism

Moving Away from Cultural Essentialism

Once again, defining modernity singularly and normatively as the rise to hegemony of the egalitarian/democratic principle would help us to view the process as less alien but the unavoidable native of all cultures. Modernity within the non-European (also in European) context is mostly discussed in terms of culture, cultural change and even cultural displace- ment, in short culturalism. The trajectory of the present essay on the other hand is to shift the discussion to power configuration or better to the unpacking of culture itself as the reified form of contested power.

Within colonial and nationalist anthropologies, culture is mostly presented as a monolithic, rounded-up whole, distinct from all others, having singular attributes in contrasting binaries – spiritual/material. Individualist/communitarian, rights-based/duty-sensitive, linear/circular etc., in other words as essentialised. But, developments in Sociology of cul- ture, Cultural Marxism and Cultural Studies have helped us to interpret culture as discursively constituted and held in dynamic equilibrium. Putative cultural wholes are seen today as negotiated and tentative settlements of the conflicting movements of dominance and resistance. Actual power-realisation within societies has always been asymmetrical, tension-ridden and conflictual and the notion of culture has helped to project them other-wise. But when this culture is deconstructed, we could see the criss-crossing of conflicts of interests within, all of which fall in the broad categories/ forces of hierarchicalisation and equalisation. If power was held asymmet-rically within pre-modern societies, based on ascriptivity, then there was also the pressurising presence of resistance, demanding equalisation and re-constitution. However, by and large these latter forces could not gain ideological hegemony, hence the visibility almost everywhere in pre-modernity of ascriptivity-based social hierarchies. And as resistance was largely subsumed into seeming consensus, the harmony of a single cultural whole could be projected in the interest and insistence of the dominant.

Rejecting Modernity

Modernity dawns on such a scenario, either as an eruption from within as it is claimed to have been in Europe or as a provocation from without as in the erstwhile colonies. Consequently, the sequence of changes in the two sce-narios has been vastly different, leading to much confusion or even camou-flage of the nature of the multi-layered power process. In the latter context of 'provocation from without', in which modernity was seen to have been injected through the dubious agency of Colonialism, the dominant response was to identify the agency with the phenomenon itself at the level of cul-ture: Colonialism represents the imposition of the Western on the local and its distortion/displacement and hence ought to be rejected. This clearly was a cultural-essentialist argument, that is, taking culture, both of the provoked and provocator, at its face value. That this is so could be derived from the fact that the response to Colonial modernity everywhere has been deeply fissured. The response of the dominant itself was ambiguous, for while there was a running rhetoric against it, in practice it was being swallowed as mate-rial culture indiscriminately. But, it is with the response of the subaltern everywhere we are concerned. Though academically non-problematised, the subaltern response to Colonial modernity has been distinct, and also confronting that of the dominant. The subaltern groups more or less every-where found a peculiar resonance to the oncoming modernity, despite its medium of Coloniality. Even avoiding glorified accounts, it could be said that the general realisation was that of the dawn of a new age, arrival and legitimacy. Their hitherto muted aspirations and struggles towards equality and inclusiveness came to acquire a new meaning and salience. In and through their efforts, the meaning and implications of culture, as projected by the dominant, came to be contested in every aspect. The realisation among the aspiring subalterns was that, in the name of culture, power was being denied to them by their own elite and therefore the culture question at least to the extent it referred to them was a question indeed of power and power sharing. The call of culture was then perceived as the peremptory command for the preservation of the asymmetrical power realisation of pre-modernity (Aloysius, 1997). Aspirations for equality of the subalterns could only be suppressed and delegitimised by calling them foreign, alien, undesirable and Colonial culture. Sure enough there was much in the Colonial imposition that was peripheral, unnecessary and even obnoxious. But the core point of contestation clearly was about the principle of egalitarianism or democratisation. Modernity in this sense was not at all Western, but the reawakening of the potential/muted embedded within every culture. While one could concede that it was in the West that the logic of modernity was first formulated, this does not make the substance itself Western or culture-specific. While much modernity could be imported, unless the egalitarian tendencies within are released, anchored and dovetailed with what is being imported, the situation could never be held to be modern. For, all genuine modernity is an eruption from within, however, much of its concrete unfolding is abetted or obstructed by forces from without.

Pluralising Modernity

While the dominant rhetoric of anti-modernity cannot be said to have abated within South Asia, it has certainly been supplemented recently with the 'nuanced' formulations of alternative, multiple and unique modernities. Pluralising modernity at least in this part of the world is a curious combination of the resurgent and reaffirmed traditionalism on the one hand and the rise of post-modernism elsewhere. It is said that how different societies grapple with modernity cannot be brought within and much less judged from a single, more often than not 'hegemonic' – read, normative – framework. Diverse socio-historical formations should be seen not comparatively or evaluatively, but each on its own basis. The rejection of modernity as singular and normative is unambiguous here, though formulated as the broadening of the study of modernity itself. Despite its academic sophistication, it needs to be said however, that this formulation also does not escape cultural essentialism and discusses modernity still within the cultural register.

Expressions of equality/inequality, however, are historically evolved and culture-specific. And transition to modernity, therefore, requires the dismantling of the historically evolved culture-specific expressions of inequality and replacing them with expressions of equality and inclusiveness also culture-specific and historically evolved. We are talking here basically of a process which is mostly internal, though supplemented to a more or less extent with external forces. And again, though the process is conceptually singular, in concrete, there are as many dismantling/re-mantling of expressions of inequality/equality as there are cultures. While re-valorisation and institutionalisation of the values of democracy and equality would bring about unity of peoples to some extent, deletion of diversities is nowhere on the agenda. While the normative is singular-universal in ideal, its actualisation is indeed multiple particulars. But, these multiple particulars, if to be termed modern at all, would have had to initiate the process of dismantling the historically evolved forms of inequality and re-mantle equality and not otherwise. The point is whether singular, plural or unique, to be modern one cannot escape the normative-democratic, which, at least conceptually, is singular and universal. In fact, historically speaking, it is in modernity that it is in and through the actualisation of the democratic principle that cultures have become self-consciously plural and not otherwise. The singular-normative egalitarian principle as the foundation of global modernity would actually promote and not suppress the diversity of cultures. By merely terming the present day concrete cultures, societies and nation-states as many modernities the academic attempt seems to be, to wriggle out of the normative-egalitarian ideal, ward off criticism from the vantage point of democratisation, and the mass aspired for social change, and still claim the intellectual-moral privileges of being part of the modern community of nations. Alternative, multiple or unique modernities will always be perceived at least by the subaltern majorities not as an expression of concern for cultural diversity but academic justification of social power status quo, if they are not firmly and ideologically at least set on the path of comprehensive dismantling of inequality as an internal trajectory.

Global Modernity and Social Contestation

Negotiating with the major controversies, this intervention has sought to do three things: one, defining the core of modernity as the rise to hegemony of the egalitarian/democratisation principle; two, explaining the paradox of modernity as the contestation this application of the democratic, that is, power-reconfiguring principle has triggered off; three, shifting the discussion of modernity to the realm of power and its contestation and locating such contestation as internal to all cultures.

Now, if our search is for global modernity, that is, which the entire globe could in consensus, look upon, appropriate and nurture as its own, there cannot be a better candidate than normative democratisation. Such a modernity cannot be rejected as foreign or alien. Positing plural/alternative/unique modernities is no way out either. As a demand for egalitarian power reconfiguration within, modernity releases antagonistic forces engendering ambiguities, paradoxes and even plain human disasters. This however does not justify its rejection but calls forth intensification of efforts to complete the incomplete project of normative modernity.

If this volume represents an attempt to comprehend within a single axis both the affirmation and negation of the more significant contemporary power-realisation as well as power mobilisation, then the Enlightenment principle of ascriptive non-discrimination is still the best candidate. As a normative principle, this brings to sharp relief the dichotomy between the actual and the ideal. Such a dichotomy indeed provides a vast and multilevel space and scope for the launching of equally complex social contestation everywhere. As suggested above, the most significant mobilisations of contemporary times such as anti-racism, anti-casteism, feminism and environmentalism, all are indeed concerns of ascriptive non-discrimination and its extensions. Reading modernity is not a mere mapping out of the actual and the existent in presumed neutrality. It is also a de-bunking of the actual, highlighting what could be as well as what should be within the very logic of the situations. It is simultaneously a reading as well as a call for action for a cause which cannot in any meaningful sense be gainsaid.

References

Aloysius, G. (1997). *Nationalism without a Nation in India*. Oxford: Oxford University Press.

Aloysius, G. (2009). *The Brahminical Inscribed in Body Politic*. New Delhi: Critical Quest.

Blum, J. (1998). *The End of the Old Order in Rural Europe*. Princeton: Princeton University Press.

Chatterjee, P. (1997). *Our Modernity*. Sephis – Codesria, Internet.

Cohn, S.K. (2006). *Lust for Liberty: The Politics of Social Revolt in Medieval Europe 1200–1425*. Cambridge, MA: Harvard University Press.

De Moor, T. (2008). Silent Revolution: A New Perspective on the Emergence of Commons, Guilds and other forms of Corporate Collective Action in Western Europe. *International Review of Social History*, *53*(Supplement), 179–212.

De Tocqueville, A. (2011). *The Ancient Regime and the French Revolution*. Cambridge: Cambridge University Press.

Duby, G. (1980). *The Three Orders The Feudal Society Imagined*. Chicago, IL: University of Chicago Press.

Gaonkar, D.P. (2001). *Alternative Modernities*. Durham: Duke University Press.

Greenfeld, L. (2006). *Nationalism and Mind: Essays on Modern Culture*. Oxford: One World Publications.

Guinard, P. (2001). *Alexis De Tocqueville, the Visionary of Modernity*. Retrieved 16 June 2014, from http://cura.free.fr/docum/10toc-en.html

Haferkamp, H. and Smelser, N.J. (Eds.) (1992). *Social Change and Modernity*. Berkeley, CA: University of California Press.

Harpham, G.G. (1994). So…What is Enlightenment? An Inquisition into Modernity. *Critical Inquiry, 20*(3), 524–556.

Heller, A. (1999). *A Theory of Modernity*. Oxford: Blackwell.

Kozlarek, O. (2006). Theodor W. Adorno and Octavio Paz: Two Visions of Modernity. *Culture, Theory and Critique, 47*(1), 39–52.

Read, C. (2003). National History as Social Critique? Tocqueville's Unconventional Modernity. *Studies in Social and Political Thought, 8*.

Saler, M. (2006). Modernity and Enchantment: A Historiographic Review. *The American Historical Review, 111*(3), 2–37.

Sieyes, E.J. (1963). *What is the Third Estate*. London: Pall Mall Press.

Sullivan, R.J. (1989). *Immanuel Kant's Moral Theory*. Cambridge: Cambridge University Press.

Taylor, C. (1992). Modernity and the Rise of Public Sphere. *The Tanner Lectures on Human Values*. Delivered at Stanford University, 25 February, 1992. At tannerlectures. utah.edu/_documents/a-to-z/t/Taylor93.pdf

Taylor, C. (1995). Two Theories of Modernity. *The Hastings Center Report, 25*(2), 24–33.

Tjomsland, M. (1996). *A Discussion of Three Theoretical Approaches to Modernity: Understanding Modernity as a Globalising Phenomenon*. Working Paper 2, Chr. Michelson Institute of Development Studies and Human Rights.

Van Der Veer, P. (1998). The Global History of 'Modernity'. *Journal of the Economic and Social History of the Orient, 41*(3), 285–294.

Wallerstein, I. (1995). The End of What Modernity? *Theory and Society, 24*(4), 471–488.

5

Vicissitudes and Possibilities of Critical Theory Today

José Maurício Domingues

Defining Critical Theory

The goal of this text is to evaluate the directions of critical theory today and its relations in particular with sociology, with concrete reference to the contemporary world. It is not a matter of restricting critical theory to the tradition of the so-called Frankfurt School and its offspring, nor circumscribe it to what has been named 'Western Marxism'. I would rather focus on critical theory in a more *ecumenical* way, supposing that other authors and currents are included in it more broadly, sharing, however, some common presuppositions. This takes us to a discussion about some trends that could contribute in the direction of a renewal of this theoretical field. Before doing so, nevertheless, it is necessary to define the extent to which and how a theoretical approach can be brought within the critical tradition, without aiming at a systematic discussion of all currents that could at present be seen as part of this intellectual field. Let me concentrate on some fundamental strands of the contemporary debate.

Ambivalence in relation to the evolution of modernity, in its multidimensional aspects, which include capitalism, without being restricted to it, characterizes much of European social theory since at least the mid-eighteen century until, especially, the last decades of the twentieth century. Freedom and domination loom large in several of such analyses as the poles in which modernity is substantiated and frustrated, since its promises are actualized in a partial and unilateral way by means of institutions that to some extent embody the values of the modern imaginary, but simultaneously establish patterns of social relations rooted in new forms of domination (Domingues, [2002] 2006: Chapters 1–2). Some, as Weber, take critique very far. This may not, however, really amount to what I want to define ecumenically as critical theory. Weber did not go beyond resignation as to a highly bureaucratized society, deprived of freedom, in which the values of liberalism could no longer, he believed, be realized (Cohn, 1978).

Critical theory stands here, therefore, as a strand of questioning of modernity that supports not only its values, against present institutions, but that also endeavours to find in it, as well as in the agents that move within it, the potential, the elements and possible subjects of the emancipation promised by modernity. These values cannot of course be merely a derivation of the ideas of the critical theoretician, rather consisting in conceptual extrapolations of themes and tendencies that emerge and linger on in the actual social world of modernity in its successive transformations. That is, it is an *immanent critique* that aims at *transcending* social conditions that prevent the actualization of the values of modernity and the demands social agents effectively critical bring to the fore of intellectual and political disputes (Benhabib, 1986: 328–329; Browne, 2008). There are many ways and 'models' of doing critical theory even in the more circumscribed tradition of the Frankfurt School (Müller-Doohm, 2005). It must be clear that it is not the case of abiding only by the conceptions of justice that appear in social movements, nor of looking exclusively for incipient moral elements that articulate them on the basis of suffering or that may come to articulate them morally, but all these factors as well as others. This means I disagree with both Fraser and Honneth (2003). If that demand furnishes clear criteria, on the other hand it is plain that reality is not pure. More complicated is Habermas' (1981) straightforward substitution of social analysis and immanent social impulses towards change by the idea that the core of critical theory resides in the very structure of human communication and by a somewhat fuzzy idea of a strategy of conceptual 'reconstruction', which he has applied differently to several phenomena.

Nobre (2008) for instance has insisted on a claim of 'no competition', since Marx, but especially with reference to Horkheimer's founding text, between 'traditional theory and critical theory', an outlook that would reach at least to a certain period of Habermas' work. I see here some ambiguity: it is not clear if no competition is to be posed in terms of parallel developments, although critical theory can embody the findings of traditional theory, or if it would be really superior to the latter due to its cognitive standpoint. Only according to this last angle do I think that the perspective of no competition would be valid in Marx and Lukács. More generally, the critical standpoint, linked to emancipation, can claim pre-eminence only insofar as it is rooted in the transcendence of the present through the recognition of the emancipatory elements to be found in it at least in nuce.

I would like to suggest, however, that it is not in a methodological perspective that we must ground critical theory, but rather on the social immanence of a core value, which has not lost at all its potential, although it can become dormant when some social goals of emancipation are achieved. I refer to *equal freedom*, that is, the demand that every and each one has the same social *power* and is at liberty to choose his or her own path in life, individually and collectively, beyond systems of domination – or that imply control – and the false liberal dichotomy of negative and positive freedom. This has been the substantive historical core of critical theory since Marx, through Adorno, to Habermas (Domingues, [2002] 2006: Chapters 1–2).

That said, what about the whereabouts of critical theory in a more strict sense? Twenty years ago, when democracy started to decay in the western world, after decades and even centuries of difficult and conflictive strengthening, its outstanding approaches supported the idea that the expansion of 'civil society' or the 'public sphere' – and procedural and deliberative democracy – would occupy centre-stage in emancipatory politics (Cohen and Arato, 1992; Habermas, 1992). No capitalism, no neoliberalism, no de-democratizing changes of the state. In this respect, although there were already problems in Habermas' (1981) main work, in particular, due to his adoption of systems theory and a tacit affiliation to neoclassical economic theory, his ulterior discussion of democracy moved to fill a gap, albeit in an arguable way, that was highly problematic for critical theory. Nevertheless, it also meant a retreat from a broader conceptual standpoint. His last relevant intervention in this debate took on important discussions about the encroachment of eugenic neoliberalism upon life politics (with reference to biotechnology) (Habermas, 2001a, 2001b); and, more recently, it evinces perhaps the beginning of the acknowledgment of the possibility of de-democratizing processes, exemplified concretely by the present fate of Europe (Habermas, 2011). Honneth, after insisting on the centrality of recognition politics – which can offer an interesting middle-range theory, but should not be blown out of proportion – seems to have concluded, in his contribution with Martin Hartmann, that critique lost its immanent transcendent core. This would be due to the capacity of contemporary capitalism to take up the demands of the 1968 generation, with its aesthetic and social critique, at most remaining, as an element of tension, the 'paradoxes' generated by the inevitably incomplete and somewhat illusory realization of such values (Honneth, 2010), although, in what is his main opus thus far, freedom, as the general principle of modern *ethical life*, is re-affirmed (without however an at least more explicit recognition of its egalitarian thrust, as a value, in this civilization), and as if it had been basically institutionalized (Honneth, 2011). Global conceptions of justice have also recently drawn the attention of authors within this tradition, in relation, however, to individuals, not countries or collectivities, nor in what concerns the dynamic of capitalism or democracy at the national and global levels (cf. Fraser, 2009).

In order to weave part of his recent arguments, Honneth draws upon the work of Boltanski and Chiapello (1999), whose diagnosis of modernity holds great interest, when they deal with what they consider the 'new spirit of capitalism', although they excessively emphasize morals and motivation (in variance, in fact, with Weber's view). This is a problem that also harms Habermas' and in particular Honneth's works. More seriously, Boltanski, the group's 'chef d'école', chose later on an amorphous and unspecific definition of critical theory, which excessively stresses moral issues, his arguments fuming away, moreover, in a rhetoric in which power is absent as an issue (Boltanski, 2009). His theory does not give pride of place to, or even vents, crucial developments undergone by European countries at present, the selection of models of critique that he carried out formerly with Thévenot, all egalitarian-meritocratic, leaving no room to relations of domination, which rarely come to the fore morally in modernity (Boltanski & Thévenot, 1991). Furthermore, despite their mobilizing of several authors of political philosophy, arbitrarily selected, they do not aim at a 'critical sociology' but rather at a 'sociology of critique', paying no attention to the main values that we can surely find in the multiple lifeworlds and their daily criticism, which compose the core of the modern imaginary (Boltanski & Thévenot, 1991). That is, the polarization of classes, racist demagoguery, the decay of democracy, neoliberalism, nothing of the kind turns up in Boltanski's writings, although crucial aspects of capitalism are actually present in his joint study with Chiapello (Boltanski & Chiapello, 1999).

At the same time, some Marxist authors, such as Harvey (1990, 2009), have critically presented interesting and relevant discussions about the contemporary world, proceeding, however, as though it was enough basically to resume Marx's theoretical scaffoldings, something that is not plausible after so much change in the world and in theory in the last decades. Some 'post-Marxist' writers jumped into the world of 'discourse' and, despite interesting conceptual discussions, have been treading a cloudy sphere, which has limited capacity to understand the present in its multidimensionality (cf. Butler et al., 2000). A reductive concentration on the West comes out, moreover and once more, also in these currents.

On the other hand, there is 'post-colonialism'. We still have to wait to see which will be its concrete innovations, beyond the idea that it is necessary to thoroughly reinvent social theory, beyond Eurocentrism, as if this had never been carried out and the social sciences and the humanities had never been capable – for instance in Latin America, where in a way or another 'critical thought' has thrived, but also elsewhere – of proposing solutions to the problems of intellectual dependency and conceptual lack of adequacy which they denounce. This is patently absurd (see Debés

Valdés, 2012). More interesting are actual pieces of work in this direction and with a perspective close to post-colonialism, such as those of Nandy (1978), whose work already is – or should be – a global reference. His is a rare example of a partially non-modern critique of modernity, although at the same time it stands as already modernized alterity (therefore as part of modernity), centred around the question of freedom and blending European influence with a transformed heritage of the Indic civilization (Domingues, [2010] 2011). Concrete analysis of the contemporary world, about so-called post-colonial societies, are absolutely missing in such approaches – apart from Chatterjee's interventions (1993, 2004), whose fixation on the ideas of 'community' and the secundarization of the struggle for rights are rather arguable, indeed close to a subrepetitious – and unintentional – acceptance of problematic elements of present day *status quo*. In Latin America, Mignolo (2000, 2005) stands out in this regard. His work is centred on the exclusion, through 'coloniality-modernity', of original peoples and the search for a savage rhetorical articulation, against western rationalism and official rationalization. It is the world of discourse, dear to the criss-cross of post-modernism and post-structuralism, that underpins much of this restrict 'post/de-colonial' standpoint, notwithstanding the relevance of a number of problems they emphasize (a shining example of which is Spivak, 1988).[1] In any case, although these are surely relevant issues – diversity of the global social world as well as epistemological and political challenges must be tackled – critique cannot by any means stop at this. Besides, such a discussion is not an exclusivity of post- or de-colonial thought: many in Latin America and elsewhere, for instance the Egyptian Marxist Samir Amin (1973, 1988), were attentive to these issues, either substantively pointing out the role of imperialism or with a straightforward critique of 'Eurocentrism', whether we think he hit the mark or not.

There are several relevant elements in those approaches, but they are, in my view, limited. The world faces increasing problems, and modernity is driven in a direction of ever greater social polarization while democracy is sapped, a process which in Latin America we have at least resisted with some success. This is a fundamental aspect of what I have been calling the third phase of modernity, in what it has of more perverse and more con- nected to the defeat of emancipatory projects. Let us examine the issue more closely in order that we understand what can be said of critical social theory at present. Here, we must speak of an ecumenical theory and of rescuing intuitions, empirical and theoretical, that surfaced in the origins of this tradition. An incisive sociological approach, rather than philosoph- ical, has much to offer in this regard, keeping, in any case, the clash between modern values and institutions at its core. There are obviously other authors, as well as a legion of themes, such as patriarchy and sexism, racism and the destruction of the environment, which have their own critical lineages. I do not aim at dealing with them all here, much less to exhaust the multiple and ever more specific themes that a social life in exponential complexification throws up. It matters here only to outline what would be the fundamental axes of a critical diagnosis of the present, pointing to emancipatory forces at this historical stage, a crucial theme for the very legitimacy of critical theory, as well as throwing light on research alleys that seem relevant in this connection.

Contemporary Modernity

In the last three or four decades, there has been a radical change in the position of countries across the globe. Capitalism has changed its patterns of accumulation and regulation, as well as of consumption; that is, it has deeply altered its 'mode of development', to draw upon French regulation school. Neoliberalism is an expression of that, as much as the changes in the form of organizing production and consumption in what has been conventionally known as 'post-Fordism'. A globalization of such processes came about in all countries of the world, in a 'uneven and combined' manner, along with its fragmentation: through *just in time* and *lean production*, through outsourcing and networks between firms, by the pluralization and segmentation of consumption markets, as well as by a further concentration and centralization of capital, and by an increased polarization between social classes, or between poor and rich, from a phenomenological standpoint. Social liberalism has also slowly gained strength, with sectorialized and targeted policies (especially for the poor). This has marked, contingently, let me stress, the passage from the second phase of modernity – organized to a large extent by the state – to the third one, of greater social complexity, in which the state draws back to other governmentality tasks, leaving the economy, now much more globalized, to be increasingly regulated by the market, with a predominance of finance capital over it in the framework of so-called 'American empire' (Boyer, 1986; Harvey, 1990, 2009; Piketty, 2013; Domingues, 2008, 2012, 2013).

There was, nevertheless, the expectation that democracy would flourish – or there was at least a normative perspective about the democratic question. The hope of the aforementioned dominant sectors within critical theory stemmed from that. This did not happen overall. Instead, the democratic elements of those political systems have shrunk – in relation to the thrust of citizens in the behaviour of state incumbents, as well as in what concerns the space for participation and their protection, when they do participate (Tilly, 2004: 7–30, 2007). It could be suggested that the

problem is localized in the countries of the old 'Third World' and in those
which lived under 'real socialism', China, Cuba or Russia. However, this
is patently false: democracy is restricted and retreats exactly in those countries in which it originally emerged in the West, in Europe and the United
States. Participation, respect to the electoral mandate conferred by the
population, the articulation with the organized forces of society, respect
for human and other rights, freedom of press, tolerance in relation to distinct ethnic and religious groups, over all this hangs a question mark produced by explicit electoral fraud, an accentuation of the repressive side of
the state, the indifference to the mandate received by parties and 'leaders'
to carry out the policies defined in their campaigns, the official use of torture and kidnapping, the growth of secrecy and of secret and surveillance
services, official and open racism, the instrumental and selective use of
justice, the growing strength and independence of executives vis-à-vis par-
liaments (and within these, of central banks), frontal attacks against the
press if it is critical of the *establishment*, whereas the mass communication
means become ever more monopolistic and connected to global neoliberalism (notwithstanding the growth of alternative media). Unfortunately,
very little has been, critically or not, theorized in this regard (for some
aspects of this, see American Political Science Association, 2004; Crouch,
2004; Sassen, 2006; Pierson and Skocpol, 2007; Streeck, 2011, 2013).[2] To
a certain extent, the formal continuity of liberal democratic systems fore-
closes discussion of the theme. It is obvious that we should not forget
either that what could called the de-exceptionalization of the 'state of
exception', which marks the evolution of liberal political systems since
their own emergence in the nineteenth century and today (Agamben,
[2003] 2005), has reached its pinnacle, underpinning the strengthening of
executives to the detriment of popular sovereignty and the parliament.

In this respect, although facing difficulties and shortcomings, Latin
America is the only region in the world that has decisively moved forward
recently, contrary to most other global regions, towards building and deepening democracy, developing what I have called a 'molecular democratic
revolution'. It is true that a 'transformist' project has had great sway over
Latin American societies, in particular with neoliberalism in the 1990s and
that, economically, the situation is problematic due to processes of repri-
marization or 'commoditification' that reiterate, even in the case of industrialized Brazil, its peripheral or semiperipheral vocation. It is also true
that, overall, the strengthening of the executive happens in the region.
However, a project of greater 'social cohesion' is visible, to a greater or
lesser extent, in most Latin American countries. It has refused the increase
of polarization and differentials of income and wealth, the hallmark of the
contemporary world. This is clear in the case of Brazil, although speaking

of a new middle class, defined according to income only, does not make sense. In reality, in any case, a general increase of acquisitive power and of social mobility has been going on. This has led to some extent to what may be a new wave of mobilization, which has started with huge demonstrations in 2013, with a demand of universal social rights (Domingues, 2008, 2013). This does not mean that the politico-administrative systems of domination – sovereignty and governmentality – are not powerful in these countries and that their control by the citizenry has become less important than elsewhere. We should not forget the Weberian, and also Foucaultian, lessons about domination, even the rational–legal one that today has the imprint of more or less democratic elements in the design of the political system, as well as sometimes with good social-civilizatory intentions.

Where has been so-called critical theory on the face of it all? Adrift, at best. The critical theory of Marx centred on a discussion of liberal modernity, its first phase; with Adorno and Horkheimer, as well as Habermas and other members of the so-called Frankfurt School, on the second phase, state organized originally, in this case mainly on a philosophical level. This was somehow reproduced elsewhere in the post-colonial or peripheral world more generally through national liberation movements and nationalist and affirmative projects of various kinds, often harking back to the nineteenth century (Debés Valdés, 2012). Vis-à-vis the third phase, which unfolds brutally and rapidly before our eyes, it was, at least until very recently, with Habermas' intervention on a more political level, silent and aloof, or at least awkward and self-centred. In contrast, the expectations and behaviour of citizens and semi-citizens in this changed world are of deep disquiet and rejection of such models of economic, political and cultural domination, although they face difficulties to translate this outlook programmatically and into formal political systems. We often find unruly or at least restless populations, not prone to deference (which, it is worth noting, not always finds virtuous practices, especially when democracy and well-being are denied to them, sometimes unravelling in criminality and blind violence). This is as true of France and Spain as of Egypt and Thailand today (Therborn, 2009; Pleyers, 2011; Castells, 2013). Overall, the demand of equal freedom as to democracy, the rejection of neoliberalism, and the defence of social rights and plural social lifestyles has resumed centre stage. Demonstrations, new social movements and uprisings have expressed this across the globe, despite the rise of milder social liberalism and the fact that reactionary right-wing tendencies come up in this context too.

While traditional twentieth century social movements have become weaker, this new situation becomes theoretically plausible once we focus on the destruction of ties of pre-modern personal domination (of which the extinction or radical change of the old peasantry is an expression), by the expansion of capitalism, as well as the generalized reach of the state into society, and the loss of legitimation of social hierarchies all over the world. These populations seem to have at least partly fathomed that the idea of 'elites' is merely a justification for a bigger and illegitimate power, as well as curbing the equal freedom that modernity has promised. That is, the mechanisms of disembedding set in motion by the radical modernization of the contemporary world, in multiple directions (with western neoliberalism and a variant of capitalism to be found in particular in East Asia standing out), have been promoting the constitution of a popular subjectivity which, despite the use of several models of 'governmentality' (implying subjectivization and control), is socially much freer than at any other moment since the beginning of the Neolithic revolution and the fixation of nomadic groups through agriculture. What is left of control are the tough restrictions to global immigration. Nevertheless, this is often a disorganized mass, whose political mobilization and horizons of change are frequently short, without well-defined projects. Hence, some are willing to talk about the 'multitude' (Hardt & Negri, 2000) with a positive sign, overlooking, however, the serious shortcomings that underlie its movement. In this regard also Latin America has been at variance with much of the world, since its social movements have been pivotal for democratizing changes, recent events in Brazil perhaps pointing in a distinct direction, though (Domingues, 2008: Chapters 1 and 3, 2013). In fact, account taken of the restrictions to participation and the lack of adequate answers to their demands, it is possible to expect even a toughening of the forms of rebellion that marked the closing of the political space in Europe and elsewhere (Tilly, 2004: 27–28), with the present decay of democratic practices by the state.

It is important to note that the systems and projects of domination that characterize the first and second phases of modernity to large extent hinged on attempts at homogenization of social life. This happened through the generalization of the market, through citizenship, in its several dimensions, through nationalism, through mass production and consumption (especially in the Fordist era). In the same sense, the projects of emancipation were launched through the homogenization of classes – especially the working class, but sometimes also the peasantry – as agents of change, through the demand of shared citizenship status in social democracy, through a certain emphasis on freedom and the defensive and emancipatory nationalisms of the periphery. Admittedly, a certain level of social pluralism and of projects always subsisted within these proposals, which, moreover, when victorious, could not be thoroughly implemented, above all due to the resistance of society itself. All the critique of Adorno and Horkheimer ([1944–1945] 1984) as well as of their intellectual offspring, centred on the violent homogenization promoted by the 'Enlightenment', was rooted precisely in those tendencies and modernizing moves. They understood this through a philosophical reading of history that denounced its 'logocentrism', which reached its apex with the final solution of the elimination of the irreducible particularity (*Besonderheit*) of the Jew by Nazism. Yet, heterogeneity is no longer scary. If it cannot be controlled, in fact it underpins now new projects of domination, segmentation, exclusion and cooptation, by the market, politics and social policy, which we can see as a new phase of modern civilization (Cohn, 2003). It can certainly come along with demands of homogenization, as in the populist racism drawn upon by the European extreme-right and now also centre-right ruling circles, as well as in the US evangelical right, constituting modernizing moves that contain contradictory tendencies and elements, all articulated, however, so as to reinforce or resume the vigour of state systems of domination that would allow for a new sustained offensive of the ruling groups of Europe and the US on the face of an economic crisis whose overcoming has been difficult.

This is true too in what concerns, for instance, India and China, with fast developments of capitalism, increasing inequalities (notwithstanding the overall decrease of poverty), overarching and very exclusivist nationalisms, the fragmentation of the market, the destruction of nature and the entrenchment of the rich not only as rich, but also of a middle class that moved apart from the poor and lives now the dream of boundless consumerism. The latter is one of the crucial elements of its differentiation, alongside other mechanisms that characterize lifestyles, which have fault lines in dwelling places, habits, attitudes, vis-à-vis the mass of workers and even the lower layers of the middle classes, defeated and connected to services and social rights. Indifference, such as in China, or spite, as in India, for democracy – which is, however, in this last country enthusiastically celebrated by the popular classes and the subaltern castes – completes the framework for the insertion of such middle classes within their countries. This depiction points to the third phase of modernity, cut across by heterogeneity, polarization, market nixes and threats or blockages to democracy (Abaza, 2006; Lange & Meier, 2009; Domingues, 2012). As already noted, although Latin America partakes in many of these characteristics, it has moved in the last years in the opposite direction. To which extent this is sustainable in the long run is a question that only the future shall answer.

In this regard, it is understandable that the 'autonomism' that has affected some Latin American social movements for a good while has led to impasses (Svampa, 2008), although their resistance to bend to sometimes authoritarian tendencies even within the left and centre of the left is understandable. We need also to question Chatterjee's (1993, 2004) theoretical views, elsewhere in the world, which in principle identifies, indeed celebrates, 'political society', which would exist besides law, declining from a demand of rights, and opposed, according to him, to the 'civil society' of the middle classes, a line of argument that ends up commending the idea of an autonomous 'moral community'. Today this has very little effect on systems of domination that are well pleased to maintain society divided in watertight compartments, insofar as the so-called 'excluded', the new 'dangerous classes', are under control. On the contrary, for present-day systems of domination such arrangements can be highly favourable, moving away from any universalist principle of social cohesion, which demands a broader solidarity, as well as several levels of individual and collective subjectivity, which cannot stop at the level of micro-mobilizations. It is necessary to avoid the paroquialism of mobilizations which do not go beyond the local level, which are by the way typical of mobilizations carried out under more radically authoritarian regimes (Tilly, 2004: 30) – making no sense to reproduce such a strategy in particular when there is greater room for participation, even though democracy may be limited.

It is difficult to predict the sustainability of this mode of capitalist development, with markets relatively shrunk by design, especially inasmuch as a crisis of overaccumulation and overproduction charges the horizon, what becomes graver due to the fact that China is an industrial export juggernaut whose internal consumption is, however, rather restricted (its rate of savings remaining very high) (Brenner, 2006; Hung, 2008). More interesting, however, is – at the same time that we emphasize emancipatory potentials, at this point expressed in a still defensive way in the West – to draw attention to the issue of real citizenship, in what it is distinguished from the formal citizenship extant in many countries, in the material and symbolic aspects. It is not a matter of denouncing that actually unequal social agents, in terms of class, gender and other structures, underlie the exercise of such citizenship. This is absolutely true, but I would like to underline that the very exercise of citizenship is threatened by the deepening of social fractures and the piecemeal destruction of the common status of citizen. This was the historical achievement of social democracy especially in Europe, which was reproduced in the US by possibilities of social ascension and market inclusion which no longer exist. After all, since this has been a crucial theme for political theory since Aristotle, we must not forget who, concretely, is the citizen, how he or she can exercise its citizenship, with which reach (Dun, 1979). Even in Latin America, which present telos is of advancements, we may easily lose the momentum that pushes in this direction, floundering or stopping half-way in the process of democratization that has been unfolding in the last decades. It is also important to think how different countries are placed in the global system today, for which, even though in need of important revisions, the par excellence Latin American critical theory, the structuralism of the Economic Commission for Latin America (ECLA) of the United Nations (UN) and some versions of the theory of dependency, remain a source of inspiration and analysis (Domingues, 2008: Chapter 2). This affects all dimensions of social life, to start with by the issue of global justice, from a collective standpoint.

Can we move further than that at present, beyond the imaginary and the institutions of modernity, but also beyond rhetoric? 'Trend-concepts' (see Domingues, 2014), for the diagnosis of the times as well as for the identification of possibilities of development beyond modernity – the 'real movement of things' as it was once referred to, have always been a staple of critical theory. But such efforts were simply abandoned in favour of a reading of history that places too much stress on contingency, with few exceptions (such as Habermas' former theorizing of new plural social movements, or those which point to that unspecific encompassing agent, the 'multitude', as the great emancipator of the post-modern age). This is not at all clear right now, and probably the level of complexity of social life has foreclosed absolutist and excessively generalized statements about agents of emancipation, let alone abstractly globalized affirmations about such far-reaching historical trends (though the power of corporations seems increasingly pervasive and scary, not emancipatory at all). Moving away from certainty, its underlying sociological and epistemological underpins, was indeed necessary. Perhaps, however, we need to resume this more systematically, even if necessarily in more a modest (and not necessarily optimistic) frame of mind. Of course sociology can and must play a crucial role in this.

Renewing Critique

The multidisciplinary project of Adorno's and Horkheimer's Frankfurt Institute for Social Research continues to offer an interesting model to follow. A general theory of modernity cannot but demand a joint and multidisciplinary effort. Moreover, the gamut of problems that requires attention of what would be critical perspectives, necessarily plural, is very large and carries on widening. I would like to suggest, however, that, in order to understand this contemporary social universe, there is nothing better than sociology, a discipline whose identity seems to wither away, torn by the colonization of its field by neighbouring or adversarial disciplines. It is not a matter of demanding purity of sociology, of course, instead of stressing the analytical legacy of the sociological tradition, in relation to the imaginary, to social practices and institutions. It is to a good extent upon this that I believe it is possible and necessary to search once again for an ecumenical and vital critical theory. It does not have in the restless populations of the planet its object, subject or destination, but rather finds in the broad and decentred collective subjectivity which is critical in actual social life the agents with which it must be capable of dialoguing and whose ways, in its multiple and manifold directions, it can analyze, discuss, criticize, without a claim to superiority, but without uneasily feeling smaller just because it restricts itself to the intellectual practice that constitutes its own continent. Getting rid of awkward questions, of free thinking, not immediately practical, has in addition been the consistent project of the ruling collectivities of the third phase of modernity. There is no reason to compromise with that. On the other hand, the specific forms that modernity and, within it, systems of domination take on today contaminate all spheres of social life, wherever in the planet, something that requires special attention.

It is therefore necessary to move from philosophy, without leaving it aside, overcoming themes and concepts of the critical tradition, recovering others and extracting from them all that remains of their 'rational kernel', seriously discard provincialism and the exclusive concentration on a single country (usually that of the author him or herself), trying thus to systematically outline the specific elements of what I have called the third phase of modernity. Sociology, both professionally and publicly (Burawoy, 2005), can critically investigate and bring into the open the impasses, iniquities, injustices and possibilities of this social universe. This is necessary whether we use this concept or any other that grasps the far-reaching changes that cut across the contemporary world, its systems of domination as well as emancipatory aspirations and practices, whose core, as argued above, remains equal freedom as an orienting value. Critical theory, despite the historical troubles it has faced and faces at present, can and must renew itself in order to cope with the greatness and misery of contemporary modernity, contributing to its discovery of the alleyways of progressive social change.

Notes

1   Providing we keep equal freedom as an orienting value, hence do not lose sight of the future as transcending the limitations of the present, and universalist standpoints, Santos' (2002) demand that we concentrate on the present and search for alternatives which emerge across the planet also can help reaffirm a critical view, although he seems to discard too easily the propelling force of modernity as a global and partly frustrated emancipatory telos, which still holds as a horizon, problems to be discussed below notwithstanding.

2   Curiously and strangely, in his book about democracy, Tilly (2007) does not in any moment refers to twentieth century United States and only rarely and obliquely does so as to Europe, often supporting, despite the advances his work represents, a formalist position once the liberal-democratic institutions are established.

References

Abaza, M. (2006). *Changing Consumer Cultures of Modern Egypt: Cairo's Urban Reshaping*. Leiden and Boston: Brill.

Adorno, T.W. and Horkheimer, M. ([1944–1945] 1984). *Dialektik der Aufklärung*. Frankfurt am Main: Suhrkamp.

Agamben, G. ([2003] 2005). *State of Exception*. Chicago: The University of Chicago Press.

American Political Science Association – Task Force on Inequality and American Democracy (2004). *American Democracy in an Age of Rising Inequality*. Retrieved on 19 June 2014 from www.apsanet.org

Amin, S. (1973). *L'Imperialisme et le development inegal*. Paris: Minuit.

Amin, S. (1988). *L'Eurocentrisme*. Paris: Economica.

Benhabib, S. (1986). *Critique, Norm and Utopia: A Study of the Foundations of Critical Theory*. New York: Columbia University Press.

Boltanski, L. (2009). *De la Critique. Précis de sociologie de l'émancipattion*. Paris: Gallimard.

Boltanski, L. and Chiapello, E. (1999). *Le Nouvel esprit du capitalisme*. Paris: Gallimard.

Boltanski, L. and Thévenot, L. (1991). *De la Justification. Les économies de la grandeur*. Paris: Gallimard.

Boyer, R. (1986). *La Théorie de la regulación. Une analyse critique*. Paris: La Découverte.

Brenner, R. (2006). *The Economics of Global Turbulence: The Advanced Capitalist Economies from Long Boom to Long Downturn, 1945–2005*. London and New York: Verso.

Browne, C. (2008). The End of Immanent Critique? *European Journal of Social Theory*, *11*(1), pp. 5–24.

Burawoy, M. (2005). For Public Sociology. *American Sociological Review*, *70*(1), pp. 4–28.

Butler, J., Laclau, E. and Zizek, S. (2000). *Contingency, Hegemony, Universality: Contemporary Dialogues on the Left*. London and New York: Verso.

Castells, M. (2013). *Networks of Outrage and Hope: Social Movements in the Internet Age*. Cambridge: Polity.

Chatterjee, P. (1993). *The Nation and Its Fragments: Colonial and Postcolonial Histories*. Princeton, NJ: Princeton University Press.

Chatterjee, P. (2004). *The Politics of the Governed: Reflections on Popular Politics in Most of the World*. New York: Columbia University Press.

Cohen, J. and Arato, A. (1992). *Civil Society and Political Theory*. Cambridge, MA: MIT Press.

Cohn, G. (1978). *Crítica e resignação. Fundamentos da sociologia de Max Weber*. São Paulo: TA Queiroz.

Cohn, G. (2003). A sociologia e o novo padrão civilizatório. In C. Barreira, (Ed.). *A sociologia no tempo*. São Paulo: Cortez.

Crouch, C. (2004). *Post-Democracy*. Cambridge: Polity.

Debés Valdés, E. (2012). *Pensamiento periférico. Una tesis interpretativa global*. Santiago de Chile: Idea-Usach.

Domingues, J.M. (1995). *Sociological Theory and Collective Subjectivity*. London and New York: Macmillan and Saint Martin's Press.

Domingues, J.M. ([2002] 2006). *Modernity Reconstructed*. Cardiff: University of Wales Press.

Domingues, J.M. (2008). *Latin America and Contemporary Modernity: A Sociological Interpretation*. London and New York: Routledge.

Domingues, J.M. ([2010] 2011). Ashis Nandy e as vicissitudes do self. Crítica, subjetividade e civilização indiana. *Teoria crítica e (semi)periferia*. Belo Horizonte: Editora UFMG.

Domingues, J.M. (2012). *Global Modernity, Development, and Contemporary Civilization: Towards a Renewal of Critical Theory*. New York and London: Routledge.

Domingues, J.M. (2013). *O Brasil entre o presente e o futuro. Conjuntura atual e inserção internacional*. Rio de Janeiro: Mauad.

Domingues, J.M. (2014). Global Modernity: Levels of Analysis and Conceptual Strategies. *Social Science Information*, 53(2), 180–196.

Dun, J. (1979). *Western Political Theory in the Face of the Future*. Cambridge: Cambridge University Press.

Fraser, N. (2009). *Scales of Justice: Reimagining Political Space in a Globalizing World*. Cambridge: Polity.

Fraser, N. and Honneth, A. (2003). *Redistribution or Recognition: A Political-Philosophical Exchange*. London and New York: Verso.

Habermas, J. (1981). *Theorie des kommunikativen Handelns* (Vols. 1–2). Frankfurt am Main: Suhrkamp.

Habermas, J. (1992). *Faktizität und Geltung*. Frankfurt am Main: Suhrkamp.

Habermas, J. (2001a). *Die Zukunft menschilichen Natur*. Frankfurt am Main: Suhrkamp.

Habermas, J. (2001b). *Glauben und Wissen*. Frankfurt am Main: Suhrkamp.

Habermas, J. (2011). *Eine Verfassung Europas. Ein Essay*. Frankfurt am Main: Suhrkamp.

Hardt, M. and Negri, A. (2000). *Empire*. Cambridge, MA: Harvard University Press.

Harvey, D. (1990). *The Condition of Postmodernity*. Malden, MA and Oxford: Blackwell.

Harvey, D. (2009). *The Enigma of Capital and the Crisis of Capitalism*. New York: Oxford University Press.

Honneth, A. (2010). *Das Ich in Wir. Studien zur Anerkennungstheorie*. Frankfurt am Main: Suhrkamp.

Honneth, A. (2011). *Das Recht der Freiheit. Grundrisse eine demokratischen Sittlichkeit*. Frankfurt am Main: Suhrkamp.

Hung, H. (2008). Rise of China and the Global Overaccumulation Crisis. *Review of International Political Economy*, 15(2), 149–179.

Lange, H. and Meier, L. (Eds.) (2009). *The New Middle Classes: Globalizing Lifestyles, Consumerism and Environmental Concern*. Dordrecht: Springer.

Mignolo, W.D. (2000). *Local Histories/Global Designs: Coloniality, Subaltern Knowledges, and Border Thinking*. Princeton, NJ: Princeton University Press.

Mignolo, W.D. (2005). *The Idea of Latin America*. Oxford: Blackwell.

Müller-Doohm, S. (2005). How to Criticize: Convergent and Divergent Paths in Critical Theories of Society. In G. Delanty (Ed.), *Handbook of European Social Theory*. New York: Routledge.

Nandy, A. (1978). Towards a Third World Utopia. *Traditions, Tyranny, and Utopias: Essays in the Politics of Awareness*. New Delhi: Oxford University Press.

Nobre, M. (2008). Teoria crítica hoje. In D.T. Peres et al. (Eds.), *Tensões e passagens. Filosofia crítica e modernidade*. São Paulo: Singular.

Pierson, P. and Skocpol, T. (Eds.). (2007). *The Transformation of American Politics: Activist Government and the Rise of Conservatism*. Princeton, NJ: Princeton University Press.

Pleyers, G. (2011). *Alter Globalization: Becoming Actors in the Global Age*. Cambridge: Polity.

Piketty, T. (2013). *Le Capital au XXIe siécle*. Paris: Seuil.

Santos, B.S. (2002). Para uma sociologia das ausências e uma sociologia das emergências. *Revista crítica de ciências sociais, 63*, 237–280.

Sassen, S. (2006). *Territory, Authority, Rights: from Medieval to Global Assemblages* (2nd ed.). Princeton, NJ: Princeton University Press.

Spivak, G.C. (1988). Can the Subaltern Speak? In C. Nelson and L. Grossberg (Eds.), *Marxism and the Interpretation of Culture*. Urbana, IL: University of Illinois Press.

Streeck, W. (2011). The Crisis of Democratic Capitalism. *New Left Review, 71*.

Streeck, W. (2013). *Gekaufte Zeit. Die vertagte Krise des demokratischen Kapitalismus*. Frankfurt am Main: Suhrkamp.

Svampa, M. (2008). *Cambio de época. Movimientos sociales y poder político*. Buenos Aires: Siglo XXI and Clacso.

Therborn, G. (2009). *From Marxism to Post-Marxism*. London and New York: Verso.

Tilly, C. (2004). *Contention and Democracy in Europe, 1650–2000*. Cambridge: Cambridge University Press.

Tilly, C. (2007). *Democracy*. Cambridge: Cambridge University Press.

Part II
Rethinking Social Contestation through Modernity

6

The Global Age: A Social Movement Perspective

Geoffrey Pleyers

Introduction

The coordinators of this volume propose to explore the links between social movements and 'a general view of contemporary social processes' or a 'social configuration', to take Elias' concept. Following Touraine (1981), they consider that specific generations of social movements correspond to specific types of society. After the workers' movement in the industrial society and 'new social movements' more oriented towards cultural struggles and recognition in the 'post-industrial society', they raise the question: 'Is there a new generation of social movements that correspond to a new phase of modernity (late modernity)?'

I would like to develop this question in two directions. First, while most chapters of this volume consider a new stage of modernity, I suggest that we have entered an era that is neither modern nor post-modern and that Albrow (1996) calls 'the global age'. The limits of the planet and of natural resources impede pursuing the modern project based on permanent growth and represent a major challenge for humanity. Secondly, I will draw on an agency-centred approach, combining two major questions: 'Who are the social actors who challenge the normative orientation at the core of modernization and promote alternative values and practices that may contribute to the rise of a global age, or may embody glimpses of a global age society?' and 'Can we grasp some dimensions of life and society in the global age *by studying current social movements?*'

After sketching out the 'global age hypothesis' and the need for an agency-centred approach, I will briefly explore how the global age perspective sheds a new light on the meanings and potential of four movements (indigenous and small farmers' movements, local and convivial initiatives in Western cities and climate justice [CJ] NGOs) and, conversely, how these actors provide insights for a better understanding of the global age and social agency in and towards it.

Social Agency in the Global Age

The Global Age Hypothesis

The successive reports by the International Panel on Climate Change lead to a clear statement: The modern way of life is not sustainable. It alters fundamental geological and chemical cycles, generates global warming at an increasing pace and depletes natural resources. This assertion deeply questions modernity itself, as the modern worldview is built on the perspective of an ever-expanding world and infinite natural resources – that allows economists and corporations to consider nature as a 'free good' (JB Say) and to exclude 'externalities' from economic considerations – and on the idea of permanent growth, that is supposed to lead humanity towards progress and better living standards (IPCC, 2013).

In the first part of the 21st century, we may experience a shift from *Globalization* – defined as the expansion of modernization and driven by the idea of growth– to what Martin Albrow (1996) has called *the Global Age*. It may be synthetized as *a social configuration* (Elias, 1969) in which life and society are deeply shaped by an increasing reality and consciousness of (a) the interdependence at the scale of humanity and (b) the finitude of the planet.

Rather than a comeback to post-modern positions, whose hyper-cultural perspectives have been criticized (Best & Kellner, 1997), Albrow argues for the specificities of a new age that is neither modern, nor post-modern, but 'global'. The modern project is incompatible with the limits of the planet and its natural resources.

The global age is both *an objective and a subjective reality*. The objective reality of the global age is notably illustrated by the 'anthropocene perspective' (Crutzen, 2002) and by global warming. Its subjective reality is both the rising consciousness of the finitude of the planet and the resulting worldview (*Weltanschauung*). The rise of global dangers and challenges (nuclear, climate change) has increased the consciousness of a shared destiny at the scale of humanity and expanded a sense of cosmopolitan identity (Albrow, 1996; Beck, 2007). However, these objective and subjective realities of the global age do not always correspond. Elias (1991: 214) pointed out a significant delay: 'Compared to the relatively rapid change of the integration shift, the pace of the corresponding change in the social habitus of the individuals concerned is extraordinarily slow'. For instance, the oil peak in 2006 represents a considerable threat to modern economy and way of life (Urry, 2012). However, most policy makers, citizens and social scientists live and work as if the oil peak did not exist. Thus, modernity and the global age co-exist in the subjective and objective reality of our time.

Taking into account the finitude of the planet contradicts the modern project of perpetual expansion and improvement of living standards through new technologies and science. It sheds a new light on contemporary debates on development (Escobar, 1995), world system (Smith and Wiest, 2012), growth (Latouche, 2011; Jackson, 2008) and raises major challenges for society and its actors, from global institutions to the sense of responsibility of ordinary people. It deeply transforms the way individuals and communities consider and experience life, society and the world.

Social Change in (and towards) the Global Age

As social scientists, we can neither deny the reality of the impact of human activities on climate and the environment, nor endorse the idea of a determinist social transition resulting from an environmental crisis. Future scenarios in a world affected by climate change and the finitude of the planet are numerous (Urry, 2013). A 'business as usual in the midst of climate deregulation' scenario is far from excluded. It actually dominates current policies and habits and is supported by powerful actors, which makes it the most probable option as long as the main resources (and oil in particular) remain of relatively easy access.

The 'redemption catastrophe' scenario has recently gained impetus among intellectuals and activists. The founder of the transition movement (Hopkins, 2011) and some of the most protagonist ecological actors and thinkers (e.g., Cochet et al., 2012) maintain that a catastrophe is needed to push humanity to adopt the required changes. Such a direct link between major crises and social change is questionable. The multiplication of hurricanes in the US and the heavy pollution smog in Beijing (see Zhang & Barr, 2013) have not impeded the governments of the two most polluting countries to maintain their energy and industrial policies[1] largely unchanged. The Fukushima major nuclear disaster has not prevented the Japanese government from restarting its nuclear power plants.

My point is not to deny that a crisis may represent an opportunity for social agency. Nevertheless, no matter how large it is, the crisis itself does not generate social change. The latter depends on the capacity of social actors to highlight the questions spawned by the situation and to successfully promote alternative political visions and economic rationality. Moreover, actors who manage to impose their interpretation of the crisis and foster an alternative political and economic rationality are not always the progressive ones (Klein, 2008).

Developing perspectives for a better understanding of social agency in and towards the global age thus constitutes a major challenge for social scientists. It requires analyzing both progressive and conservative actors, as well as the actors and mechanisms that foster the apathy in most individual and collective actors.

Social Movements as a Heuristic Tool

Studying social movements and the meanings and conflicts they raise provides us with two main ways to grasp elements of an upcoming social configuration with empirical data: social agency, on one side subjectivity and prefigurative action on the other side.

First, social movements contribute to the transformation of society[2]. Following Alain Touraine (1978), the concept of 'social movement' refers to a particular meaning of action; when actors challenge major normative orientations of a society and contribute to the transformation of this society. A good illustration was provided by Castells (1997), who started the second volume of his trilogy on the age of information by analyzing two movements that allowed him to understand some of the major transformations and influential actors of the next decade: the Zapatistas in Mexico and the Patriots in the US. The Zapatistas prefigured both the rising impact of indigenous movements in Latin America and the alter-globalization movement. The American Patriots and the grassroots conservative movements became the social constituency of Georges W. Bush government and of the Tea Party.

In addition to struggling for a different society, some social movements seek to embody it in their action and subjectivity. Prefigurative activism and the quest for more consistency between one's values and one's practices have become a central dimension of activism in many movements (Epstein, 1991; McDonald, 2006; Pleyers, 2010). It is notably the case among various sectors of ecological activists. The study of some environmental activists may thus provide us with empirical data about the impact of acute awareness of global interdependency and of the constraints of a limited planet on individual subjectivity and her sense of responsibility.

An agency-centred approach of the link between social movements and a general social configuration thus leads to the following question: 'Which actors challenge the normative orientation at the core of modernization, show the glimpses of a global age society and promote alternative values and practices that may contribute to the rise of a global age?'

Progressive Movements Towards the Global Age

While scientists and the International Panel on Climate Change have accumulated data alerting on the magnitude of climate change and its devastating consequences, more cars have been built old in 2014 than ever before[3] and economic growth remains the main preoccupation of all governments. The challenges of the global age are huge and urgent, but changes in individual and collective behaviours have remained very limited so far. This paradox of social agency in the global age may however only be apparent. The panorama is different when we look at grassroots actors. While actions and worldviews of policy makers remain largely shaped by the modern context, challenges and constraints, elements of a different social configuration are experienced, lived and produced in the shadow of everyday life, local initiatives and citizen debates.

Indigenous People Movements

In the last two decades, Latin American indigenous movements[4] have contributed to changing governments and shaping major public debates, laws and new constitutions (Cortez, 2011; Le Bot, 2009). They have implemented alternative social and political organizations in their communities in the Americas, India (Srikant, 2009) among other regions of the world. They have become leading protagonists of major global movements, inspiring thousands of activists over the world, as it is notably the case of Zapatista rebellion and community organization (Holloway, 2002).

Indigenous movements impact is even wider among current ecological movements as it was on the global justice movement. Indigenous movements have revisited traditional cosmovisions to propose alternative perspectives of development, happiness and relations with 'nature' that are far more compatible with the constraints of a limited planet than current policies and worldvision. Among the most widespread concepts, the 'Buen Vivir' ('good life', 'Sumak Kausai' in Quetchua) draws on Bolivian and Ecuadorian indigenous cosmovisions. This epistemological, cultural and economic paradigm proposes an alternative conception of development and happiness that focuses not on growth, accumulation and mass consumption but on a 'good life', defined as a cultural expression of shared satisfaction of human needs in harmony with nature and the community (Kowii, 2012; Cortez, 2011). Its core principles are the following ones (Gudynas, 2011): a quest *for harmony, and not for growth and endless development;* the respect of· 'Mother Earth' and of nature, to which humans are part of; the primacy of the community over individualism; a focus on complementarity, rather than competition; a de-commodification process in opposition to the *'monetarization of everything'*. It challenges core principles of modernity, such as the quest for a permanent growth and accumulation, the separation of nature and culture, and the primacy of expert knowledge.

However, indigenous people who implement this perspective as a personal and collective philosophy and in their community's daily life are seldom visible in national and international public arenas. Their perspectives have been connected to an international audience through events, brokers (Tarrow, 2005) and 'translaters' (Sousa Santos et al., 2014). The 2009 World Social Forum in Belem and the 2010 People Forum on climate change in Cochabamba have contributed to diffusing their world-views and their plea for more respectful relations with nature. Combining insights from the post-colonial studies and inspirations from indigenous traditional knowledge that was often little formalized, progressive intellec-tuals (Gudynas, 2011; Houtart, 2010; Acosta & Martinez, 2012) have brought perspectives inspired by the 'buen vivir' into intellectual and polit-ical arenas, often based on an idealized perspective of indigenous commu-nities and missing some of their complexity and their philosophical and cultural dimensions (Kowii, 2012). In the current global debates about an 'ecological transition', these perspectives oppose the 'scientific ecology' and the market and engineer solutions to deal with climate change, consid-ered as rooted in a narrow Western perspective and do not deal with the roots of the problem.

Small Farmers

Small farmers were also supposed to disappear with modernization and its urbanization and industrialization processes. The capitalist and sovietist systems as well as Indian – so called – 'green revolution' and most non-aligned countries development projects sacrificed family agriculture on the altar of modern industrialization. After the fall of the Berlin Wall, agro-industry and food corporations have figured among the main winners of corporate globalization. In this context, it was unexpected that small farm-ers' movements would become major protagonists of global movements.

Founded in 1993, La Vía Campesina has become the most globalized movement network, claiming 200 million members in 88 countries. It has been a leading actor of the struggle against the World Trade Organization, the alter-globalization movement and World Social Forums. Its role is even more central among environmentalist movements towards a global age. La Vía Campesina's organization, discourses and aims actually embody the two main features of the global age (the integration and interdependency at the scale of humanity and the challenges of a limited planet). It has suc-cessfully framed itself – and small farmers in general – as a global actor and an indispensable stakeholder in dealing with climate change and envi-ronmental challenges. Therefore, they relied on a double strategy.

First, La Vía Campesina has been particularly successful in combining various scales of actions (Bringel, 2014), from the local to the global, while maintaining 'a balance between local realities and global action'

(Desmarais, 2007: 135). Agrarian movements put forward an alternative development model that relies *on relocalization, re-peasantization and de-commodification.* Their claims for local agroecology and food sovereignty directly challenge the corporate globalization and the global food system. At the same time, it has projected itself as a global actor, adopting as one of its main slogans 'Globalize struggle, Globalize hope' building international alliances to claim the right to food sovereignty (Claeys, 2012; Bringel, 2011). It has kept its focus not only on its grassroots constituency and on 'relocalization' as a main target, jealously guarding the autonomy in the inclusions of its grassroots voices, but it has also invested the World Social Forum and a number of UN arenas (Claeys, 2012; Gaarde, forthcoming). La Vía Campesina has contributed to building the global scale by its struggles and by integrating UN arenas. It has also reshaped the local scale, as a scale that is not opposed to the global nor pre-modern, but that may contribute to dealing with some challenges of the global age by the rescaling of life, production and consumption.

Secondly, rather than presenting their claims as a corporatist defence of small farmers, la Vía Campesina has successfully framed them as public interest of humanity and major contributions to dealing with key challenges of the global age: to feed the planet, to protect the environment and to limit global warming.

> We must go beyond the anthropocentric model, we must rebuild the cosmovision of our peoples, based on a holistic view of the relationship between the cosmos, mother earth, the air, water and all human beings. Human beings do not own nature but rather form part of all that lives. The small farmers, peasants and indigenous agriculturalists hold in their hands thousands of solutions to climate change (Vía Campesina's final declaration at the 2010 Summit on Climate in Cancun).

Indigenous communities and small farmers were previously considered as anachronistic leftovers of a pre-modern era that would disappear with the modernization process. They now inspire citizens and intellectuals worldwide and are widely considered as frontrunners of the global age. As summarized by an activist during the 2008 Social Forum in Mexico City, I was always taught to look at the North and the West. But today, if we want to change things, we have to look towards the South and towards the indigenous people'.

Indigenous cosmovisions and community and small farmers' alternatives are not much different from what these actors proposed a few decades ago, but the rise of the global age has provided a new space for small farmers and indigenous peoples' identity and agency and to the recognition of their contribution to humanity. While their claims and projects did not fit in the modern project, they now *resonate* with the aspirations of thousands worldwide and with the objectives of international institutions.

Critical Consumption and Convivial Movements

The aspiration to build a world based on more self-reliant local communities is shared beyond indigenous communities and small farmers. It has recently gained a new impetus all over the Western world. 'Relocalization movements' were particularly active in Australia, the US and the UK in the mid-2000s. Hopkins (2011) has given a new impetus to local and ecological 'transition initiatives' in the UK and abroad. 'Voluntary simplicity' (de Bouver, 2009) has gained momentum and thousands of local food networks and 'community supported agriculture' have been created in the last decade. They question the industrial food system rationale that is responsible for one-third of human induced greenhouse gas emissions (Gilbert, 2012) and promote family farms. Critical consumption is understood as the deliberate and conscious attention paid to consumption choices in order to reify political positions connected with moral conceptions and global responsibility (Pleyers, 2011). Its rapid expansion (notably in the food sector) testifies the consciousness of some constraints of the global age has reached far beyond classic environmental activists. Moreover in the aftermath of the economic crisis, thousands of Southern Europe citizens have turned to local initiatives both to address their needs outside of failed market economy and to foster local solidarity (Sánchez, 2012; Conill et al., 2012). Particularly insightful intellectual and activists' spaces have rescued the concept of 'commons' to think and implement alternative management of common resources beyond state and market, and beyond the false dichotomy of institutional regulations and personal choices (Boiller, 2014).

Everywhere, activists[5] recycle and reuse objects, travel by bike and public transports, reduce their consumption, grow vegetables, buy local food and set up local currencies. They claim to change the world through prefigurative activism, by implementing alternative practices in their daily lives and local communities. Personal commitment to the global age and a more sustainable planet also involves considerable subjective dimensions such as personal resistance against the 'constant formatting by advertisings and the rule of a consumption, competition and constant comparison society' (a young activist in Belgium, interview, 2013)[6]. These activists call themselves 'objectors to growth and speed', and question the economists' monopole over the determination of well-being on the basis of GDP growth (Méda, 2013).

While decreasing consumption and restraining one's choices is constraining in a consumption society, activists put much energy *in reframing it (and living it) as happy experience.* To be involved in food or environmental movements does not require sacrificing part of one's life for a cause, they insist. On the opposite, activists claim they live 'more intensely' and enjoy 'more authentic pleasures' and happiness. 'It is important to explain to people that it is not a sacrifice. On the contrary, life will actually become better.' (an activist from Sustainable Flatbush, New York City, 2010).

Likewise, 'voluntary simplicity' practices do not only aim at decreasing personal carbon footprint, but also reduces working time and fosters convivial human relations (Schor, 2010; Caillé et al., 2012). Activists seek to 'replaces productivity by conviviality' (Illich, 1973: 28), the anonymity of (super-)market relations by the authenticity of direct relationships between consumers and local producers; the widespread social disaffiliation (Castel, 2003) by renewed social fabric in collective gardens or among bikers.

Analyzing these actors allows us to gain access to some elements of both subjectivity and agency in the global age. On one side, local and convivial environmental movements show glimpses of the internalization of the rules and constraints of the emerging social configuration. We may well expect cultural transformations connected to a shift to the Global Age to be more visible among these activists, prior to a possible dissemination into a broader population. Interviews and fieldwork[7] with young environmental activists have shown how deeply their subjectivity and daily experience are reshaped by the consciousness of the global age and its challenges. It transforms daily practices as private as showers, diets and transport. They share tips to 'micro-shower' and reduce the use of water, eat local and season vegetables. Many have become vegetarians and avoid (or reduce) the use of cars and planes. We may also analyze the impact of an acute awareness of global interdependency and of the constraints of a limited planet on an individual subjectivity and her sense of responsibility. These actors testify to the rise of an ethics of responsibility specific to the global age and essential to a sustainable life on a limited planet (Jonas, 1984; Arnsperger, 2011). It includes more sustainable bonds with nature, along with a different concept of the self and of one's connection to the world.[8]

On the other side, these actors explore various paths of social agency that put life and experience rather than policies at the core of social change. These movements oppose modernization and top-down development perspectives. They rescale life and production, re-thinking the meaning and extend of consumption. From their local territories, these small and local actors contest core values of our society and thereby manifest a global relevance. Local and personal changes and the internalization of constraints of the global age constitute an indispensable element of the adaptation to the global conditions of life on a limited planet and provide social actors with paths for concrete social agency in a global age.

However, pointing to the significance of local movements does not dispense a critical analysis of empirical and structural limits of these forms of social agency. Empirically, the impact of these initiatives and movements remains limited when confronted to a consumer society that seduces millions of newcomers in emerging countries. Analytically, the connection between local or personal change and social transformations at the national and global scales usually remains a blind spot for activists (Pleyers, 2010). Can the world be changed only by multiplying individual conversions or building local 'resilient' communities? Will the multiplication of 'alternative islands' in an ocean of modern capitalist societies manage to alter the system? Or will actors also have to tackle more institutional and political struggles?

Climate Justice NGOs

The 'Climate Justice Movement' is often used as an umbrella for designating the whole set of ecological activists. In this section, I focus on professional activists working in NGOs, endowed with a strong expertise, monitoring and research capacity, but who maintain a contentious perspective on environmental issues and oppose the market-based proposals to deal with climate change.

Climate justice activists' main objective is to *'repoliticise' climate and environmental issues*. They do so by pointing to the strong connection between climate issues and social justice, and by focusing on advocacy and global regulations while claiming some admiration for grassroots struggles and actors. Climate justice (CJ) NGO activists are thus at the crossroads of two confluences which results in tensions and concrete dilemas: social and environmental claims; grassroots and institutional perspectives on social change.

Red and Green: 'Change the System, not the Climate'

The CJ movement emerged from a confluence of social and environmental struggles. It is partly rooted in the 'environmental turn' of the alter-globalization movement in the second half of the 2000s (Bullard and Müller, 2012; Pleyers, 2010: 251–256), which generated lively and committed expert networks and initiatives such as the 'climate action camps'. The repeated clashes between pro- and anti-'market solutions' to global warming among civil society organizations also propelled the birth of the 'climate justice movement'. The 'Climate Justice Now!' network was founded at the UN conference on climate in Bali, in 2007, in opposition to the stance held by the 'Climate Action Network'. The latter was rejected on the grounds that it is dominated by international (mainly Northern)

NGOs that consider carbon trade and market-based solutions as a step towards a more sustainable development. On the contrary, CJ activists denounce carbon trade as a further financiarization of nature (e.g., Durban Declaration on Carbon Trading, 2005), and virulently condemn agrofuels (Houtart, 2010; De Schutter, 2013), 'green washing' and 'green capitalism' (Müller & Passadakis, 2009; Featherstone, 2013). As stated in their main slogan 'System change, not climate change', CJ activists consider that global warming requires structural changes in the economic and development model, rather than adjustments at the margins.

Albrow's global age hypothesis, most of the ecological transition thought (Hopkins, 2011) and some cosmopolitan theories point to a rather consensual shift towards a rising awareness of the unity of humanity. Likewise, scholars and activists maintain (Chakrabarty, 2009) that global warming and environmental damages affect humanity as a whole and consequently lead to a focus on the common destiny of humanity rather than class and national divides. In the opposite, CJ activists point to the contentious dimension of the shift to the global age and to rising social conflicts linked to environmental challenges (Svampa & Antonelli, 2009). They insist that all human beings do not share the same responsibility in global warming and in the destruction of the environment.[9] They point to a differentiated responsibility for industrialized countries and to the richest (7 per cent of mankind account for 50 per cent of the greenhouse gases emissions). Hence, they consider that to tackle global warming and the environmental crisis requires dealing with inequalities, North/South relations and neoliberal globalization.

CJ activists and committed intellectuals merge climate and environmental justice with anti-capitalism frames (Guerrero, 2011; Löwy, 2011; Ceceña, 2013) and often contribute to build a master frame that points to a 'civilization crisis' (Ornelas, 2013) provoked by the capitalist and industrial system or the 'productivist ideology'. Like the Global Age analytical perspective, they maintain that the current environmental challenges cannot be dealt with in the modern economic and development paradigm and requires deep reshaping in the economic system as well as in societies and global governance.

Institutional Civil Society with an Eye of the Grassroots[10]

CJ NGOs are also at the crossroads between institutional and grassroots approaches. On one hand, CJ NGO activists consider perspectives that focus on local change and individual purchasing habits as illusory and limited in scope. CJ 'radical NGOs' invest much of their energy in some of the typical functions of institutionalized civil society actors. They raise public awareness, monitor international institutions and negotiations, draw

up expert reports and conduct advocacy campaigns to convince governments to adopt regulations.

On the other hand, CJ activists constantly denounce 'big environmental
NGOs' and oppose both their very top-down institutional approach and
their support of market-based solutions. They re-assert the conflictual
dimensions of their claims and repeatedly refer to – often idealized –
'grassroots struggles', preferably from the global South.

Their conflictual stance stems from two main sources. First, successive
international summits on climate change and the environment (Bali, 2007;
Copenhagen, 2009; Cancun, 2010; Rio, 2012…) favoured confluences
among North-based environmental NGOs and social movements from the
global South, including small farmers, indigenous peoples and delegates
from local struggles protesting against state 'development' projects (mines,
dams, big plants, highways…). Indigenous peoples' participation and
insights from Southern movements were particularly strong at the 2009
World Social Forum in Belem and the 2010 'Peoples' World Conference
on Climate Change and the Rights of Mother Earth' that gathered 25,000
people from 147 countries in Cochabamba, Bolivia.

The second root of this positioning lies in the activist career (Fillieule,
2009) of 'young adults' now turned into professional NGO activists. A few
years ago, they protested against international summits and implemented
a horizontal 'alter-activist' culture (Pleyers, 2010: Chapters 2–4). Now
working as professional NGOs' activists, they however maintain some
suspicion towards 'big environmental NGOs', develop a more contentious
approach and contribute to a 'gradual SMO-ization of environmental
NGOs… with a growing tendency to participate in less conventional forms
of collective action and to express increasingly explicit criticism of EU
policies' (Della Porta & Caiani, 2009: 172).

The failure of the UN negotiations on climate in Copenhagen became a
new unifying reference for the CJ movement and an apparent turning point
in its strategy. The path toward institutional change led by the UN being
blocked, CJ activists have decided to focus on the support to grassroots
alternatives and struggles against infrastructure projects and extraction
industries. However, by claiming that 'change will not come from institutional agreements but from grassroots' actors', CJ NGOs put themselves in
an uncomfortable position. First, CJ NGOs *raison d'être* is precisely the
conviction that local solutions are not sufficient to deal with global challenges. Secondly, NGOs, even radical ones, are not grassroots actors. They
may provide occasional support, expertise or media coverage of local
movements, but with the web 2.0, grassroots networks often do not need
intermediaries.

The role of CJ NGOs lies in their capacity to connect local environmental struggles (e.g., water movements, protests against a dam…) to international struggles and institutions. '*We have to make them feel that their local struggle is part of something wider*' (a CJ NGO professional, Focus Group, Brussels, 10/2013). This process transforms both the scale (from a local to international) and the meanings of the struggle (from the defence of a local livelihood to environmental justice). Thus, and contrary to many of their discourses, CJ NGOs and activists have not stopped monitoring and lobbying UN and European institutions. The next major governmental Climate Summit in Paris in 2015 is in everyone's head, hopeful it will be conducive to a better tackling of climate justice, or at least that the urgency of environmental challenges will gain impetus thanks to the coverage of the event. In the meantime 'there is one key question: How do we build a global movement for climate, locally based but also global appeal and strategy' (final assembly, 2013 WSF Climate Space).

Conclusion: From the Global Age to Social Movements and Back

The panorama of progressive actors that foster a more responsible shift towards the global age is far from complete. This chapter restrained the scope on some environmental actors, ignoring actors who focus on challenges of democracy or economic regulations in the global age (see Pleyers, 2010). Even among environmentalists actors, green parties and policy makers (Richardson & Rootes, 2006), networks of heterodox economists, local resistances to development projects (mines, dams, airports…) (Svampa & Antonelli, 2009; Srikant, 2009) and 'grassroots environmental alliances' would have deserved a proper analysis.

The aim of this chapter was, however, to illustrate a two-sided heuristic connection between a social configuration and social movements. The global age hypothesis has shed a new light on specific meanings of environmentalist actors. Conversely, analyzing these social movements and their claims provide us with two sources of empirical elements to grasp elements of life, society and public debates *in* this global age, and social agency *towards* the global age.

On one hand, prefigurative movements show the glimpses of life and society in a global age. The shift towards a global age is not only a matter of international negotiations and institutions. While actions and world-views of policy makers remain largely shaped by the modern context, challenges and constraints, elements of a different social configuration are experienced, lived and produced in the shadow of everyday life, local initiatives and citizen debates. They suggest the rise of an ethics that better corresponds to the global age. On the other hand, by combining expertise and agency in international negotiations and institutions, with grassroots struggles and bottom-up strategies, environmentalist activists explore innovative strategies to promote habits and public policies more consistent with a finite planet. They provide elements for a multi-dimensional and multi-scalar approach to social change, from local to global, from personal change to institutional regulations.

However, these movements' impact on international negotiations and public policy remains limited compared to the urgency of the challenges. Environmentalist movements are now widespread, but they have not significantly reduced mass consumption and the depletion of natural resources. The economic crisis and quest for economic growth has lowered the interest for environmental issues among Western countries and the rise of China as an economic superpower and environmental super polluter brings about new challenges (Zhang & Barr, 2013). Indeed, there is no system or determinist force sparking towards a smooth and untroubled adaptation to the constraints of the global age and social agency plays on both sides. Counter-movements require a particular attention. Conservative movements promote a modernization perspective and are effectively engaged in maintaining the mainstream model. Urry (2013: Chapter 4) evokes the efficiency of US conservative movements and car and oil companies lobbies in organizing a backlash against environmental movements and values in the 1970s. More recently, the same actors have massively founded climate-sceptics think tanks (Brulle et al., 2013).

The CJ movement also contributes to a major renewing of critical perspectives in a time increasingly shaped by the global age. CJ activists transform the claims of both social and environmental justice. Social justice should include intergenerational justice, environmental and climate debts, redistribution policies at the global level and an *aggiornamento* of Western welfare state, relying on the economic growth that destroys nature and on the exploitation of workers in the South. Therefore, they stress both the need for international regulations and institutions, and inspirations from non-Western knowledge. The combination of these critical approaches and the global age perspective suggest that what is at stake in the current crisis and social movements is modernity itself, both as a utopia, a social organization and an ethos based on a permanent growth. A renewal of the critical perspective thus requires an epistemological shift from the modern roots of social sciences and mainstream worldview (Echeverría, 1995). Empirical studies of actors who prefigurate and foster a transition to a global age thus provide us insightful perspectives to rethink society, regulations, solidarity and emancipation in the 21st century.

Notes

1   Vasi's (2011) excellent book provides a rigorous analysis of the impacts and failures of green movements' strategies on national governments.

2   'Social movement' is a heuristic concept and not an empiric reality. It is 'neither an empirical reality, nor a transcended reality. It is a sociological concept. Historic actor can neither be fully identified to it, nor understood outside of their relation to it' (Touraine, 1965:70).

3   An expected 85 million (see Ramsey & Boudette, 2013).

4   Only a minority of indigenous people and communities are actually involved in initiatives for an alternative way of life (Fontaine, 2006).

5   Many citizens who contribute to these initiatives do not actually consider themselves as 'activists'. 'I do not see it as activism. It is just a change in our way of life' (a Swedish student, 2012).

6   The assertion of activists' subjectivity and authenticity against consumption society plays as a permanent repetition of the Habermas' confrontation between the Lebenswelt and the System.

7   Interviews in France (2009–2012), New York City (2010–2011) and Rio de Janeiro (2013) and sociological interventions (series of focus groups) with young environmentalists in Belgium (2013).

8   Elias' (1969) interdependency between the self and social configuration.

9   See notably the Declaration of the 2002 Climate Justice Summit in Delhi.

10   This section relies notably on the results of a sociological intervention I conducted with Christian Scholl and Priscilla Claeys, both from the University of Louvain, on climate justice activists working in NGOs around the European institutions in Brussels in 2013.

References

Acosta, A. and Martínez, E. (Eds.). (2012). *El Buen Vivir*. Quito: Abya Yala.

Albrow, M. (1996). *The Global Age*. Cambridge: Polity.

Ariès, P. (2012). *Le socialisme gourmand*. Paris: La Découverte.

Arnsperger, C. (2011). *L'homme économique et le sens de la vie*. Paris: Textuel.

Beck, U. (2007). *The Cosmopolitan Outlook*. Cambridge: Polity.

Best, S. and Kellner, D. (1997). *The Postmodern Turn*. New York: Guilford Press.

Boiller, D. (2014). *Think Like a Commoner*. Gabriola Island: New Society Publishers.

Bringel, B. (2011). 'Soberanía alimentaria: La práctica de un concepto. In P.M. Osés. (Ed.), *Las políticas globales importan. Informe Anual de Social Watch 2010*. Madrid: IEPALA, pp. 95–102.

Bringel, B. (2014). *O MST e o internacionalismo contemporâneo*. Rio de Janeiro: EdUERJ.

Brulle, R., Carmichael J. and Jenskins J. (2013). Institutionalizing Delay: Foundation Funding and the Creation of US Climate Change Counter-Movement Organizations. *Climatic Change*, 1–14. doi: 10.1007/s10584-013-1018-7. www.drexel.edu/~/media/Files/now/pdfs/Institutionalizing%20Delay%20-., Numéro du volume?

Bullard, N. and Müller, T. (2012). Beyond the 'Green Economy'. *Development, 55*(1), 54–62.

Caillé, A., Humbert M., Latouche S. and Viveret P. (2012). *De la convivialité*, Paris: La découverte.

Castel, R. (2003). *Transformation of the Social Question*. New Brunswick, NJ: Transaction.

Castells, M. (1997). *Power of Identity*. Oxford: Blackwell.

Ceceña, A.E. (2013). Subvertir la modernidad para vivir bien. In R. Ornelas (Ed.), *Crisis civilizatoria y superación del capitalismo*. Mexico: UNAM.

Chakrabarty, D. (2009). The Climate of History: Four Theses. *Critical Inquiry*, *35*(1), 197–222.

Claeys, P. (2012). The Creation of New Rights by the Food Sovereignty Movement. *Sociology*, *46*(5), 844–860.

Cochet, Y., Dupuy J.P. and Latouche S. (2012). *Où va le monde? 2012–2022: une décennie au devant des catastrophes*. Paris: 1001 Nuits.

Conill, J., Castells, M., Cardenas, A. and Servon, L. (2012). Beyond the Crisis: The Emergence of Alternative Economic Practises. In M. Castells, J. Caraça and G. Cardoso (Eds.), *Aftermath. The Cultures of the Economic Crisis*. Oxford: Oxford University Press, pp. 65–84.

Cortez, D. (2011). *La Constrcucción Social del Buen Vivir en Ecuador*, Quito: PADH.

Crutzen, P. (2002). Geology of Mankind. *Nature*, *415*, 23.

De Bouver, E. (2009). *La simplicité volontaire*. Charleroi: Couleurs libre.

De Schutter, O. (2013). *Note on the Impacts of the EU Biofuels Policy on the right to Food*. New York: United Nations Human Rights.

Della Porta, D. and Caiani, M. (2009). *Social Movements and Europeanization*. Oxford: Oxford University Press.

Desmarais, A.A. (2007). *La Vía Campesina: Globalization and the Power of Peasants*. London: Pluto.

Durban Declaration on Carbon Trading (2005). Climate Justice Now! The Durban Declaration on Carbon Trading. Available at www.durbanclimatejustice.org/durban-declaration/english.html (accessed on 9 September, 2014).

Echeverría, B. (1995), *Las ilusiones de la modernidad*. México: UNAM/El equilibrista.

Elias, N. (1969). *Le processus de civilisation*. Paris: Fayard.

Elias N. (1991). *La société des individus*, Paris: Fayard.

Epstein, B. (1991). *Political Protest and Cultural Revolution*. Berkeley: University of California Press.

Escobar, A. (1995). *Encountering Development*. Princeton: Princeton University Press.

Featherstone, D. (2013). The Contested Politics of Climate Change and the Crisis of Neo-liberalism. *ACME*, *12*(4), 44–64.

Fillieule, O. (2009). Carrière militante. In O. Fillieule, L. Mathieu and C. Péchu (Eds.), *Dictionnaire des mouvements sociaux*. Paris: Presses de Sciences Po.

Fontaine, G. (2006). Convergences et tensions entre ethnicité et écologisme. *Autrepart*, *38*(1), 63–80.

Gaarde, I. (forthcoming). *La Vía Campesina Occupying Global Policy Space*, (Ph.D. dissertation). *École des hautes études en sciences sociales*, Paris.

Gilbert, N. (2012). One-Third of Our Greenhouse Gas Emissions Come from Agriculture. *Nature News*. doi:10.1038/nature.2012.11708.

Gudynas, E. (2011). Tensiones, contradicciones y oportunidades de la dimensión ambiental del Buen Vivir. In H. Farah and L. Vasapollo (Eds.), *Vivir bien*. La Paz: CIDES.

Guerrero, D. (2011). The Global Climate Justice Movement. In M. Albrow, H. Anheier, M. Kaldor and H. Seckinelgin (Eds.), *Global Civil Society*. London: Palgrave.

Holloway, J. (2002). *Change the World Without Taking Power*. London: Pluto.

Hopkins, R. (2011). *The Transition Companion*. Devon: Green books.

Houtart, F. (2010). *Agrofuels*. London: Pluto.

Houtart, F. and Daiber, B. (Eds.). (2012). *Un paradigma postcapitalista: El bien común de la humanidad*. Panama: Ruth.

Illich, I. (1973). *La convivialité*. Paris: Seuil.

IPCC. (2013). *Fifth Assessment Report: Climate Change 2013*. New York: United Nations.

Jackson, T. (2008), *Prosperity Without Growth: Economics for a Finite Planet*. New York: Earthscan.

Jonas, H. (1984). *The Imperative of Responsibility: In Search of an Ethics for the Technological Age*. Chicago: Chicago University Press.

Klein, N. (2008). The *Shock Doctrine*. New York: Metropolitan books.

Kowii, A. (2012). *El Sumak Kawsay*. Quito: UASB.

Latouche, S. (2011). *Vers une société d'abondance frugale*, Paris: Mille et une nuits.

Le Bot, Y. (2009). La grande révolte indienne. Paris: Laffont.

Löwy, M. (2011). *L'écosocialisme*. Paris: 1001 Nuits.

McDonald, K. (2006). *Global Movements*. Londres: Blackwell.

Méda, D. (2013). *La mystique de la croissance*. Paris: Flammarion.

Melucci, A. (1996). *Challenging Codes*. Cambridge: Cambridge University Press.

Müller, T. and Passadakis. (2009). Another Capitalism is Possible? From World Economic Crisis to Green Capitalism. In K. Abramsky (Ed.), *Sparking a World-wide Energy Revolution*. Oakland: AK Press.

Ornelas, R. (2013). *Crisis civilizatoria y superación del capitalismo*. Mexico: UNAM.

Pleyers, G. (2010). *Alter-Globalization. 'Becoming Actors in the Global Age'*. Cambridge: Polity.

Pleyers, G. (2011). *La consommation critique*. Paris: DDB.

Ramsey, M. and Boudette, N. (2013). Global Car Sales in 2014. *Wall Street Journal*. Available at http://online.wsj.com/news/articles/SB10001424052702304858104579262412636884466

Richardson, D. and Rootes, C. (2006). *The Green Challenge*. London: Routledge.

Sánchez, M. (2012). Losing Strength? An alternative Vision of Spain's Indignados, Reflections on a Revolution. Retrieved on 20 June 1994 from http://roarmag.org/2012/06/losing-strength-an-alternative-vision-of-the-indignados/

Schor, (2010). *True Wealth*. New York: Penguin.

Smith, J. and Wiest, D. (2012). *Social Movements in the World-system*. New York: Sage Publications.

Sousa Santos, B. and Meneses, M.P. (2014). *Epistemologies of the South*. Boulder, CO: Paradigm.

Srikant, P. (2009). Tribal Movement in Orissa: A Struggle Against Modernisation? ISEC Working Paper No. 215, ISEC, Bangalore.

Svampa, M. and Antonelli, M. (Eds.) (2009). *Minería transnacional, narrativas del desarrollo y resistencias sociales*. Buenos Aires: Biblios.

Tarrow, S. (2005). *The New Transnational Activism*. Cambridge: Cambridge University Press.

Touraine, A. (1965). *Sociologie de l'action*. Paris: Seuil.

Touraine, A. (1981). *The Voice and the Eye*. Cambridge: Cambridge University Press.

Urry, J. (2012). *Climate Change and Society*. Cambridge: Polity.

Urry, J. (2013). *Societies Beyond Oil*. London: Zed Books.

Vasi, I.B. (2011). *Winds of Change*. Oxford: Oxford University Press.

Zhang, J. and Barr, M. (2013). *Green Politics in China*. London: Pluto.

7

Social Movements and Contemporary Modernity: Internationalism and Patterns of Global Contestation

Breno M. Bringel

Introduction

Modern social movements have been understood as practically synonymous to national social movements. The labour movement – despite the creation of the many different 'Internationals', which is one of the main starting points for militant internationalism and cross-border activism – was identified and ultimately associated with a government and a nation. This idea frequently reflected up in the study of social movements. Even though there is a broad consensus that the 1960s was a moment of academic institutionalization of the social movement debate (with the development of discussions on the resource mobilization theory, political process, new social movements, etc.), the narrowing of the field during this period corresponds, strictly speaking, with a second phase of the study of social movements (Bringel, 2011).

The first phase involves the interpretations of sociological 'classics' and is premised upon a deep relationship between emerging social movements in industrial societies and the characterization of the elements, dynamics and values of modernity. The debates on liberty, equality, justice and emancipation, which were extremely important in that period, are proof of this. In fact, by placing conflict and collective action at the center of the social structure and devising an interpretation of class as a political subject and of organization, Marx provides us with the first theory on social movements compatible with a broader theory of modernity and labour internationalism (Bringel & Domingues, 2012). However, since Marx and up to the 'new social movements', despite many theories connecting the actions of social movements and broader societal changes (Blumer, 1951; Touraine, 1965), as well as a clear concern with international articulation, these connections were, to different degrees, mediated and centralized by the nation-state.

It was only in the 1990s, which coincides with what I consider to be the third phase of social movement studies and the rearticulation of its practices during contemporary modernity (Bringel, 2011) and with what José Maurício Domingues calls the 'third phase of modernity' (Domingues, 2012; see also the introduction of this book), when the theories on collective action and social movements started to try to capture, in a more systematic fashion, the cross-border overlapping of politics and activism. It was also a moment when modernity (or modernities) became highly complex, which coincides with what other authors prefer to call 'post-modernity', or any other number of labels, such as 'liquid modernity' and others.[1] We find here many profound societal and geopolitical changes, which lead to a globalization, unparalleled in history, of processes, structures and social flux, as well as a profound restructuring of social actors' articulation and contestation practices and dynamics.

This does not mean that the 'transnational activism' and 'global movements,' which emerged in this particular moment, are the exclusive outcome of the effects and the response to neoliberal globalization and new 'global governance' (Tarrow, 2005; Pleyers, 2010). Far from it, what happened was a larger interaction between scales and actors, as well as a greater decentring of the nation-state as a hegemonic reference for protests and the configuration and articulation of social actors, forcing a redefinition of internationalism and transnational solidarity. One can even take a step further: there is a *progressive de-nationalization of contemporary internationalism* (Bringel, 2014b; Cairo & Bringel, 2010), which is expressed in the decentralization of solidarity with a state/nation (as was common, for example, in the mid-20th century with Cuba, Nicaragua under the Sandinistas, or various other 'new African states' during decolonization) towards a growing solidarity with a cause, movement and/or experience. The same holds true as to other specific and organizationally decentred causes, as has been common in the recent protest cycle led by the so-called 'indignados' in Portugal or Spain. If contemporary transnational capitalism's dynamics have become much more complex, the same is true for social contestation.

In the last couple of decades, a vast amount of literature has attempted to describe and examine the scale shift, the different cycles of global contestation and the actions of social movements in the international scenario. Studies such as those by Smith et al. (1997), Keck and Sikkink (1998), Brysk (2000), Waterman (2001), Della Porta and Tarrow (2005), Tarrow (2005), Santos (2006), McDonald (2006), Khasnabish (2008), Pleyers (2010), von Bülow (2010) and, more recently, Castells (2012) and Featherstone (2012), among others, sparked pioneering discussions concerning a 'new' transnational activism that transcends national borders.

These authors define the phenomenon in different ways: 'transnational activism', 'global collective action', 'transnational social movements', 'global civil society', 'networks of the outrage', 'global left', 'new inter-nationalism', or 'complex internationalism'. However, opening up the field of social movement studies beyond the territoriality of the nation state does not mean starting with similar theoretical-methodological assumptions, nor common epistemological and normative-political hori-zons. This is how the wide range of practices and conceptual possibilities of the subject often leads to homogenizing views of social actors acting globally in the current stage of modernity. This can lead to generalizations about 'global activism' from a specific type of global action carried out by social actors. This point seems to be quite problematic. For example, the recent literature on transnational advocacy networks often analyses this *specific type* of global action carried out by social actors practically as a synonym *of* transnational activism and *of* contemporary internationalism in general terms.

In this chapter, I seek to characterize and analyse the main patterns of contentious collective action utilized by social actors who acts globally in the current stage of modernity. It is important to distinguish, in analytical and political terms, the diversity of forms of action, their geographic scope, the variety of actors and their projects, their concepts of social change and their critical views on modernity itself. Based on my previous work on the antiglobalization movement (Bringel & Echart, 2010; Bringel, et al., 2009), rural social movements' transnational networks (Bringel & Falero, 2008; Bringel, 2014a; 2014b), and more recent research on the current geopolitics of global outrage (Bringel, 2013), I suggest that since the fall of the Berlin Wall up until today five main patterns of global contestation have coexisted: the persistence of a more 'classical' standard of interna-tionalism; the internationalization of territorialized social movements; the transnational advocacy networks; the antiglobalization movement; and, finally, a more recent pattern of global outrage.

There are tensions and overlappings among these different patterns, which despite not exhausting the possibilities for globally oriented conten-tious collective action in the current stage of modernity, are quite represen-tative of the diversity of expressions and tendencies of activist contemporary internationalism. I will examine the main characteristics of each one of these patterns comparatively, utilizing a set of four variables: the first, a spatial one, evaluates its geographical scope and the ways it articulates the scales of political action (in the local–global continuum, including the intermediate stages) and the territory-network dialectic; the second variable expresses a temporal profile and associates each one of the pat-terns analysed to a specific cycle of global mobilization; the third variable seeks to define the social actor or collective subject underlying each one of these patterns; and, finally, the fourth and last variable analyses the main forms and repertoires of collective action utilized by these different patterns. Although it is possible to include other variables in a more significant manner (among them, how each one employs new information and communication technologies), in this chapter my focus is limited to transversal dimensions such as space, time, actors and the action itself.

Transformation and Persistence of Solidarities and Militant Internationalism

As a modern concept, the notion of solidarity (which is frequently confused with fraternity or brotherhood) was discussed by all of the 'founding fathers of sociology' since the mid-19th century: from the Comtean interpretation of solidarity related to continuity to Durkheim's well-known vision on solidarity as one of the normative mechanisms that integrate members into society, going through Weber's more micro-oriented interpretation of character, relating it to social action and emphasizing the importance of interests and honours. The theoretical realm aside, it is a fundamental element and strongly rooted in political and religious practices and projects of different stripes. The practice of solidarity is ancient, and vis-à-vis pre-modern societies peasant communities are frequently used as examples to illustrate the importance of reciprocity and loyalty.

In a more articulated analysis, Marx is the one, once again, who would connect the realm of ideas and the one of practical politics. When formulating his own vision of class solidarity, he was influenced by previous formulations, such as Charles Fourier and Pierre Leroux's early 19th century contributions, possibly the first ones to shape the notion of solidarity politically and socially. Fourier, often considered the founder of utopian socialism and cooperativism, put forward a very programmatic proposal based on the creation of self-sufficient rural communities, the *phalanstères*, in which between 1,500 and 1,600 people would live in harmony, with social and collective solidarity essential for its functioning. Leroux began with a harsh criticism of Christian charity, the idea of a social contract being the foundation of a society, and the concept of society as an organism in order to conjure up his conception of solidarity as a relationship.

Within the context of capitalism's first great crisis and the 1848 revolutions, the term solidarity is expanded and we observe how an 'I' and an 'us' is created, as well as an 'us' and a 'them' (Stjernø, 2004). One issue that is particularly interesting for the initial delimitation of solidarity and modern internationalism is that, although the construction of this 'us' as labour class referenced the identification of a common situation and common enemy, similar political practices and physical proximity, the restriction to a specific group (class) was not assumed to be confined to the territory of a nation-state. However, this opening is ambivalent since ultimately what was at stake with most of the Internationals, with the exception of the more radical anarchists, was an internationalist solidarity which sought to challenge the states, regardless of how diverse their projects for the post-extinction period of the capitalist state.

The First International emerged in 1864, with the motto 'workers of the world, unite', and driven by the ideal of labour's cohesive action in the struggle for the abolition of class society and economic emancipation, singles out the state, an outcome of a Marxist vision that breaks with the Bakunists, as an important reference for the articulations of labour parties. It is, in a nutshell, an *internationalist interstate* articulation. With quite different perspectives and ideas, and of a social democrat character, in 1889 the Second International unfolded and, in the 20th century, the triumph of the Russian Revolution led to the creation of the Communist International (the Third International), which became a network of communist parties of different countries whose objective was to spread the revolution globally. If in the Social Democrat International we saw a tension between the alignment with the interests of the nation-state and the more separatist perspective of labour internationalism, in the Communist International we see a strong uni-directionality of the internationalist diffusion, a product of the idea of broadening the process initiated in the Soviet Union, to other national and state units in the construction of socialism.

The crisis and disputes within the Communist International after the triumph of fascism in Europe led many activists, guided by Trotsky, to create in 1938 the Fourth International, whose banner was the 'Transition Program,' which considered the crisis of human civilization to be a crisis of labour leadership. It is important to point out that Trotsky's vision reiterated original beliefs of the First International, namely, that only a permanent global revolution seeking to spread socialism could overcome a rigid identification between socialism and the territoriality of the nation-state, and reverberates in many emancipatory experiences and later global contestation processes that understand that resistance must be as global as capital. Sections of the Fourth International still exist in many places, especially in Latin America and Europe but, while they are still loyal to many of its foundational principles, they are also engaged with the new manifestations of internationalism born after the fall of the Berlin Wall and the radicalization of neoliberal globalization. Somehow, the creation of a global party for labour revolution lost momentum to the timely and/or permanent convergence between multiple parties and social movements seeking emancipation.

Many groups, from Trotskyite dissidents in the 1940s to more recent initiatives by the former Venezuelan president Hugo Chávez, discussed and suggested the creation of a Fifth International. It seems unlikely that the social forces opposed to capitalism in the current stage of modernity will come together in this kind of space/movement. This may seem paradoxical, since the internationalist resistance to capital is increasingly broader and more diverse and the power of capital deeper and far-reaching. Be it as it may, we must consider contemporary capitalism's transformations (in its productive and financial manifestation, but also in its social, political and cultural capillarity) as well as the changes in the left and in global resistances (which include an important debate about its past and its views on the future, the metamorphosis of utopian and ideological references, among many other elements).

In many cases, in the contemporary literature 'new internationalism' is pitted against 'classic internationalism'. The 'novelty' has scant explaining power for it is not a category of analysis, as was made clear during the debate on 'new social movements'. Still, it is important to contemplate the transformations and permanence of the solidarities and activist internationalism not only in terms of a continuum of articulation practices but also in terms of broader changes within a new geopolitics of resistances which redefines key issues, such as: Who are the political enemies? What differentiates this century's left from last century's left? What does activism and being an activist mean today? How can we understand current social transformations? A thought experiment of this kind is beyond the scope of this chapter, but I can put forward at least three general comments.

Firstly, in classical internationalist solidarity, the *international* was almost always opposed to the *national*, while the contemporary internationalism of the 'Zapatista and Seattle generation' breaks with this binary logic to incorporate a broader sense of political solidarity, which transcends the territoriality of the nation-state and flows between the local and the global (in a greater activation of politics of scales and different actors), without creating a new binary, essentialist opposition. With these new possibilities to explore human solidarity in the global community using multi-scalar interactions, contemporary social actors have partially displaced traditional forms of solidarity, which are currently more decentred (as are forms of organization) and intermittent, forcing new conceptualizations. The notion of *inter*national itself can no longer be understood in a strict sense, as an interaction and solidarity between nations, but as solidarity among peoples.

Secondly, we need to observe the spatial–temporal displacement of solidarities as well as the political projects that practice them, in different places with distinct ends. The classic Internationals responded to a concrete historical process where solidarity initially expanded from Europe or the Soviet Union to other parts of the world. However, while not opposed to modernity and its values, the processes and dynamics of internationalist solidarity within the Global South also existed during the same period, becoming stronger around the mid-20th century with the decolonization struggles in Asia and Africa, which sparked solidarity among groups of different Latin American countries. For example, there were many transnational connections between Chilean, Cuban, Angolan and Congolese activists and between leftist groups in Brazil and the revolutionary processes of Angola and Mozambique. This leads us to consider that international solidarity and transnational networks do not operate in an abstract dimension, but respond to certain geostrategic and geocultural agendas which, to a great extent, operate in a more regional rather than strictly global fashion (Cairo & Bringel, 2010).

Lastly, the global scenario after the fall of the Berlin Wall set the stage for 'complex internationalism' (Della Porta & Tarrow, 2005) where social actors, political projects and mobilization repertoires create spaces for convergence, grievances, identities and increasingly overlapping and transversal forms of diffusion. There is a generational shift, intimately connected to a technological revolution which allows for a dynamic of more constant and faster local/national/global exchanges and leads to an undermining of activisms among different collectives, networks and initiatives which generate a sense of multiple belongings and more flexible identities. A pattern of more 'classical' internationalism still persists in articulations and political projects that seek to keep alive strategic debates, elements of the anticapitalist struggle, some basic ideological beliefs, values and modern ideals, as well as political references that were created in the last two centuries and were adapted to the current period. Many parties, labour unions and movements still keep the flame of 21st century internationalism alive by updating a curated heritage of the Internationals and the workers' international struggle. However, other patterns of globally oriented collective action have emerged and are forcing a redefinition of internationalism, which should be understood as a social practice of solidarity among peoples connecting worldwide struggles in different moments and places.

The Internationalization of Territorialized Social Movements

One of the main innovations of contemporary internationalism is the consolidation of a new pattern of globally oriented contentious collective actions, different from the preceding one: the internationalization of territorialized social movements. The main collective subject here is not the urban proletariat but peasants and indigenous populations, which can leave many modernity interpreters perplexed, since, imbued with a modernizing conception, they frequently associated rural communities with tradition, backwardness, apathy and the inability of possessing a transformative agency. Based on neo-modernizing views, many social theorists kept reinforcing, though in a more attenuated manner, these sorts of ideas, updating them based on the demographic situation and the contemporary urban issue. The apparent paradox presents itself in the following manner: How can rural social movements be one of the most deeply rooted in places and communities, and at the same time one of the most active in the map of contemporary global contestation?

What is more, this perplexity harbours a teleological, eurocentric and modernizing view of progress and a broad spectrum of binary and dichotomous logics, typical of Western modernity and the globalizing mindset, which greatly limited the comprehension of social and political life. In other words, there is no contradiction in the fact that a social movement is deeply rooted in one place and at the same time very active in the international scenario, as there is no absolute contradiction between the local and the global (though there often might be inherent tensions), which are not completely separate spheres of political action.

The fact that social movements are *located* in territories does not mean they are *localists*. There is a growing 'global sense of place' (Massey, 2005) in these movements, which articulate in a complex and relational fashion, places, networks, scales, experiences and dynamics of diffusion (Bringel, 2014a). The more well-known examples are the Zapatista Army of National Liberation (EZLN), whose uprising in the beginning of 1994 in the Lacandona forest of Chiapas was an important turning point for global action and internationalism, and the Brazilian Landless Workers' Movement (MST), one of the most territorialized and internationalized rural movements in the world, each following different paths to global action. In fact, in the last few decades, the EZLN and the MST have converted themselves into references for a whole generation of activists around the world, creating networks, new types of solidarities, pedagogical-political practices, and ways to understand social transformation.

In the EZLN case, it is possible to state that the practices and messages coming out of Chiapas into the world assumed a rupture with the discourse of 'there is no alternative' based on a profound criticism of the new world order. Beyond this charge, the EZLN contributed by fostering new internationalist political ideas, repertoires of disobedience and rebelliousness, alternative ways to construct the (counter)power and social change as a process. With their strategy of communicative guerrilla and emphasis on the creation of transnational spaces for convergence like the intercontinental and 'intergalactic' meetings, the global scale became a main player in localized resistances, creating also a series of long-lasting transnational exchanges.

In the MST case, four internationalist levels of action allowed for a constant articulation with other players and with other scales of collective action: (a) the articulation with other rural social movements in different parts of Latin America (coordinated by the Latin-American Coordination of Countryside Organizations – CLOC) and the world (through the Via Campesina); (b) the political solidarity of Support Committees, also known as 'Friends of MST', in different places, especially in the centre of the world-system, particularly in Europe and North America; (c) the political-economic cooperation with various actors; (d) the participation in networks, international events and transnational spaces of convergence (the case of Scream of the Excluded, the campaign against the FTAA and for ALBA, etc.).

Both cases refer to a cycle that emerged with impetus in the beginning of the 1990s, while the more invisible and informal internationalist articulations of both movements had been happening before. There are also in both cases other integral elements of this broader pattern of global action by territorialized movements: the importance of internationalist brigades, the flow of people and face-to-face activist interactions which allow for a deeper knowledge of other experiences and realities; the understanding of internationalism as a fundamental principle for social struggle; the formative/educational and communicative/counter-informative programs; the internalization in the interior of territorialized struggles of life, learning, and internationalist experiences; and the primacy of direct action and grassroots activism.

Transnational Advocacy Networks

If the territorialized movements emerging in the 1990s sought to have their own voice in the international arena, it is impossible to ignore another pattern of global collective action, whose main task is mediation and pressure, which in some cases loops back into cycles of territorialized struggles, and in others is strongly criticized by them: the transnational advocacy networks.

The literature that interprets this type of collective action tends to represent a more instrumental and organizational view of transnational activism, whose central dimensions of analysis are political articulations, international campaigns and strategic coalitions. The expertise of 'professional activists'

(Pleyers, 2010), the definition of governments and institutions, be they national or international, as adversaries and/or interlocutors, are also characteristics of this type of action, embodied mainly by non-governmental organization (NGOs) and more institutionalized actors, who have sufficient economic and cultural resources to discuss and mediate situations and demands.

The 'boomerang' metaphor used by Keck and Sikkink (1998), one of the main studies on this pattern of transnational activism, represents a somewhat rigid vision of the multiscale action of these social actors who, faced with a narrowing of political opportunities in the national scenario, activate supranational networks to influence the domestic sphere. In this manner, even though we are dealing with a type of transnational action, the state is still a main interlocutor, because the members start pressuring their own states and, when necessary, other organizations which in turn also pressure the state. The information and communication work among members, as well as their capacity to expand the reach of their messages and campaigns, becomes crucial.

Following this logic, the focus on *this type of transnational activism* is generally aimed at specific initiatives and campaigns. Cooperation and negotiation prevail over confrontation and social conflict. They speak of shared values but not the creation of a collective identity. Also, within this scenario, the result (the end itself) seems to be more important than the process (educational, learning, knowledge and mutual enrichment through exchange of experiences) and the subjectivities and symbolic resources created.

These transnational networks also proliferated globally in the 1990s, in tandem with the work of various international organizations (von Bülow, 2012). They are generally active in the field of human rights violations, environmental and gender issues. In my view, these actions complement rather than compete with the previous and subsequent patterns, but the relationships of cooperation and conflict depend on the type of mediation utilized, the degree of engagement with the cause and the movement one advocates, and, in sum, broader visions of politics and activism. In fact, though the relationships might be confrontational and polarizing, there are several convergences (of members/activists, agendas, horizons, objectives, etc.) and synergies and possibilities of 'cross-fertilization' in some moments and spaces (Pleyers, 2010).

Regardless, the structures, repertoires of action, the grassroots social underpinnings, the aims, the identifying constitution, the privileged scales, the landmarks and the interpretation of reality as well as the construction and definition of demands, interlocutors and political adversaries/enemies vary by degrees and should be examined carefully. Also, there are enough tensions (such as the ones happening within and outside the World Social Forums and their counter-forums dynamics, as we will see below) which demand a strictly analytical differentiation to more deeply and sociologically comprehend some of the main tensions and patterns of transnational advocacy networks.

The Antiglobalization Movement as a Global Actor

The territorialized social movements have become internationalized, as discussed above, in order to project their own voices without the need of brokers on the international stage, and at the same time established alliances with other kindred grassroots movements affected by the same enemies and dynamics of capitalism. The transnational advocacy networks' fundamental tool is the ability to exercise pressure in national and international institutional arenas. These two modes of action converge, but they are also superseded by another type of globally oriented collective action that marked the new century: the antiglobalization movement.

All of them challenge the distance between the decision-making centres and the regular locales of citizen participation. However, in the specific case of the antiglobalization movement, we can say that, unlike the previously mentioned cases, we are dealing with a complex and diverse actor, already emerging as a global actor, with global proposal and protests that are publicized and organized globally. Beyond this, the antiglobalization movements surface partially because of the incapacity of NGOs', actors which many were trusting upon, in previous years, to resolve the situation of increasing global inequality. They do offer, however, an alternative: The mobilization and construction initiated by the grassroots in what I would like to call 'globalized grassroots', criticizing the co-optation by NGOs and their mode of negotiation and collaboration with political financial institutions. Still, the emergence of antiglobalization movements is also related to the crisis of the neoliberal economic model and the struggle against globalization, making it possible to identify several stages of global mobilization.

In previous texts (Bringel & Echart, 2010; Bringel et al., 2009), I have suggested, in analytical terms, the need to differentiate among the various cycles and sub-cycles of this movement: there is, very generally speaking, a first phase (embryonic or initial) which begins in the end of the 1980s, with the first protests in Europe and the definition of some global interlocutors against those that are protesting; a second phase is characterized by the definitive entry of social actors in international deliberations, the creation of more solid and permanent global coordination mechanisms (Peoples' Global Action), and the consolidation of global interpretative groups and new global enemies (especially transnational corporations). The 1994 Zapatista uprising and the celebration of the First Intergalactic Meeting against Neoliberalism and for Humanity are important events for the convergence of various antiglobalization social movements. This phase would end in 1999, with the public emergence of the movement in Seattle, inaugurating a third stage, which lasted until 2001, marked by many protests and increased intensity in social conflicts. The year 2001 suggests a pause for reflection since, although global protests were still the main mode of operation, their intensity lessened after the repression of the mobilization in Genoa, and afterwards we notice a more proposal-oriented branch of the movement being fleshed out in the following years, constituting a fourth phase, with the consolidation of the World Social Forum.

The issues encompassed and the regionalized scope of the World Social Forum make it possible to extend the meeting to all regions of the world and accommodates more specific domains of action (education, migration and many others), but in the course of the 21st century this model starts nearing exhaustion and the main weaknesses of the antiglobalization movement become visible. During this period, the main modes of collective action vary: counter-summits held in front of international financial institutions (IMF and World Bank), at the first stage; parallel summits to the official ones, even if the agendas proposed were similar (as in the 'Earth Summits' held in 1992 in Rio de Janeiro), at a second one; counter-summits with autonomous agendas, largely possible thanks to the use of the Internet by different groups and collective, in the third stage; and finally the creation of spaces of convergence for protests and global proposals in the fourth stage.

On the one hand, the success of the antiglobalization movement is beyond debate when we look at the vast repertoire of articulations and protests, and proposals formulated as a critique of the pernicious effects of neoliberal globalization. On the other hand, one cannot deny the paradox that lies in the fact that after unmasking neoliberalism and its social, economic and environmental consequences, the movement itself is not capable of coming up with a convincing answer in the face of a system marked by the multidimensional crises of globalizations that had already been identified by antiglobalization protests. The financial crisis that exploded in 2008 was not followed by a global contestation capable of rearticulating the manifold issues and regional axes, which, 10 years before has spatialized the antiglobalization movement throughout the globe.

Facing the absence of coordinated global contestation, each axis of action and the participants of the movement (also known as the 'movement of movements') diluted and proceeded to apply their own repertoire of protests and proposals during times of crisis, with particular emphasis on environmental, peasant and indigenous movements, but also encompassing youth in dire conditions in the case of Europe. This dispersal means that it is possible to identify differentiated trends between North and South. In the first case, the majority of protests copes with the immediate after effects of the financial crisis, fighting with 'reactive repertoires' (defence of historically acquired rights), in the terminology of Tilly (1978). In the second case the struggle sets out to establish ownership of natural resources and common goods in the face of the new strategies of capital devised for times of crisis in central countries, in some places as in almost all Latin American countries, with 'proactive repertoires' (the defence of newly acquired rights, or acknowledged but as yet immaterialized).

The decline of unified action, the disarray of more structured and global manifestations and the political and discursive reappropriation of many of the antiglobalization movements claims led to the exhaustion of a model and another cycle of global mobilization. Protests would resurface in many parts of the world after 2011, yet following a quite different pattern from the antiglobalization movement and those of global collective action already analyzed above: thus, a new geopolitics of global outrage emerges in the second decade of the 21st century.

The New Geopolitics of Global Outrage

Indignation or outrage is not a social movement. It is a state of being (Bringel, 2013). As such, it can be expressed in a variety of ways. In Southern Europe, for example, the feeling of social indignation over the last years had multiple sources, but one of the main themes was the refusal to pay for the direct consequences of the crisis, which should instead be assumed by those responsible. Bankers and speculators thus became the main targets of social mobilizations. In the United States, 'occupiers' directed their outrage at these same actors, bolstered by the argument that the 1 per cent – far removed from the concerns of the general populace ought not to determine the future of the 99 per cent. In Brazil, Egypt, Senegal and many other countries, a mixture of uprising, political experimentalism and anger shook the streets.

According to Pleyers and Glasius (2013), despite some differences, this new global cycle is characterized by three aspects, namely, the call for democracy, social justice and dignity. These are some overlapping themes that take on diverse meanings and materialize as particular grievances in different scenarios. The diffusion and resonance of mobilizations and some of their symbols is clear (think only of the 'V' sign standing for Vengeance or Anonymous), yet operates in a fashion quite distinct from other patterns of global contestation hitherto analyzed: the repertoires, messages and calls for action travel in vertiginous speed and disseminate virally, and are redefined and adapted with stunning facility. Global actions and opinions are easily shared through Facebook and other digital social media, while is it significantly harder to share, as in the case of territorialized social movements and the antiglobalization movements, the permanent transnational spaces that allow for a deeper knowledge of the struggles, collectivities, subjectivities and realities that occur elsewhere.

The outrage movements initially were diffused and polarized, above all a manifestation of society bursting at the seams. The participants, many of which had no previous activism experiences, converged in public spaces in many cities throughout the world bearing grievances and mobilizing manifold significations. The rejection of political systems, traditional political parties and conventional forms of political organization cut through all expressions of this cycle of global outrage which, in many cases, revived the values and assumptions of the other patterns mentioned above, although without explicitly mentioning them. In this sense, what stood out was a longing for horizontality, the negation of representation and the rejection of formal leadership.

Collective action as well underwent change: There is a greater protagonism of individuals and public squares. Tahrir, Sol, Taksim and Zuccotti Park were epitomes of this new cycle and public space became both the place into which mobilization was channeled as well as a grievance on its own right (this is clear, for example, in the cases of Brazil and the protests for better public transport and of Turkey and the opposition to the construction of a shopping mall on Taksim Square). The relationship with other traditional social movements and with other patterns of global mobilization is often marked by tensions; likewise, the organization operates in a fashion far more decentred and articulated according to affinity groups.

New Information and Communication Technologies (NTICS) were used in new ways compared to the other patterns of global collective action. Territorialized movements innovated in the use of communication webs and lists; transnational advocacy networks used the internet to facilitate mediation and contribute to the visibility of political and social pressure (expanding repertoires to include digital subscriptions); the antiglobalization movement appropriated NTICS for mobilization and for the construction of counter-information platforms (with the motto 'Be the Media' leading to the creation of the Indymedia). In this cycle of global outrage, digital social networks (whether corporate or alternative) are opposed to mediation by third parties and allow for greater personal engagement and protagonist roles and to a decentralization of global calls for action, a phenomenon that is behind many of these actions.

If in the other patterns of global action the events of contestation were, in general, always framed within a broader process, current events have become, many times, an end in itself. However, international solidarity becomes more relational and contingent than before (Juris, 2012), and at the same time less mediated by states and more focused on events rather that broader movements or experiences. Lastly, although global adversaries and interlocutors have been established in the current cycle of global indignation, this is not as pronounced as in the case of the antiglobalization movements, while states re-emerge as the main actor being questioned.

This could lead to a relativization of the global reach of this pattern and it would in fact be possible to frame it as an internationalist experience. In other words, the following question begs to be answered: *how global are global movements*? Despite 'Third-Worldism', classic internationalism was by and large a Western experience and was constituted as integral to the geopolitical modern imagination. This means that social struggles became international and became relatively more 'global,' yet this was conjured up from a particular position in the world, with accompanying values and ideals and the construction of representations and hierarchies and the pre-eminence of the connection among territorial states. After the fall of the Berlin Wall a new global geopolitics and a new stage for social contestation emerged, in which the process of framing the global scale unfolds rather distinctly in the geopolitics of power and resistance: the reach of cross border interactions of social actors has become far more global; the crystallization of internationalists practices are more decentred (and they emerge not only in Europe, but also, with increasing momentum and force, in peripheral countries – and among them); the relationships between scales of action overlap and are inter-dependent; solidarity and diffusion dynamics are more relational and contingent; and local/localized social struggles are potentially more visible at the global level.

Today, in sum, movements and contestations, as well as modernity *per se*, are increasingly global. Hence, it becomes crucial to analyze how the global operates in terms of space–time in the constitution of actors and collective actions that transcend established borders. In the case of globally oriented social movements and collective actions, the focus of this chapter, several paths can be followed, each one corresponding to different patterns that determine global action in the current stage of modernity: the claims and grievances made by ideologies and subjects that have a global reach despite not being universal; the advocacy and the pressure on international institutions designed to regulate capitalism; the globalization of resistances, the internalization of supranational references and the localization of global practices and imaginations; the dialectical relationship between networks/flows and territories; and the social construction of scales of political action.

Notes

1 For a more conceptual discussion about contemporary modernity in different fields, see the chapters of the first part of this this book.

Acknowledgment

Breno Bringel would like to thank Sidney Tarrow and José Maurício Domingues for suggestions and comments on this chapter.

References

Blumer, H. (1951). Collective Behavior. In A.M. Lee (Ed.), *New Outline of Principles of Sociology*. New York: Barnes and Noble.

Bringel, B. (2011). A busca de uma nova agenda de pesquisa sobre os movimentos sociais e o confronto político: Diálogos com Sidney Tarrow. *Politica & Sociedade, 10*(18), 51–73.

Bringel, B. (2013, July). Brazil within the Geopolitics of Global Outrage. *Global Dialogue*, Newsletter of the International Sociological Association.

Bringel, B. (2014a). MST's Agenda of Emancipation: Interfaces of National Politics and Global Contestation. In J.N. Pieterse and A. Cardoso (Eds.), *Brazil Emerging: Inequality and Emancipation*, New York and London: Routledge, pp. 89–126.

Bringel, B. (2014b). *O MST e o Internacionalismo Contemporâneo*. Rio de Janeiro: EdUERJ.

Bringel, B. and Domingues, J.M. (2012). Teoría crítica e movimentos sociais: Intersecções, impasses e alternativas. In B. Bringel and M. da Glória Gohn (Eds.), *Movimentos sociais na era global*. Rio de Janeiro/Petrópolis: Vozes, pp. 57–76.

Bringel, B. and Echart, E. (2010). Dez Anos de Seattle, o Movimento Antiglobalização e a Ação Coletiva Transnacional. *Ciências Sociais Unisinos, 46*(1), 28–36.

Bringel, B., Echart, E. and López, S. (2009). Crisis globales y luchas transnacionales. In P. Ibarra and E. Grau (Eds.), *Crisis y Respuestas en la Red, Anuario de Movimientos Sociales 2009*. Barcelona: Icaria, pp. 210–220.

Bringel, B. and Falero, A. (2008). Redes transnacionais de movimentos sociais na América Latina e o desafio de uma nova construção socioterritorial. *Caderno CRH, 21*(53), 269–288.

Brysk, A. (2000). *From Tribal Village to Global Village: Indian Rights and International Relations in Latin America*. Stanford: Stanford University Press.

Cairo, H. and Bringel, B. (2010). Articulaciones del sur global: Afinidad cultural, internacionalismo solidario e iberoamérica en la globalización contra-hegemónica. *Geopolítica(s), Revista de estudios sobre espacio y poder, 1*(1), 41–63.

Castells, M. (2012). *Networks of Outrage and Hope: Social Movements in the Internet Age*. Cambridge: Polity Press.

Della Porta, D. and Tarrow, S. (Eds.) (2005). *Transnational Protest and Global Activism.* Lanham: Rowman & Littlefield Publishers.

Domingues, J.M. (2012). *Global Modernity, Development, and Contemporary Civilization: Towards a Renewal of Critical Theory.* New York and London: Routledge.

Featherstone, D. (2012). *Solidarity: Hidden Histories and Geographies of Internationalism.* London: Zed Books.

Juris, J.S. (2012). Reflections on #occupy Everywhere: Social Media, Public Space, and Emerging Logics of Aggregation. *American Ethnologist, 39*(2), 259–279.

Keck, M. and Sikkink, K. (1998). *Activists Beyond Borders: Advocacy Networks in International Politics.* Ithaca: Cornell University Press.

Khasnabish, A. (2008). *Zapatismo Beyond Borders: New Imaginations of Political Possibility.* Toronto: University of Toronto Press.

Massey, D. (2005). *For Space.* London: Sage.

Pleyers, G. (2010). *Becoming Actors in the Global Age.* Cambridge: Polity Press.

Pleyers, G. and Glasius, M. (2013). The Global Moment of 2011: Democracy, Social Justice and Dignity. *Development and Change, 44*(3), 547–567.

Santos, Boaventura de Sousa. (2006). *The Rise of Global Left: The World Social Forum and Beyond.* London: Zed Books.

Smith, J., Chatfield, C. and Pagnucco, R. (1997). *Transnational Social Movements and Global Politics: Solidarity Beyond the State.* Syracuse, NY: Syracuse University Press.

Stjernø, S. (2004). *Solidarity in Europe: The History of An Idea.* Cambridge: Cambridge University Press.

Tarrow, S. (2005). *The New Transnational Activism.* Cambridge: Cambridge University Press.

Tilly, C. (1978). *From Mobilization to Revolution.* New York: Random House.

Touraine, A. (1965). *Sociologie de l'action.* Paris: Seuil.

Von Bülow, M. (2010). *Building Transnational Networks: Civil Society and the Politics of Trade in the Americas.* Cambridge: Cambridge University Press.

Waterman, Peter (2001). *Globalization, Social Movements and the New Internationalisms.* London: Continuum.

8

Global Modernity, Social Criticism and the Local Intelligibility of Contestation in Mozambique

Elísio Macamo

Introduction

Sociology is modernity in other words. It saw the light of day as a language that fulfilled the task of describing a type of society emerging out of very specific historical circumstances, and it rendered that type of society visible through its descriptions. Arguably no sociologist has expressed this relationship better than Emile Durkheim (1984, 1988) whose key concepts are better understood as performative social descriptions, i.e., as ways of producing reality through description (see also Macamo, 2011). Doing sociology, therefore, is an engagement with modernity. The question for someone who deploys sociological tools primarily to make sense of social action and relationships that come into fruition in parts of the world that sociology did not necessarily have in mind at its own inception is a very complex one. It is the question whether the assumptions underlying the language which seeks to render modern society intelligible is adequate enough to account for social action and relationships away from the geographical, historical and economic context that produced the vocabulary that makes up sociological language.

Modernity is an important concept and anyone seriously engaging in sociological work is primarily concerned with laying bare the elements of modernity that are constitutive of social reality everywhere. Modernity constitutes in and by itself a challenge. Things do not get easier if one qualifies it with the adjective 'global'. Arif Dirlik (2004) may be right in claiming that global modernity is a turning moment that marks the beginning, and not the end, of a kind of history that is less narcissistic than history as told by Western science and wonderfully described and dissected by Jack Goody in his *The Theft of History* (2006; see also Escobar, 2004). But misgivings concerning the usefulness of the notion of 'global modernity' are in order. They are informed by three kinds of difficulties. These are epistemological, methodological and analytical. Indeed, while one must acknowledge the compelling power of global structural forces acting on every corner of the world and on every individual upon the earth, forces we can legitimately articulate with modernity, however, we may define it, one can still wonder how conceptually and theoretically liberating a new perspective can be that makes the intelligibility of local action an artefact of structural factors. To put it simply, the question is whether we can claim to understand social phenomena in the rest of the world – and in this case, in Africa – by accounting for it with reference to the very rationality of modernity.

This chapter addresses these issues. First of all, the chapter will formulate its claim on the tension underlying the use of concepts and theoretical frameworks developed in a given setting to a different kind of setting. This should not be read as a claim of incommensurability. Rather, it should be read as a word of caution on the scope and reference of concepts. To illustrate this, the contribution will discuss the notion of 'social movement' and with reference to Imre Lakatos describe its study as a research programme. In other words, the study of social movements will be understood as a dynamic set of theories seeking to make sense of a given class of phenomena (Lakatos, 1978). Doubts will be raised concerning the usefulness of this notion to the study of protest in the African context. This discussion will pave the way for the second step which will consist in drawing on a discussion of Michael Walzer's (1989) ideas concerning morality to argue that they offer points of anchorage for the grounding of the study of protest in society and its constitutive processes. The idea behind this will be to find a vocabulary that is sensitive to local settings. Finally, the argument will be illustrated with an empirical case from Mozambique.

The Social Movements 'Research Programme'

Studying social movements carries positive connotations. It describes the collective challenges thrown against a central authority on behalf of interest groups without much formal political clout (Tilly, 1978; McAdam et al., 2001). The positive elements in the notion shine through in the belief that a social movement can only earn this status if it fulfils three conditions, namely (a) solidarity among its members, (b) commitment to standing up for a cause against a common enemy and (c) deployment of means of contestation that go beyond the acceptable limits within a given polity (Melucci, 1989). Studying social movements, therefore, is nearly akin to taking the right side and setting about describing the right (or wrong) course taken (or to be taken) by history. The elements entailed in the study of social movements can be described as related theoretical propositions concerning legitimate and necessary social change undertaken by social groups with legitimate grievances against the dominant political order. The assumption of a necessary social change driven by legitimate grievances constitutes the hard core of the research programme. The identification of phases and types in the historical evolution and geographical spread of social movements would correspond to what Lakatos thought a positive heuristic should be able to deliver. It gives instructions to the researcher on the kinds of phenomena to look at in order to maintain a fruitful balance between theoretical propositions and empirical reality.

While research on social movements has made important contributions to our understanding of history, particularly, social and political history (Tilly, 1978), traditions of resistance around the world (e.g., Abbink et al., 2003; Ahikire et al., 1994 for Africa; Wickham-Crowley, 1992 for Latin America), it can still be argued that its usefulness can be questioned, particularly, as far as Africa is concerned. The notion has not been absent from attempts at describing social processes in Africa. It has been variously used to describe peasant actions and ethnically motivated uprisings and millenarianism. In more recent years, the notion has been deployed as a catch-all phrase to account for civil society groups mobilizing against what they perceive to be the onslaught of neo-liberal thinking on African countries as represented by structural adjustment policies of the World Bank and the International Monetary Fund[1]. The sense of the appropriateness of the notion of social movement when it is applied to phenomena observed in Africa feeds on the plausible assumption that groups described as social movements are standing up collectively against a common enemy with a view to heralding a better social order.

The shortcomings of the notion in the African context can be reduced to three main problems. The first is epistemological. The suggestion that there is something positive about how the social movement notion is deployed in research calls attention to the danger of teleology. Social movements point to the articulation of collective claims against a common enemy and against the background of knowledge of what a just and better society is. Under these circumstances, any research that describes any form of contention as a social movement runs the risk of confusing its own theoretical assumptions with empirical reality and, beyond that, of forcing empirical reality into the straightjacket of its own theoretical frame. Generally speaking, the normative nature of the definition of social movements gives researchers considerable leeway with regard to what should count as a social movement. Any form of contention that falls under the analytical gaze of the researcher of social movements becomes, by virtue of the researcher's attention and conceptual framework, a social movement.

The second problem is what Mahmood Mamdani (1996), in another context, described as 'history by analogy' which consists in looking at African historical phenomena with reference to European historical development. History by analogy takes place when concepts and theoretical implications derived from a very specific context are used to describe a completely different context without due attention being paid to local specificities on both sides. Given that the history of social movements has been extensively studied in Europe, all that remains to be done seems to be to document instances of the phenomenon elsewhere. Cause for concern emerges when research is transformed into the study of what Africa lacks in order to fit into the ideal-type represented by Europe. In the study of social movements, this can happen at many crucial analytical junctures. For instance, since research on social movements in Europe has shown that these reveal internal solidarity, commitment against a common enemy and deployment of non-conventional means of protest, absence of any or all of these features from anything that convention has agreed to assign the label of a social movement in Africa might lead to a search for the reasons why Africa fails to live up to the model.

Finally, the social movement research programme seems to have difficulties in articulating the genesis of the phenomenon with the general challenge of providing sociological descriptions of social phenomena that draw directly from the way society actually manifests itself. It dogged the early attempts at defining the notion of social movements in empirically useful ways (see, for example, Smelser, 1962; Castells, 1978). It is not clear under what circumstances a certain type of events warrant a description in terms of the social movement research programme. There is a historicist assumption in the hard core of the research programme. It comes into view in the implicit belief in the desirable inevitability of the change likely to be wrought by a social movement. In this connection, the research programme raises issues concerning the selected reference class. When peasants, for instance, organize to protest against the marketing board of a given country, what is the particular aspect of their action that allows a researcher to claim that he or she is dealing with a social movement? When youths take to the street to protest against unemployment or food price increases, what is the particular aspect of their desperate action that warrants the social movement description? These questions reveal, perhaps, the difficulty of establishing a convincing link between the reality of social life and the explanatory claims of the concept itself.

These three problems deserve serious attention. They call for a bracketing off of the notion of social movements, while an account of the nature of contestation is attempted that seeks to engage with social life and reality. The American philosopher Michael Walzer seems to offer a useful point of entry into this particular challenge. While he is not directly interested in protest, he offers useful insights on the nature of morality and the place and role of social criticism. These can be used to construct an argument that links social movements to empirical social reality.

Social Criticism and Local Intelligibility

In seeking an explanation for instances of contention in settings different from those within which the concepts and theories used to account for them emerged, we may be talking about our own concepts and theories, and not necessarily about local events. There is more to social phenomena than just what our concepts allow us to say. My suggestion is that we think of protest and contention as a form of social criticism. This re-conceptualization can perhaps help us to identify further dimensions that are closer to local settings and do not turn local action into an artefact of our conceptual schemes. Walzer argues that a sense of good and evil plays a significant role in explaining how individuals within and across communities can be moved by the fate of others. He distinguishes two basic forms which morality can take. More specifically, Walzer is interested in the role played in debate by the answer to the question concerning the kinds of obligations we have to others. The first form, which he calls thin morality, has no specific individual in mind. It refers to a universal obligation to recognize the humanity of those who may be too far away from us. It is this sense of universal obligation that enables each one of us to feel solidarity with those fighting for their freedom and justice without committing us to accepting the exact details of which give substance to their sense of those values.

Thick morality, in contrast, refers to the obligations individuals have towards others who share local conditions and circumstances placing them into the same community of fate and values. A simple sense of what makes individuals human is not enough to account for the obligations they must have towards others. A common historical experience, which can find expression in a common language and a common set of cultural values, binds each and every individual to a rich web of meanings which are more likely to be immediately intelligible within a specific local setting. Thick morality is local, whereas thin morality is global. Individuals draw from their sense of thick morality to understand and feel sympathy towards the moral claims made by others in far-away places. What enables them to develop this sense of obligation is the general recognition of the right held by every individual to be respected in their dignity as humans. Walzer is making a plea for a discursive perspective on morality that assumes that what comes to count as the morally right way to behave towards others is the outcome of debate within a normative community. Furthermore, the recognition of distinct forms of moral language does not imply that all that individuals who are far away from others can do is simply to accept the legitimacy of others' local values.

Walzer discusses and develops ideas concerning social criticism. He lays emphasis particularly on what he considers to be the interpretative path to criticism. The main claim is that morality is something over which members of a society argue. Moral argument addresses the question concerning what the right thing to do may be. In order to answer this question individuals have to consider the society in which they live, the means individuals have at hand, the opportunities open to them and many other structural aspects that constrain or enable action. According to Walzer, the answer has to do with the meaning which the way of life of a given community has to individuals. At the end of the deliberations individuals have to be able to say what the right thing to do is as far as they are concerned. Social criticism, therefore, represents the different positions which individuals articulate and express in moral debate. Such positions reflect different understandings and interpretations of social order and the place which different individuals should have in it.

Social criticism, therefore, offers an adequate point of entry into the politics of contention. Unlike the notion of social movement, which packages contention into a normative frame of reference that lends normative and teleological legitimacy to protest, social criticism does not pass judgement on the societal relevance of contention. It simply bears witness to how individuals position themselves with regard to social order while at the same time intimating the possibility that such positioning may harbour different interpretations of how a society should be organized and what life chances it should be able to make available to its members. Contention is in this sense a critical commentary on the nature of society given by its members. Social criticism is where protest originates as contention. Societal members offer critical commentaries from different stations, different perspectives and different existential experiences. A useful way to address the challenge of uncovering the local intelligibility of protest in Africa, therefore, is to spell out the conditions under which social criticism takes place, for it is in those conditions that the types are to be found which offer heuristic models for the study of protest.

The basic sociological impulse underlying contention is, therefore, social criticism. It constitutes itself on the back of moral argument, i.e., debate about the obligations members of a community feel towards other members of the same community. The conditions under which moral argument takes place are important in any attempt at drawing analytical consequences which can inform a study of protest in African settings. These conditions are important because negotiating whether they should exist, and how, is part of the moral argument. This applies, by extension, to the rules governing the behaviour of participants in a moral argument. These rules have to do with how dissent, difference of opinion, support and agreement are expressed. Again, the point is not that such rules should be laid down before moral argument can take place. The point is, rather, that the way in which such rules emerge and are agreed upon is part and parcel of the moral argument. Jean-Godefroy Bidima's (1997) insightful discussion of the African practice of 'Palaver' and how its progressive disappearance has impoverished the African public sphere brings to the fore the constitutive role played by argument over how to argue in moral debate.

'Bread-Riots' in Maputo: The Local Construction of Grievances

Two violent mass protests took place in recent years in Mozambique. The first one was on 5 February 2009, in Maputo, Mozambique's capital city. Young people went on the rampage, as it were, protesting against increases in the fare prices of public transport as a result of increases in the price of petrol. They converged on the streets, set up road-blocks, burned cars and looted shops. The police reacted violently and killed some demonstrators. The city came to a standstill for two days as people were afraid to leave their homes. A little over a year later, on 1 September 2010, there were riots again in Maputo and for the same reasons. These two instances of violent protest had been practically the first in Mozambique since independence in 1975. From 1975 to 1990, Mozambique had a one-party Marxist political system that had no room for the expression of public grievances through demonstrations. All demonstrations that took place during this period were controlled by the ruling party and were in line with its own political agenda. They usually took place on specific days, for instance on 1st of May, and looked more like parades to extol the virtues of socialism, revolution and international solidarity with down-trodden peoples. Things began to change in the early 1990s, especially after the first multi-party elections in 1994, when workers used the 1st May parade to actually vent their dissatisfaction. Up until then it had been official practice for the Head of State and his Cabinet to attend these parades. Parading workers would file past him and at the end he would give a speech during which he would seek to rally support for his political agenda. This came, however, to an abrupt end when a very specific group of workers with very specific grievances not only gave vent to them, but actually insulted the Head of State[2] accusing him of being corrupt and a thief.

In this section, I want to look at the recent protests in order to illustrate the theoretical argument developed further above. I want to probe these violent protests as an instance of a form of contention that owes its intelligibility to local morality. I will draw from research which I conducted in Maputo in 2012, i.e., two years after the events. The research focussed on the events of 1 September 2010, and consisted mainly of interviews with, on the one hand, newspaper and television journalists who reported on the events and, on the other, with four youths who participated directly in the riots. The analysis here will draw from one of the two group interviews that were conducted with these youths[3]. The group interview was conducted in a loose form of a focus group discussion. It consisted in questions about the youths' recollections of what they did on the day of the riots, why they did what they did and what they thought to have achieved with their actions. The structure of the group interview owed more to my interest in the tropes underlying the youths' recollections of their protest experience than to the group interaction itself.

Methodologically, I draw from discourse analysis, especially as spelt out in the work of James Paul Gee (2011). Of particular importance to my purpose in this contribution is what Gee (especially, 150–184) describes as the theoretical tools that inform discourse analysis from a linguistic perspective. He identifies five tools, namely (a) situated meanings, (b) social languages, (c) intertextuality, (d) figured worlds and (e) what he calls 'Big D' discourse. These tools bring to fruition Gee's contention that discourse analysis is the study of language in use and how language can be used to do things in the world. It is this contention that informs my decision to approach the group discussion from the perspective of discourse analysis. Indeed, the aim of the analysis is to contend that what the youths said during the group discussion not only gives an account of their participation in the riots, but is also a statement of how they construct their life-worlds, a process which in itself is an important guide into the factors that render contention locally intelligible. Briefly, the five theoretical tools suggested by Gee help us to appreciate the extent to which the accounts given by the youths can be deployed to reconstruct the rationale of the riots which is locally embedded (Fine, 2010).

The tools draw attention to three interrelated ideas. The first idea refers to the social identities which social actors produce with their accounts. The specific meanings which words and utterances have in context, the main gist of the idea of 'situated meanings', as well as the manner in which language can be used as a marker of identity or even as a way of enacting an identity – which is the deeper meaning of the idea of 'social languages' – draw attention to how and what the youths said during the group discussion can be construed as the way in which they mark their place in society. More specifically, both the situated meaning and the social languages spoken by the youth may provide useful insights into the social world that makes people like themselves possible while at the same time placing them in the position of producing those same worlds. I will explore these aspects in more detail when I discuss the group interview. The second set of ideas concerns the normative frameworks that account for what the youths say and do. These can be elicited in particular both from the idea of 'figured worlds', i.e., the assumptions about the world which render, or more appropriately, which they think render their utterances intelligible, and perhaps even reasonable, as well as from the general idea of discourse, namely, the extent to which the youths form a particular speech community that defines them as a kind of people in terms of what they say and do. Finally, the third idea concerns the way in which the youths draw from other discourses and frames of reference to articulate their experience as part of the larger scheme of things.

I find theoretical sustenance for this methodological decision in the work of scholars who have been emphasizing the importance of narrative and, in particular, the attention which they advise researchers to pay to the ways in which individuals 'emplot' their lives. I am actually trying to read the group interview as an instance of an 'enacted narrative' (Czarniawska, 2004), drawing from the idea that social life is a narrative consisting of events and actions which social actors put together to render their own experience coherent to themselves (Clandinin et al., 2006). To achieve this I will focus my attention precisely on the relationships among the three sets of ideas mentioned above, namely, the social identities underlying the youth accounts, the normative frameworks accounting for the utterances and the frames of reference embedded in those accounts. Through their lively participation in the discussion the youth translated what they knew into a story[4] that I want to pick up to make sense of the 1 September 2010, riots in Maputo.

Going through the interview certain words and phrases stand out as words which can only be understood within the right kind of context. Three sets of words and phrases are particularly relevant. The first one concerns words like *o próprio* (the man himself), *o dono* (the owner) and *o mais-mais*' (the highest of them all, this is a literal translation of a slang term) which describe the Head of State[5]. The second set of words refers to the event itself which is described as *greve* (a strike) and *estereca* (a strike – appropriation of the English word 'strike' by the *Ronga* vernacular spoken in Maputo). The third set includes several words such as *infiltrados* (fifth columnists), *agitadores* (agitators), *mafiosos* (unreliable people), *malfeitores* (evil people), *pessoas que fazem maldade* (people who do bad things) and *pessoas que vandalizam* (people who commit acts of vandalism). This vocabulary points to a local setting which has a clear view of the world. Those who command authority are perceived as individuals who are beyond reach and who can only be accessed through dramatic action such as a riot. At the same time, the 'we' that constitutes the local world is described in normative terms, i.e., by identifying those who excluded themselves from the community through their objectionable behaviour.

In terms of social languages the situation is quite straightforward. There are quite a few words and expressions which mark a particular register, namely, the register of young people in Mozambique. This includes the use of derogative terms to describe situations, people and things. This is the case with the word *porcaria* (pigstry, rubbish) which is used to refer to tear gas used by the police, but also to describe moments when the riots fell out of the control of the youths or to describe people coming from other neighbourhoods and held to be responsible for the rioting. This youth language includes also loan words from English 'high', 'easy' to describe the cost of living in South Africa and Mozambique, but also words like 'boss' (addressed to the researcher as a sign of respect), 'white' to refer to foreigners with a higher standard of living and favoured by the government in the youths' perception. There is also a conspicuous use of Ronga[6] phrases in the flow of conversation which define the youth as people who live in the less privileged neighbourhoods of the city.

The normative frameworks come to light in what I coded as 'figured worlds' in the interview. These, as indicated above, refer to socially and culturally constructed realms of interpretation (Gee, 2011) that enable individuals to tell a coherent story under the assumption that their interlocutors share a common normative framework. In the group interview, the underlying narrative emphasizes two key aspects. The first aspect concerns the event itself. The youths try to make sense of it within the context of the structure of their everyday life. When asked to describe the eventful day, almost all of them started by saying '... num belo dia'[7], a way of describing the day which emphasizes two related ideas. The first one is the idea of a routine day, a day like any other day, uneventful, unexciting and basically normal. The second idea, one that is perhaps even more important, is the impression which the normalcy of the day conveys concerning the youths' agency. They did not wake up looking for trouble. Troubles happened and they reacted to them and in that way things took their course. These two ideas recur in their narrative. The day starts just like any other, they join a march (Marching gingerly...) and then they come back home to have their food (We returned home and ate peacefully...). Much more happens, of course, but this is the initial account which the youths give of their experience of the protest. They are not part of the violence which takes place and forces them to retreat (and then we retreated, we went home...), an interesting choice of word as it is associated with military language.

The second aspect addresses the reasons for their participation in the protest. These are not given directly, they simply pop up in the account, but framed in such a way as to stress the obligations which others have towards them while portraying themselves as victims. It is in this sense that the youth talk about the high cost of living. Interestingly enough, when they talk about these things they do not offer them as reasons for the protest. They simply mention them and they expect the researcher to draw his own conclusions. Here is an example:

> And one more thing: they said that in order for us to board the mini-bus, and... so you see, everybody 'no, you can't' because my salary doesn't really help. Somebody who gets paid 2,500, what's that, two and a half, that's nothing. What does a bag of rice cost? You see, that's when people said the price of the mini-bus must go up, so we said no, let's do this, we must speak to the president.

When the issue of violence crops up, as indeed it should since the protests were characterized by violence, they youth shift the responsibility to others. They even mention a man who is supposed to have funded the protest by feeding the protesting youths and buying tyres for burning on the road. The way they refer to him is as someone whose goals and motivations are mysterious to them[8], which in the context of the overall account makes the youth less accountable to their own deeds. They talk about the obligation of the government to talk to them and in this way they offer a reason for the destruction of property and confrontations with the police, for these are the only means through which they can make themselves heard. Inequality plays a major role in their accounts. It is the sort of inequality that refers to how the cost of living is experienced differently by people and, most importantly, how racial minorities with a higher standard of living seem to receive preferential treatment from the government. Interestingly enough, the link between the youths' violent protest and the obligations of the government is not established in a direct manner. It is always a suggestion which the listener can pick up to draw conclusions as to the legitimacy of the means which they chose to articulate their grievances.

Finally, what the youths' accounts articulate are not isolated results of individual experiences. Individual accounts are the expression of a collective experience which pitches the youths and the communities to which they belong against an invisible other who can take many forms. The

youths and their suffering communities are pitched against the government – those who do not care about them – well-off members of society
who can afford the kinds of things which the majority cannot and, generally speaking, those who may be like them, but fail on their obligations
towards them. This is particularly the case with local political and administrative officials who ask for bribes to do their job[9]. This opposition renders the youths' accounts coherent[10]. While they do not actually say it,
their account constructs them as a moral community which is grieved by
those who fail to honour their own obligations.

This is a brief discussion of a single interview conducted to ascertain
the tropes which are constitutive of the narratives of youths who participated in the protests – which actually became riots. The lessons which can
be drawn from them are of necessity yet limited in scope. However, they
do give an indication of what the local intelligibility of protest and contention could mean. Michael Walzer's suggestion that what constitutes a community are the ties which bind individuals to one another through moral
obligations may provide a useful framework within which to begin to
make sense of what protests are about. Three issues seem relevant for the
reconstruction of this local intelligibility, all of which point towards social
criticism as the sociological essence of protest and contention.

The individuals who descended on the streets of Maputo to articulate
their grievances were first and foremost enacting social identities. In the
particular case at hand, i.e., the accounts of the four interviewed youths,
the descent on the street rendered them visible as youth whose social identity was determined by a sense of despondency. This is an important aspect
that can be surmised from how they report on their own experience of the
protest. They are individuals whose social profile is sharpened by the failure of others to honour their obligations towards them. They have no
employment and are part of a community that is a victim of circumstances
created by others too far away to be made accountable. They accept their
predicament up to a point, and if at times they convey the impression that
they do not that is because it is not even possible to reach across to those
they would wish to engage morally. The youth reduce the world to moral
categories whose action and inaction only allows for types of interpretation which point to the failure to honour moral obligations. While they do
not actually formulate these moral obligations it is obvious that what they
resent most is the absence of a sense of community.

The second issue that comes to the fore is the way in which their account
tries to weave together political narratives that are spontaneous, vernacular
and do not commit them to a political programme of any sort. What is
political is constituted by the sense of responsibility which should underlie
the relationship between the youths and the communities within which

they are integrated on the one hand and those who have the duty to listen to their grievances on the other. It is no accident that the account provided by the youths does not go to any great length in identifying clearly those that they pit themselves against. A simple description of the youths' predicament is enough to draw the lines that mark the political space. Politics is not something that is part of everyday life. Everyday life is normal, by which it is implied that economic deprivation, insecurity and lack of opportunity are part of one's life. They only become issues when for whatever reason the opportunity arises for individuals to articulate their grievances. But even here there are hedges that can always be brought up to limit the political scope of these grievances. The grievances are presented as descriptions of everyday life which engage the listener to draw conclusions concerning the legitimacy of whatever course of action is taken to express them. All the while, the youths can always exit out by claiming to having been victims of some form of external instrumentalization. They became violent because the police was violent, or because people from other neighbourhoods came intent on causing trouble or even because someone with obscure ends incited them to violence.

Ultimately, however, and this is the third issue that emerges from the group interview, what the youths are engaged in is an effort to make sense of their own action. Their narrative constructs that sense, i.e., the sense is not prior to the narrative. In fact, their account chronicles the day (getting up in the morning, going to the bakers, finding people in an uproar, joining the march towards the residence of the President, facing up the police, 'retreating', eating and drinking at the expense of someone else). All the while, the account seeks to represent that eventful day in ways which enable the listener to imagine a normal day in the life of a harmonious community which is brought to an abrupt end by actions which suddenly lend a political meaning to their lives. The key resource which they use to bring this chronicle and the mimesis together into a coherent narrative is a plot – Czarniawska calls this an 'emplotment' – i.e., the production of characters in conflict and representing good and bad (the youth and their communities versus the police, government and unreasonable members of the community), an attribution of a function to the events of the day (which consists in sending a message signalling a wish for more dialogue) and a theme to interpret their participation in the day's events (we were drawn into something that gave us the opportunity to vent our anger).

What lends protest and contention a local texture is the potential for social criticism which they seem to host. Social criticism is made possible by the extent to which individuals manage to represent their relationships with others in terms of moral obligations. These moral obligations are not prior to protest and contention. They are constituted by protest and contention, for it is in the context of the articulation of grievances that individuals are able to formulate the obligations that are owed to them. Modernity may be understood as a global phenomenon with a vocabulary that may be appealing to individuals wherever they may be. However, it is also domesticated locally through the ability of individuals to articulate it with locally intelligible grievances. Tilly (2007) had drawn attention to the extent to which contentious politics could not be linked intrinsically to democratic outcomes. This analytical caveat is relevant also to the study of the local texture of contention.

Conclusion: Global Modernity and Local Voices

I agree with the general gist of the argument underlying the idea of a global modernity. There is a strong sense in which we are witness to the end of a narrative hegemony that should make it possible for us to recover voices hitherto unheard. While I share the view that we have a duty to refuse being part of ethnocentric discourses, I feel strongly about replacing such ethnocentric discourses with frameworks which are not sufficiently sensitive to local views. The test which alternative conceptual schemes should pass is the test that determines whether they allow us to appreciate local intelligibility. What I have tried to do in this contribution is to discuss ways of recovering local voices through the identification of the ways in which social action and phenomena become intelligible to the people who make them possible. Social criticism, especially as an extended commentary on moral obligations, seems to be a relevant social mechanism through which the local can make itself visible to sociological analysis. Relevance in this context means the extent to which the notion can be usefully applied to gaining insights into the constitution of society. To start with, moral obligations are the key properties of social relations. They point to a condition displayed by individuals when, for whatever reason, they are strongly unhappy about a given state of affairs. The existence of this moral frame is of crucial importance. Traditionally, protests have been studied within the theoretical and conceptual framework laid down by the notion of social movements. Social movements are generally understood as manifestations of dissent that translate into collective claims making through relevant repertories of collective action. To the extent that protest is a form of dissent and collective claims making it is only logical that its study should be pursued within this conceptual framework. The starting point for the discussion proposed here is the claim that dissent and claims making are made intelligible within moral frames. In this sense, moral frames are central to the conditions of possibility of protest. In fact, I want to claim that they are even more central than our overarching theoretical frameworks. Global modernity is a matter of fact; but so are moral frames.

Notes

1   The label currently in use to describe this phenomenon is 'new social movements' (see Tarrow, 2005; Pichardo, 1997; Boron & Lechini, 2005).

2   These are the so-called 'Madgerman', i.e., Mozambicans who were recruited to work in the former German Democratic Republic and, after the fall of the Berlin Wall, were sent home and have since then been campaigning for compensation from the Government of Mozambique.

3   The first interview was carried out in March 2012 and the second in September of the same year.

4   Much in the same way that White (1987, p. 1) had described narrative as the translation of knowing into telling.

5   'We want to speak with the man himself, with the owner of what happened, we were going to talk to the President himself'; the police car came, they told us, 'we were sent by the big boss, what do you really want?'

6   Ronga is the local vernacular spoken in Maputo.

7   It translates literally as 'on a beautiful day', and means something like 'on a perfectly normal day…'.

8   'That was agitation, he led us astray, he came with petrol and seemed to be saying this is not the way things should be, let us go because the government needs to be taught a lesson, let us go…'.

9   Here is a telling example: 'we submitted it here within the local authorities. We have one nearby, we submitted many applications asking for assistance because it's hard living in our neighbourhood with the kind of difficulties we face. The first thing is lack of employment, it's like there is no work, there is work. There are people who want to eat [need bribes, EM] so you must buy them first. How can I buy a vacancy if I do not work and do not do anything? Someone says "?look, I've got a vacancy here" ?. You will be paid 7,000 or more, but you should give me three to secure the job'.

10   Here is, for example, what one youth says: 'R2: There are people who live well, "when they buy a soft drink and you tell them it costs 10 they will be surprised and will say what? Only 10, I don't drink this". Where are they from? They come from there, they belong to them. They don't even know what it is to board a mini-bus. Do you know how much a mini-bus ride costs? They have four cars, he's got a car that takes him there and there'.

References

Abbink, Jon G., de Bruijn, M. and Walraven, Klaas van (2003). *Rethinking Resistance: Revolt and Violence in African History*. Leiden: Brill.

Ahikire, J., Mamdani, M. and Oloka-Onyango, J. (Eds.) (1994). *Studies in Living Conditions, Popular Movements, and Constitutionalism*. London: Brandes & Apsel.

Becker, H.S. (1963). *Outsiders – Studies in the Sociology of Deviance*. New York: The Free Press.

Bidima, J.-G. (1997). *La palabre: une juridiction de la parole*. Paris: Éditions Michalon.

Boron, A.A. and Lechini, G. (Eds.) (2005). Politics and Social Movements in an Hegemonic World: Lessons from Africa, Asia and Latin America. CLACSO, Consejo Latinoamericano de Ciencias Sociales, Ciudad Autónoma de Buenos Aires.

Castells, M. (1978). *City, Class and Power*. London: MacMillan.

Czarniawska, B. (2004). *Narratives in Social Sciences*. London: SAGE Publications.

Dirlik, A. (2004). Spectres of the Third World – Global Modernity and the End of the Three Worlds. *Third Quarterly, 25*(1), 131–148.

Elliot, J. (2005). *Using Narrative in Research – Qualitative and Quantitative Approaches*. London: SAGE Publications.

Escobar, A. (2004). Beyond the Third World: Imperial Globality, Global Coloniality and Anti-Globalisation Social Movements. *Third World Quarterly, 25*(1), 207–230.

Fine, G.A. (2010). The Sociology of the Local – Action and its Publics. *Sociological Theory, 28*(4), 355–376.

Giddens, A. (1990). *The Consequences of Modernity*. Stanford: Stanford University Press.

Goody, J. (2006). *The Theft of History*. Cambridge: Cambridge University Press.

Gusfeld, J.R. (1986). *Symbolic Crusade – Status Politics and the American Temperance Movement*. Champaign: University of Illinois Press.

Joyce, P. (2002). *The Politics of Protest – Extra-Parliamentary Politics in Britain since 1970*. Houndmills: Palgrave Macmillan.

Lakatos, I. (1978). *The Methodology of Scientific Research Programmes: Philosophical Papers*, Vol. 1. Cambridge: Cambridge University Press.

Macamo, E. (2011). Social Criticism and Protest: The Politics of Anger and Outrage in Mozambique and Angola. *Stichproben, Vienna Journal of African Studies, 11*(20), 45–69.

Mamdani, M. (1996). *Citizen and Subject: Contemporary Africa and the Legacy of Late Colonialism*. Princeton: Princeton University Press.

McAdam, D., Tarrow, S. and Tilly, C. (2001). *Dynamics of Contention*. Cambridge: Cambridge University Press.

Melucci, A. (1989). *Nomads of the Present*. Philadelphia: Temple University.

Pichardo, N.A. (1997). New Social Movements: A Critical Review. *In Annual Review of Sociology, 23*, 411–430.

Smelser, N.J. (1962). *Theory of Collective Behavior*. New York: Free Press.

Tarrow, S. (2005). *The New Transnational Activism*. Cambridge: Cambridge University Press.

Tilly, C. (1978). From Mobilization to Revolution. Reading, Mass: Addison-Wesley.

Tilly, C. (2004). *Social Movements, 1768–2004*. Boulder: Paradigm Publishers.

Tilly, C. (2007). *Democracy*. Cambridge: Cambridge University Press.

Walzer, M. (1989). *The Company of Critics – Social Criticism and Political Commitment in the Twentieth Century*. London: Peter Halban.

Walzer, M. (2006). *Thick and Thin: Moral Argument at Home and Abroad*. Notre Dame: University of Notre Dame Press.

Wickham-Crowley, T. (1989). Winners and Losers and also-Rans: Toward a Comparative Sociology of Latin American Guerrilla Movements. In S. Eckstein (Ed.), *Power and Popular Protest: Latin American Social Movements*. Berkeley: University of California Press, pp. 132–181.

Wickham-Crowley, T. (1992). *Guerrillas and Revolution in Latin America: A Comparative Study of Insurgents and Regimes since 1956*. Princeton, NJ: Princeton University Press.

Zurcher Jr., Louis A. and Kirkpatrick, George, R. (1976). *Citizens for Decency: Antipornography Crusades as Status Defence*. Austin: University of Texas Press.

9

Globalized Modernity, Contestations and Revolutions: The Cases of Egypt and Tunisia

Sarah Ben Néfissa

Introduction

The popular uprisings in several Arab countries across 2011 took the international scene by storm and surprised non-specialists, regional experts and academic research works alike. Upheavals in Tunisia and Egypt triggered what was later dubbed as the 'Arab Spring' The aim of this chapter is to build upon these cases and show how the protests that preceded the uprisings of 2011 as well as the uprising itself and its consequences must by analysed and understood within the context of globalisation.

According to Jean Baudrillard (2005), modernity is not a proper analytical concept; there are no such things as laws of modernity; there are only 'traits' of modernity. These same propositions could, at least partially, apply to the concepts of *mondialisation* or globalisation. One of the traits or phenomena[1], in the case of globalisation, is the undermining of the state's influence over societies. In the context of authoritarian or despotic states, globalisation allows for a form of 'pluralism by default' (Camau, 2006a), which leaves considerable leeway for the expression of protests as a form of action. This realisation, however, does not imply that globalisation should be considered what provoked the so-called 'Arab Spring' – far from it. It simply means that one must look at the articulation of certain phenomena linked to globalisation, especially the opening up of media spaces and collectives that claim to be part of civil society in order to understand and analyse the uprisings in the Arab world. Yet the 'Arab Spring' also expressed quite clearly a very important new phenomenon, namely, the hybridisation of political expression that upends the divide between North/South, democratic/authoritarian governments, developed/ underdeveloped countries.

Why did the popular uprising in the region catch off guard part of the academic community, notably in France? What were the impacts of the process of de-monopolisation undergone in the field of media on the protests and the uprisings in Egypt and Tunisia? How did the externalisation of social protesting, by means of civil society collectives partially modify the action and also the language of social contestation? How can the hypothesis of the hybridisation of political expression in the world enrich the current debate on the 'nature' or the 'qualification' of the Arab uprisings? Can the 'Arab Spring' be fitted into the framework of the globalisation of modernity?

How does Authoritarianism Make Itself Acceptable? A Dominant Question in the French Academic Field

The multi-sector uprisings at the scales seen in Tunisia and Egypt in 2011 remain shrouded in mystery. Those specialising in social movements have always been aware of the mysterious nature of such events. The origins of the uprising in Tunisia have been attributed to the public suicide of Mohamed Bouazizi, a street vendor, in front of a government building of Sidi Bouzid. Yet, only a few months before a young unemployed man committed suicide publicly in front of a government building in Monastir, with no consequences. Chance had it that when Mohamed Bouazizi set himself on fire, someone within the range used a mobile phone to film him and then uploaded the video to the Internet and soon enough on the same night it was being broadcasted by France 24 and Al Jazeera (Salmon, 2013). The national and international attention drawn by the incident through the media entailed a succession of protests all over Tunisia leading dictator Ben Ali to flee the country a few weeks later. Similarly, without the Tunisian precedent, which opened up the 'field of possibilities' and the 'existence of an Arab public space'[2], would it be possible to imagine that the call to descend upon the streets made on 25 January 2011 by Facebook users that created a 'We are all Khaled Saïd' page in Egypt would become so successful[3]? The general public was not alone in not being able to predict uprisings. The academic community, with few exceptions (Chahata, 2010), also failed to seriously take into consideration the transformations of protests, especially in Egypt, well before 2011. These transformations were linked to the process of demonopolisation of the media and the strengthening of civil organisations. The scientific community's attitude must be analysed in light of the extraordinary longevity of political authoritarianism in this region of the world and also of the importance of political Islam in these societies.

Compared to the different waves of democratisation that swept through eastern European countries, Latin America and Sub-Saharan Africa, the

Arab world seemed as an exception. This phenomenon has led researchers to try to explain this longevity and to analyse how political authoritarianism has become legitimated and acceptable in societies. This attitude is perfectly legitimate as it assumes that domination is a complex process that is built and reproduced *also* with the acceptance, even complicity, of those dominated, or at least of a fraction of them (Hibou, 2006; Camau & Geisser, 2003). However, for different reasons this question has become the *only legitimate question* that can be made concerning Arab societies. Moreover, interpreted literally and uncritically, it has delegitimized the opposite attitude and also acknowledged that authoritarianism was being increasingly challenged in the region.

Islamist political strands became dominant during the last three decades as the major opposition forces in Arab countries. Nevertheless, regional specialists were quick to note that the escalation of social protesting in Egypt and Tunisia was unconnected to the political opposition, especially Islamist opposition (Tammam & Haenni, 2009). Researchers hastily proclaimed their unthreatening nature and neglected to analyse the emerging language of protests, which unlike the previous 30 years, lacked Islamist overtones. Over this period, the language of protests was dominated by the call for the establishment of Islamic law, understood as a synonym for social justice and battle against corruption.

Media Monopoly Break Down, Transformation of Protest Actions and Politicisation

As in every country in the world, there have always been important social movements in Tunisia and Egypt (Bennani-Chraïbi & Fillieule, 2012). In Egypt, one need not look further than the long strikes organised by railway workers during the last decade. In Tunisia, a reminder of their significance is the broad public sector general strikes called by a large union, the General Union of Tunisian Workers, which were the part of the political scene of the 1970s and 1980s. However, long before the uprisings of 2011, protest action underwent significant changes in tandem with the transformations undergone by the field of media in Egypt. This phenomenon was particularly clear in Egypt (Ben Néfissa, 2007).

During a long time in Egypt, protest was either carried out by political opposition or by social groups with a long tradition of struggle, especially workers employed by the public sector. This phenomenon is linked to the cost of engagement. The former are relatively protected by their international recognition, whereas the latter can rely on sheer number, their tradition of struggle and engagement and the assurance of employment encourage the voicing of grievances. The novel phenomenon, starting in 2006, was the daily presence of social movements encompassing *all* social categories and especially those considered apathetic and fearful, namely the disenfranchised[4] and the less protected sectors.

The entry of these new actors in actions of protests, which were highly controlled by the Egyptian security apparatus, is an indication fear had receded. This was also accompanied by changes in the field of media, whose actors became powerful allies of contestation. Significantly, two important works on the mutations of media in Arab countries were published in 2009 (Gonzalez-Quijano & Guaaybess, 2009; Mohsen-Finan, 2009). Such changes were varied among Arab countries, and the comparison between Egypt and Tunisia is revealing in this regard. Several claims were made regarding the 'e-revolution' in the Arab world and concerning the role of the Internet and social networks in the mobilisation of protests, Facebook particularly. Mobilisation prompted by the Internet was considerably important in Tunisia since the regime of Ben Ali did not allow any freedom of expression, publishing or press. This was not the case in Egypt, despite the role of Facebook pages such as 'The Youth of April 6' and 'We are all Khaled Saïd' in exhorting the people to fill the streets on 25 January 2011.

Concerning Egypt, the studies of Guaaybess (2011) have made a significant impact. Rather than speaking of a 'digital convergence' h/she prefers to speak in terms of a 'convergence of media'[5]. According to her, what we call 'the new media' is far from replacing the traditional media. Rather, new media becomes articulated with old media. The strength of the digital still relies on strong traditional media. It is the traditional media that confers striking force to the digital. The emergence of new media consolidates more than it weakens the existing system. Bloggers alone would never have been capable of going too far without the written media's and satellite television's and the more or less ostensible role of key actors of the media intelligentsia. Guaaybess recalls as well that the mass media, regularly accessible with low costs, remains defined by television and the written press. Revolutions, she says, have been facilitated by a complex interaction among several actors on the ground and the several media that coexist.

Guaaybess's analysis can be perfectly applied to Egypt. The Egyptian media had been dominating since 2005 by the 'written press–Egyptian satellite television' duo before Internet social networks became a part of the emergence of the April 6 movement in 2008.[6] The broadcasting of talk shows on private satellite channels transferred their striking power to the written press. In reciprocation, the written press provided satellite television with not only repercussion that considerably reinforced their audiences, but also rich investigative material and articles.

The configuration of the media in Tunisia was considerably different. In the absence of independent, written and televised press, the Internet served as the only remaining channel for social contestation, despite several attempts made by the government of Ben Ali to control it. In Egypt, the impact of the media configuration on protests was manifold. It firstly lowered the cost of engagement. By using submitted photographs, written pieces or filmed reports, it protected actors engaged in contestation and also prompted public agencies to reconsider the traditional security-oriented coverage of protests. It also raised the sensitivity of the domestic public opinion regarding the causes defended by protesters. The free press and television also highlighted the discourse of actors and activists as well as their responses to government discourse.

Media coverage was also responsible for modifying modes of collective action. In many cases, it allowed information to be passed on to regions distant from the capital multiplying the number of workers on strike and encouraging those in the side-lines to join protests. The multiplication of mediatised 'sit-ins' is a clear indication that activists fully grasped the importance and power of images.[7] Similarly, the media contributed to multiply the number of social protests as media coverage was able to compensate for weakness in terms of number by the forcefulness of images and photographs.[8] In Egypt, a large portion of social movements that preceded the revolution of 25 January 2011 could be qualified as 'paper protests', recalling the term coined by Champagne (1984) in which he emphasised that protests must try to force access to media in order to obtain the acknowledgment of an issue in the public arena. Indeed, the several protests of the time were no more than the congregation of a few people for a few minutes, enough time to take a picture or to be filmed by a camera.

The choice of this form of action affected the social traits of the contesting groups, which became more diverse, as the following examples show: the members of a leisure club against the threat of closure of the club or the action of home owners against encroaching real estate developers. Mediatised protests action, therefore, multiplied the number of actions of protests because of the 'ease' provided by this repertoire of action which requires, nonetheless, certain skills and dispositions: maintaining relations with the press and other media. However, the media coverage also 'selects' certain social movements in detriment of others. The selection has less to do with the unwillingness of journalists or television producers than with the inherent constraints of the Egyptian media, defined by its centralisation in the capital and other large cities. In fact, the majority of surveys of social movements made by the press show that protests were concentrated in the larger metropolitan area of Cairo (Syam, 2010). In reality, these are biased surveys, since the media seldom covered protests in rural areas.

In Tunisia, a different configuration of the media is observed. It comes as no surprise that that digital activism was a crucial factor during the uprisings. However, in this case as well, the social media was mostly responsible for conferring 'striking power' to the new media, as showed by Salmon (2011). At the time, videos made with Smartphones, after circulating through Facebook and Youtube, became the primary material used by the satellite television, notably Al Jazeera, quickly followed by France 24, Al Arabyia and the BBC. This daily 'digital feed' linking Smartphones to Al Jazeera circumvented the usual methods of censure and control of information. It largely contributed to increasing the sympathy of those in more popular sectors and the aged who were as of yet unfamiliar with the language of the Internet.

In addition to its support to actions of contestation, the media also played an important role in the politicisation of societies in the region and particularly younger people. This trend was particularly clear in Egypt. In 2010, Al Jazeera was losing commercial ground as it faced the competition of private satellite channels that broadcasted political talk shows. Every day these programs, structured around the rich material provided by independent press and by television reporting, offered up to Egyptians the spectacle of social protests and also other political, religious conflicts that animated political and social life. Different actors were invited to expose their grievances and discuss with adversaries, mainly representatives of the state and the government's administration. Likewise, on a daily basis, television broadcasted to Egyptians self-produced images, exposing different political and social spaces and politicising the population. This was a momentous change in a society accustomed to enclosure, hierarchy and distance between different social groups.

The academic literature that has become interested in the relationship between 'associate-rivals' (Neveu, 2010), as the one that joined media actors and social movement actors, will find fertile ground in the examples of Egypt and Tunisia. The media-centrism commonly deplored by this literature is perhaps not sufficiently adapted to social and political contexts marked by despotism or authoritarianism.

Civil Society Collectives, The Weight of the 'Outside on the Inside' and New Modes of Languages of Contestation

Protest actions in Egypt and Tunisia prior to the uprisings had very few links to political opposition structures, including Islamists. However, they received a considerable boost from 'civil society' (Ben Néfissa, 2013) – in the case of Tunisia, from the local structures of the General Union of

Tunisian Workers (Choukri, 2012) and from the Association of Tunisian Lawyers. Leading figures of the Tunisian bar association, as well as a large number of lawyers, accompanied and supported the popular mobilisations (Gobe, 2011) that toppled Ben Ali in January 2011.

In Egypt, the main advocates of the social and political mobilisations for human rights were non-governmental organisations and other collective representation groups. For a long time, political mobilisations were limited to intellectual and political elites in Cairo. Closely controlled by the government because of their international connections, their domestic impact was barely perceptible. However, the background of these elites, their command of foreign languages and international experience conferred these 'rooted cosmopolitans' (Tarrow, 2007) with a certain amount of skills and resources they were able to convert domestically as expertise and support to different mobilisations.

After 2004 and 2005, when the US pressure on Moubarak's regime mounted under the doctrine for the 'Greater Middle East', the relevance of these collectives became more discernible. The *Kifaya* movement (Ben Néfissa, 2007), whose actions were premised on the promotion democracy and the opposition to hereditary succession of Gamal Moubarak to his father as the head of state was the pioneer group.

Since then the influence and clout of these networks in Egypt became harder to ignore. This plural civil society manifested itself through the creation of all sorts of collectives based on the multiplicity of 'causes' that fit the description of 'new social movements', even though their causes were specific to Egypt.

As a result, the issue of human rights became at the same time broader and more specialised: workers' rights, the rights of torture victims, legal foundations for human rights, union assistance, rights for peasants, social and economic rights, legal advice for prisoners, independence of the justice system, personal rights, social security, right to housing (Al-Tibi, 2011), the right to retirement, electoral oversight, religious freedom and so on. The topics of the international agenda also became the object of debate for domestic actors seeking to adapt them to local conditions. Some of these groups became more professional and developed the capacity to call upon the government to act based on studies, expertise and reports published by their Internet sites or as newspaper articles. The lawyers and legal experts of these groups have also taken administrative decisions to court. Another important characteristic of this civil society was its new geographic distribution: while in the 1990s these mobilisations were by and large restricted to the capital, Cairo, during the 2000s, others emerged in more faraway regions.

The increasing autonomy of civil society can be inscribed in the 'globalisation' of public space and also contributes to this process. During a long time in Egypt and perhaps in other countries of the region, because of their particular political histories and the impact of nationalistic and Islamist ideologies, the relationship with foreign countries is marked by suspicion, although, it must be said, this sentiment is often stoked by politicians. During the few years preceding the 2011 uprisings, this suspicion had decreased, allowing certain social movements to reach out for foreign investments and the support of international organisations.

But most importantly, the civil society collectives that have become true political actors introduced into the public space a new lexicon of contestation based on issues that are part of the international agenda. Paradoxically, however, governments were also responsible for the introduction of issues from the international agenda as a result of their concern in establishing an international reputation. This is what led them to promote certain 'causes' that appeared to them less risky, such as the promotion of womens' rights, the protection of the environment, fighting pollution and so on. Ultimately, these subjects became the object of particular reappropriations that helped to politicise them and confer them with a subversive load that was previously absent. The most important example was the conflict that pitted the government of Damiette against the Egyptian state regarding the construction of an extension of the 'Agruimm' industrial complex for chemical products. The mobilisation around the 'protection of the environment' brought together a plurality of actors directly, whose economic and social interests were threatened: fishermen, store-owners and real estate developers and others.

This 'externalisation' of the social movement, in general, was not carried out exclusively by the so-called 'rooted cosmopolitans' (Tarrow, 2007). The emigration from these countries, established mostly in Western countries, played an equally important role in the externalisation of certain movements, as in the case of the protracted social conflict of Gafsa in Tunisia (Dumont, 2011).

Even more importantly, the expansion of the international repertoire had the consequence of creating, at least partially, a competitor for the Islamist normative repertoire as the language of contestation. In reality, the pluralisation of the language of contestation was also the result of the emergence of a 'communitarian' language of protest. This is how the Bedouins in the Sinai revolted against the underdevelopment of their region and Coptic populations began protesting against their status as 'second rate' citizens. The Tunisian uprising in 2011 also raised the profile of 'regional communitarianism' of populations that were not benefitted by development, restricted mostly to the capital and coastal areas. This is the case of the populations of Gafsa, Sidi Bouzid, Thala, Kasserine, Jendouba, which spearheaded the Tunisian revolution before it reached the Ministry of the Interior on Bourguiba avenue in Tunis.

This communitarian language, due to its social depth, is different from the language of Islamism. It expresses itself first and foremost as a demand for social and economic development and for the renegotiation of national union models. Meanwhile, the repertoire of Islamist and nationalist grievances, facing the competition of human rights and citizenship, as shown above, was also the object of modifications. The Tunisian and Egyptian revolutions surprised the international opinion, since the language of contestation employed by these actors was evidence of the loss of effectiveness of Islamism and nationalism. This shed a light on the 'ideological hybridisation' that was slowly forming in these societies and that finally appeared on the television screen on the big day of the revolution.

Revolutions, Uprisings and the 'Global' Time of Political Expression

The analysis of the uprising in Tunisia and Egypt in 2011 is still a work in progress. The 'Arab Spring' became the object of heated debate in the media as well as within the academic world as indicated by the large number of debates, seminars and publications organised. It is important to point out that in France particularly, the *Revue Française de Science Politique* published a special number dedicated to the uprisings in the region. It brought together works interested in analysing revolutionary moments and the different processes and actors involved in their outcome, in addition to the 'causes' that triggered them.

One question, however, seems to have captivated researches and observers in general. It has to do with the *classification* of these uprisings. Were these 'true' revolutions? This question became more pressing after the first results of post-revolution elections started coming out in Tunisia and Egypt. The Islamist political forces won electoral competitions, even thought they were not the main instigators of the uprising nor the main actors of the uprisings, leading many to speak of an 'Islamic Winter' following the 'Arab Spring'.

Doubts concerning the 'classification' of the Arab Spring are based as well on the original traits of the uprisings in Tunisia and Egypt. They shared in common the absence of a leadership or an avant-garde and their logic of grievances and transformation rather that 'taking power'. This explains why after Ben Ali fled to Saudi Arabia and Moubarak's dismissal, the old political, administrative and military elites took over and, in the case of Egypt, are still managing the transition.

How to interpret the characteristics of these two revolutions? Were they instances of 'false' revolutions and merely of uprisings that were able to oust dictators only by fortunate circumstance? Regarding this argument, it is important to recall that even in the revolutions regarded as true revolutions, chance and fortune played determining roles! The 'fluid political conjunctures' discussed by Michel Dobry (2009) are characterised first and foremost by unpredictability.

In reality, the question of whether a revolution should be 'classified' as a true or false one is profoundly normative in nature. It poses the question of the 'model' or prototype revolution in the purview of the expert or researcher: 1789, 1848, 1917, the Chinese Revolution, eastern countries and so forth. Consequently, the researcher must adopt a stance of prudence, yet at the same time must approach the discourse of actors seriously. In Tunisia and Egypt alike, almost the entire majority of actors spoke of revolution and in their minds either lived or are living through a true revolution. If the researcher must not always take what actors say at face value neither must she ignore what they say. This echoes the words of Mohmed Talbi (2011), a renowned specialist in Arab-Islamic history, regarding Tunisia. In his view, the uprisings of 2011 were a practical experiment of popular sovereignty played out in the streets rather than in voting cabinets, as a capital event in the history of Sunni Arab-Islamic history, something unprecedented and a turning point that led to a *reversal of political mentality*.

Thus, building upon critiques formulated by 'transitology' (Dobry, 1995) and beyond the question of the political and institutional translation of the uprisings, it is possible to advance the hypothesis that what occurred was above all a 'political culture' revolution. An examination of the transitional episodes in these two countries supports this conclusion. One of the paradoxes of the transitional situations currently unfolding in both countries is the fact that political expression through voting coexists with the political expression of the 'street'. For Egypt, the last great mobilisation is evidently that of 30 June 2013, legitimating the destitution, led by the army, of the first democratically elected president, Mohamed Morsy. This conclusion is not unique to Egypt considering its complex and contradictory process of change. Tunisia has followed a distinct political transition trajectory. Following the first revolution of a series that swept through the region, Tunisians adopted 'the ideal path' of transition with the approval of a Constitutional Assembly elected in conditions of transparency acknowledged by international opinion. Elected in 2011 to draft, within a year, a new constitution, the Assembly, dominated by Tunisian Islamist political strands, was only able to come to a conclusion after mounting pressure from political opposition, civil society organisations[9] and also the Bardo sit-in during the summer of 2013.[10] In addition to the social mobilisations during the political transition in these two countries, social protests carried on placing emphasis on the hardships of *politically* translating the manifold social grievances at the root of the uprsising of 2011. In a certain way and according to distinct modality, both countries are in the process of experimenting with the limits of representative democracy. This is how ritualised political acts such as the vote and partisan expression combine, articulate and compete with other modes of 'alternative' expression pursued by 'civil society' such as the (new) social movements, the sit-in, the protests and the demonstrations reproduced by the media and the creation of collectives, unions and different kinds of association premised on multiple causes.

Based on this observation, one can advance the hypothesis that in reality changes in protest action prior to 2011, the uprisings/revolutions and also the current unfolding political processes make it clear that the societies in the region have caught up to the global 'time' of political expression. This is perhaps the main accomplishment of the revolutions in Tunisia and Egypt. The Islamic political forces, characterized by their strong conservatism and traditionalism rose to power at the same time when societal upheavals were under way, with societies becoming more politicised and less afraid to express themselves. Society has equally understood that democracy is not limited to casting a ballot. This world time of political expression is in fact a consequence of what Michel Camau has called 'the contradictions of democratic globalisation' (2006b), namely the democratisation of political institutions of the state at the same the time it has ceased to be the sole, not least the main, venue of political decision. If globalisation renders the contrast between authoritarian and democratic regimes starker (Camau & Massardier, 2009), it also highlights the hybridisation of modes of political action and forms of collective action. It is no longer possible today to say that violent protests are restricted to countries of the South or authoritarian regimes. Similarly, social movement are no longer exclusive to democratic countries. However, this new mode of political and social expression, liberated from the shackles of the Arab Leviathan, coexists with grievances directed towards the state demanding domestic and foreign security and also social rights. Yet again, however, this contradiction is not exclusive to the Arab region. Questioning the notion of the political exceptionality of the countries of the region was one of the main lessons of the 'Arab Spring'.

In the introduction to this chapter, it was noted that one of the main traits of globalisation was the questioning of the control of states over societies.

Globalisation has 'facilitated' the Arab Spring. But is it possible to consider as well that the globalisation and the 'Arab Spring' launched societies of the region into 'global modernity'? It is certain that countries of the South, and especially Arab ones, are experimenting political modernity for the first time in a long while and, as noted by Partha Chatterjee (1999), the normative models of Western political theory have until now been seldom able to integrate the political experiences of the South into their framework. The *values* of democracy, rights and citizenship, have been the objects of multiple and contradictory translations and re-appropriations in the societies of the region because modernity also has a subjective dimension (Martuccelli and Lits, 2009). The materialisation of the values of modernity faces several pitfalls, which are always political. It has found (and still does) what has been termed the 'communitarian question'. The will to individualise individuals has not successfully been realised due to state authoritarianism, unemployment and because the communitarian and familial protection are still more accessible for the many and have not yet been replaced by independent and neutral mechanisms of solidarity. Will this ever happen? This question is made in the context of globalisation that no longer ascribes social missions to the state. This is a fundamental question that has left its mark on contemporary social movements in Egypt and Tunisia.

Notes

1   The globalisation of markets, new telecommunication technologies and multi-level governance, international tourism, migration networks, foreign investments and so forth.

2   This Arab public space is characterised by a common language and history (whether imagined or real).

3   The organizers of the protests of 25 January 2011 were surprised by the number of people who answered to their call.

4   The most significant example refers to the protests and revolt of informal urban occupations to decry the lack of services and public goods (security, sanitation, education, access to water, heating, electricity and sewers) and the decision to expropriate many occupants from their dwellings.

5   According to Tourya Guaaybess, the digital convergence (or the disponibility of the medias that were distinguished on the same stand) gives a very important place to the electronic media (Internet and "sophisticated" mobile phone).

6   The April 6 movement was a mobilization initiated by a Facebook page in support of the strike called for by textile industry workers on the same day. This was the first show of the power of digital mobilisations. This movement was one of the many groups who called people into the street on January 25.

7   The most important of which was the long sit-in promoted by the workers of the property taxes agency in 2008 and which served as a model for the long sit in of the Tahrir Square in January 25, 3 years later.

8 From a historical perspective, Kifaya's movement was responsible for introducing this mode of action. Its first demonstration, on 14 December, 2004, brought together few people yet it received wide coverage by domestic and international media.

9 The General Union of Tunisian Workers, The Tunisian Industrial, Commercial and Craft Union, the Tunisian league for Human Rights and the bar association.

10 The Bardo sit-in was organised after the assassination of Mohemed Brahmi, a left wing, nationalist deputy.

References

Al-Tibi, M. (2011). Le droit au logement, école de la contestation. *Mouvements, 66*, 79–89.

Baudrillard, J. (2005). Modernité. *Encyclopædia Universalis*.

Ben Néfissa, S. (2013). Pour un renouvellement du questionnement sur la société civile égyptienne. *Politique et Sociétés, 3*(32), 159–176.

Ben Néfissa, S. (2007). Ca suffit? Le « haut » et le « bas » du politique en Egypte. *Politique Africaine, 108*, 5–24.

Bennani-Chraïbi, M. and Fillieule, O. (2012). *Pour une sociologie des situations révolutionnaires. Revue française de Science Politique, 5*(62), 767–796

Camau, M. (2006a). L'exception autoritaire et l'improbable point d'Archimède de la politique dans le monde arabe. In E. Picard (Ed.), *La Politique dans le monde arabe*. Paris: Armand Colin, pp. 29–54.

Camau, M. (2006b). Globalisation démocratique et exception autoritaire arabe. *Critique internationale, 30*, 59–81.

Camau, M. and et Geisser, V. (2003). *Le syndrome autoritaire. Politique en Tunisie de Bourguiba à Ben Ali*. Paris: Presses de Sciences Po.

Camau, M. and Massardier, G. (Eds.) (2009). *Démocraties et Autoritarismes. Fragmentation et Hybridation des régimes*. Paris: Karthala.

Chahata, D. (Ed.) (2010). *Le retour du politique: Les nouveaux mouvements de protestations en Égypte*. Le Caire: Ahram Press (en arabe).

Champagne, P. (1984). La manifestation. La production de l'événement politique. *Actes de la recherche en sciences sociales, 52–53*, 19–41.

Chatterjee, P. (1999). Le commerce de l'État et de la communauté en « Orient ». *Critique internationale, 2*, 75–90.

Choukri, H. (2012). Réseaux dormants, contingence et structures: Genèses de la révolution tunisienne. *Revue française de science politique, 5–6*(62), 797–820.

Dobry, M. (1995). Les processus de transition à la démocratie. *Cultures & Conflits, 17*, 3–8.

Dobry, M. (2009). *Sociologie des crises politiques, La dynamique des mobilisations multisectorielles*. Paris: Presses De Sciences Po.

Dumont, A. (2011). De Redeyef à Nantes: Mobilisation sociale et migration internationale. *Revue Tiers Monde* Hors-Série, pp. 47–66.

Gobe, E. (2011). Les Avocats Tunisiens dans la Tunisie de Ben Ali: économie politique d'une profession juridique. *Droit et Société, 79*, 733–757.

Gonzalez-Quijano, Y. and Guaaybess, T. (2009). *Les arabes parlent aux arabes. La révolution de l'information*. Paris: Sindbad-Actes Sud.

Guaaybess, T. (2011). *Les Médias arabes, Confluences médiatiques et dynamiques sociales*. Paris: CNRS Éditions.

Hibou, B. (2006). *La force de l'obéissance, Economie politique de la répression en Tunisie*. Paris: La Découverte.

Marie, A. (1997). Du sujet communautaire au sujet individuel. Une lecture anthropologique de la réalité africaine contemporaine. In A. Marie (Ed.), *L'Afrique des individus*. Paris: Karthala, pp. 53–111.

Martuccelli, D. and Lits, G. (2009). Sociologie, Individus, Épreuves. *Émulations*, *3*(5). Retrieved 25 June, 2014, from www.revue-emulations.net/archives/n-5—georg-simmel-environnement-conflit-mondialisation/martuccelli

Mohsen-Finan, K. (2009). *Les Médias en Méditerranée – Nouveaux médias, monde arabe et relations internationales*. Paris: Actes Sud Neveu.

Neveu, E. (2010). Médias et protestation collective. In O. Fillieule, E. Eric Agricoliansky and I. Sommier (Eds.), *Penser les mouvements sociaux*. Paris: La découverte, pp. 245–264.

Salmon, J.M. (2011). Les acteurs des médias dans les soulèvements. *Hommes & Libertés*. 156. Retrieved June 25, 2014, from www.ldh-france.org/H-L-156-Les-acteurs-des-medias.html

Salmon, J.M. (2013). Un soulèvement à l'heure du numérique. Le cas tunisien (17 décembre 2010–14 janvier 2011). In *Colloque Formes et dynamiques des contestations et des soulèvements dans le monde arabe, le point de vue des sciences sociales*. Rabat, 24 et 25 avril 2013 par L'observatoire des Transformations Sociales, la Faculté des Sciences de l'Education, Université Mohammed V-Souissi et l'Institut Maghreb-Europe, Fondation Friedrich Naumann.

Syam, I. (2010). La carte de la protestation pacifique en Égypte: Premiers indicateurs de la formation d'une société civile d'un genre nouveau. In D. Chahata (Ed.), *Le retour du politique: Les nouveaux mouvements de protestations en Égypte*. Le Caire: Ahram Press, pp. 51–76. (en arabe)

Talbi, M. (2011). *La Presse*, 21 April, Tunis.

Tammam, H. and Haenni, P. (2009). *Les Frères Musulmans égyptiens face à la question sociale : Autopsie d'un malaise socio-théologique*. Institut Religioscope. Suisse. Etudes et analyses, 20.

Tarrow, S. (2007). Cosmopolites enracinés et militants transnationaux. *Lien social et Politiques*, *58*, 87–102.

10

Modernity, Cultural Diversity, and Social Contestation

Luis Tapia

Social Contestation in Modernity

Modernity is a time and form of transformation of the quality of social relationships, of the structures that organize social life that has being developing for several centuries. In this regard, it is a historical time that has been configured by a set of ways of life. One of its constituent features is that it has spread at the world level, from its beginnings till today, as a process not finished, but rather in expansion.

I will, thus, sketch a distinction of types and phases of political and social conflicts and contestation in modernity, so as to be able to concentrate in the final and central part of this text on a characterization of the complexity that exists in the protest movements in the Latin American periphery. First, we can distinguish the forms of internal protest and contestation. Modernity is a type of organization of social life that has as one of its features the fact that it has generated a plural specter of lifestyles, of structural differentiation, while at the same time there goes on a more important process of homogenization of the economic structures that also becomes a process that homogenizes the patterns of social reproduction and consumption (Berman, 1988).

One of the features of modern societies is internal differentiation, not only functional but also as social division. In this sense, protest generation and social conflict stem from the class structure ingrained at the very core of modern societies. From these structures, collective subjects emerge that develop conflictive actions, in general in a corporative horizon, as well as disputes of interests in the context of the distribution of power, wealth, and positions in the economic, social and political structures as a whole (Marx, 1975).

Sometimes the forms of ideological contestation are articulated from the class core. Ideological contestation is the other type of internal contestation to modernity that does not derive exclusively from the class structure; but there have been long periods during which this has been its matrix or main source, with this articulation of class and ideology as the predominant form of generation of social and political contestation. Here, I speak mainly of the political–ideological ones.

For a long time in modern societies, the configuration of political parties has had as a main constitutional feature the fact that ideologies generate organizations and political projects that deploy force. It has been the most important form of political contestation in the heart of modern societies.

In a generic way, we can distinguish a diversity of forms of cultural contestation or cultural movements in modern times. In fact, one of the things that generates modernity, contrary to other types of society, is that it destroys previous forms of social and political unity or totality (Marx, 1975), therefore of unification of the diverse aspects of social life that, in general, tended to spread as a more homogeneous, unitary and almost closed development of the culture (although in all cultures we can find aspects of diversity and plurality).

A long time ago, in modern societies, there has appeared a diversity of cultural contestations, which implies another form of political action, not necessarily deployed through parties or unions, but through forms that turn political the aesthetic dimension, as public action through the symbolic or artistic production, or simply through the development of public spaces that are configured reflexively in relation to modern culture, or as a critique of the political and economic structures, although the unfolding of all this is also a feature of modernity.

There used to be, and there is, a second type of social contestation that is more political, relating to the configuration of colonial rule relationships since the origins of modernity. In this regard, I must first resume the characterization of modernity by Enrique Dussel (1992) as something that is constituted simultaneously to the unfolding of colonialism, in particular to the conquest of America. The main point of his argument is that colonialism is a constituent part of modernity. Hence, from the beginning of the colonial rule, relationships were configured between different social territories that modernity eventually transformed into countries.

The other form of social, political and cultural contestation that has spread with this colonial historical background is, in fact, the critique of this colonial subordination. For a long time, this has happened mainly in the form of national liberation movements, national revolutions or reform processes of a more sequential independence. We can remember and distinguish two major moments in this respect: first, the processes of independence (in particular, I speak here of not only Latin America, but also of other countries of the Third World) in relation to the former colonial power; second, the processes of national liberation generally developed against imperialism in several continents of the world.

A strong and important feature of these liberation movements is that they were inspired by modernity itself. They were contestations and processes that reformed the dominant relationships between countries and power structures within modernity, most of them based on modern projects.

Most of the processes of national liberation had as a project to build a modern nation-state that has as one of its axes a process of industrialization that, in general, translated (where the project was more advanced) into the articulation of a sector of state capitalism as the core of modernization.

Up to this point, we can consider three aspects: universality, autonomy, and sovereignty (Berman, 1988). Modernity spreads as a process of growing universalization or generalization of a certain type of quality of the condition of the social. Therefore, the modernisms or the forms of organizing symbolization, explanation and projection of this type of civilization have universal claims, something that is sustained by the material process of homogenization generated by capitalism in an expansive way in different places of the world. Autonomy has several facets. On the one hand, there is individual autonomy, which has a central place in several modern ideologies, in particular in liberalism. The idea of autonomy also moves at the level of constitution of countries, in particular in the figure of the nation-state. When we are at this political level, it connects with the question of national sovereignty. Then, we have, on the one hand, the modern socio-economic condition propelled, basically, by capitalism, which becomes generalized, although not exclusive. On the other hand, it has also strongly developed the idea of building nation-states, that is to say, political particularities in the horizon of unfolding modernity as a more general social condition. Part of this process implies national independence, either regarding persistent former colonial powers or imperialistic contemporary ones.

The third type of contestation in modernity can be framed in many ways. I will frame it here through the idea of *internal colonialism* (González Casanova, 2006). Colonization across the world was questioned not only through the independence and configuration of new countries, but had also as a main feature the persistence of a group of colonial relationships that continued to organize a good part of the productive, reproductive, political and social structures of the new countries. Independence did not put an end to all the configurations of colonialism, which persisted as an internal condition in the new independent countries. This has happened more forcefully in some countries that contain inside them a larger cultural diversity, that is to say, where colonialism did not end up destroying the cultures it conquered and subordinated.

This type of condition of internal colonialism has been questioned mainly through the configuration of anti-colonial movements within the nation-states, starting from the configuration of large community mobilizations in different historical periods. In the Andean area, there was a wave of anti-colonial rebellions towards the end of the eighteenth century, there was a new wave of anti-colonial rebellions that begun after the mid-nineteenth century and was prolonged until its end. There were several moments of anti-colonial rebellion during the twentieth century, combined with some other modern forms of political action. In what follows, I will focus on the characterization and discussion of some of the articulations of modern and communitarian forms of rebellion and social contestation in different political cycles.

Before that it is necessary to point out some lines of intersection, since so far I have just made an abstract and analytic presentation, showing things somewhat in isolation. Without taking account of everything, it is necessary to note that the wave of independence processes in Latin America, in particular in the Andean area, was preceded by large rebellion cycles. Independence in the Andean area was preceded by the great indigenous rebellion led by Túpac Katari: it was the greatest contestation of the colonial power before the wars of independence in a more strict sense. Seen in a wider perspective they include those cycles of indigenous rebellion (Thomson, 2003).

The building of a nation-state (in Bolivia and perhaps in smaller measure in Ecuador and Peru), as a product of nationalist governments that enacted an agrarian reform and, therefore, propitiated a new wave of capitalist expansion in agriculture – although under the modality of amplification of the small and medium property – made possible that during some decades they did not have important indigenous rebellions. From the 1970s onward, in some cases the 1960s, when military dictatorships begun to be established, a new wave of community and *indianista* movements begins. They generate their first political forms that are already partly a combination with modern political forms. Even when they organized political parties, one of the main features of their political life was the presence of non-modern community modes combined with modern ones, producing hybrid political forms. I will shortly concentrate on those, but before that I would like to make an intermediate synthesis that may allow me to locate theoretically the type of social contestation that emerges as a product of the questioning of internal colonialism and some new forms of neo-colonialism, that is to say, in the environment of intrastate and international relationships, as well as the consequences this has in terms of the contestation of modernity as such.

Primordial Forms as Analytic Strategy

I will sketch this horizon around an enlarged concept proposed by René Zavaleta (1982), namely, the idea of *primordial Form*, which is used to understand the relationship between the state and society and the historical articulation between them. We have, therefore, to consider them as permanently changing, hence the forms of mediation among these two poles of this divide. One could say that this is a concept that aims to explain the modern condition in general, what Marx called the split condition, basically between the state and civil society. This implies the separation between the state and economy that he later transformed into the division between the state and civil society in more political and socio-historical terms. It is in this horizon of division or separation that the first type of social contestation was configured. Some nucleuses of civil society contest the power of other nucleuses of the very same civil society as well as state politics.

Historically, the main form of historical contestation that was configured in this environment was the labor movement, with its articulations of socialist and communist movements. Another important movement is feminism, which, in historical perspective, questions not only the patriarchal structures at the heart of capitalism but also previous forms. For a long time in the colony and also for a long time in the independent republics in Latin America and in particular in Bolivia, the conquered people were kept subaltern, as they were since the Spanish conquest. They were not part of society and of the political state, and they were not recognized as part of civil society. In fact, for a long time what characterized colonial power was the distinction between the republic of Indians and the republic of Spaniards. The structures of colonial power were conceived to contain two different types of societies, disposed in a hierarchical way under the aegis of the crown.

The processes of independence did not recognize such peoples and cultures, nor did they grant citizenship to people who were born within one of the subordinate cultures. In this regard, the modern condition in a strict sense of the term characterized only part of the territories that were constituted as new countries.

In this first horizon of modernity that implies the division between the state and civil society, there is an important core that I want to point out in order to develop my argument. It consists of the constitution of labor cells of civil society: first the labor organizations with the diverse forms of solidarity which would later adopt the union form.

I want to introduce two more dimensions according to the notion of primordial form, so that I can present an analysis that contains multidimensional articulations. In the second analytical level, we could, thus, consider that in countries that have been erected on territories that experienced colonization, and where this has not destroyed the cultural diversity, we are witness to the fact that several societies are superimposed: they exist partly articulated under colonial dominance and later on by capitalism, but they have been largely disjointed. Therefore, in the notion of primordial form we can also include the type of relationships among the different societies that exist inside one country. This implies the consideration of the relationships between the modern condition and other types of societies, that is, the separation between the state and civil society, and its way of being related with another type of structures and societies in which there has not been such a separation, as is the case in a large part of the Latin American region.

Cycles of Mobilization

Construction of Nation-States in Latin America

I will use the idea of a primordial form to differentiate cycles and mobilization forms, in a selective way. The idea of the primordial form works well to differentiate mobilization forms of social protest in relation to the social and political construction processes.

The first cycle relates to the construction of the nation-state in Latin America. One of the features of the organization of social structures after independence, mainly in the Andean area, has been the fact that these countries have organized a state with some modern republican forms, division of powers, and toward the end of the century, a system of parties. However, they largely maintained the social structures and social relationships of the colonial period: a great concentration of land property, mines, and nucleuses of exploitation of natural resources as well as relationships of servitude in an extended way.

In this sense, we have countries that have territories and environments of modernity, and territories and environments of social life that are characterized by relations of servitude. One of the results of this type of configuration is a weak primordial form, because the state and the modern hubs of the economy, organized as capitalist islands, do not thoroughly articulate the country, neither all the environments of the social and productive life, nor the whole population. The political structures of the state correspond basically to very few areas of economic and social modernization. As a result, these states have been more or less repressive in relation to the population (Cueva, 1977).

This implies that for a long time most of the population was not included as citizens. In this regard, these were not very modern states, deprived as they were of nation and citizens. One could think in a generic way that the nationalist movements are articulated as contesting this condition. In general, they have tried to articulate the state and civil societies in a more continuous way, modifying those conditions. Nationalist movements, therefore, become the main form of political and social mobilization. They have also offered the main political critique during the twentieth century, mainly during its first decades.

Nationalisms are political forces that have as a project the economic and social modernization of their countries. In this sense, industrialization, the development of the internal market, and economic diversification are the components of their political projects, in the versions led by bourgeois and liberal sectors as well as in the versions articulated by labor forces and socialists.

One of the main facets of nationalisms in relation to the articulation of the primordial form links up with the creation of a nation for the post-independence states. Hence, one of their main tasks is to articulate the 'national-popular', whose composition varies from country to country.

The articulation of a nation has been made, among other things, by two means: the constitution and development of a modern civil society and the development of citizenship. Both are strongly bounded; since first an organization process is experienced at the union and corporate levels and then at the political one, through which mobilization is organized in demand of the recognition of political rights, of the broadening of citizenship. To articulate the nation or to articulate it to the state has implied citizenship, that is to say, a certain degree of political democratization (Quijano, 1989).

During the first decades of the twentieth century, one of the main objectives of political mobilization was the conquest of political rights, that is to say, citizenship amplification. The other axis in the process of articulation of the primordial form during the period of unfolding of nationalist forces connects with the relationship between the economy and state. One of the features of the economies of the Latin American countries has consisted of being strongly articulated to the world market as suppliers of natural resources, with a very low level of or almost nonexistent indexes of fiscal contribution, in a way such that the Latin American states were weak because they could neither finance the development of their institutions, nor the articulation of important mediations with the civil society.

In fact, one of the main objects of the nationalist movements' critique has been this neo-colonial character of the bond between the economy and state with the rest of the country and with the rest of the world. In that regard, one of the main objectives or elements of their political project has been the nationalization of economies and natural resources. This has been carried out by revolutions, as in the case of Mexico and Bolivia. Another important element has been agrarian reform, another modernization element vis-à-vis the relationships of servitude in the countryside. Their agrarian reforms have been made combining community components of local cultural traditions with modern elements, such as small and medium private property and production geared to the market.

There are two components in this cycle of mobilizations in relation to the construction of nation-states in Latin America. On the one hand, the presence of some ideas that correspond to central features of modernity, the ideas of industrialization and national sovereignty, the idea of the nation-state itself, in some cases the idea of representative states, that has been more strongly linked to the organization of political parties of liberal inspiration as well as socialist. On the other hand, some modalities of the combination of modernity with the community, and political and social forms, which are not modern, have been part of the articulation of these forces. This has happened more strongly in the Andean area, with more intensity in particular in Bolivia. It has consisted in a peasant transformation process linked to the formation of the labor class in the areas of mining exploitation or industrial work. This process has not been part of a more general modernization of the economic and social structures, but rather it has been developed as islands, extant in contexts of non-modern community relationships (Zavaleta, 1986).

The fact that this new labor class comes from agrarian contexts and community structures has generated a composition of modern elements – mainly introduced by socialist discourse, by unions and by anarchism, which has included the ideas of industrialization, nation-state, and sovereignty, with some elements of political culture stemming from their communitarian culture. This has entailed that the labor unions of the Andean area are characterized by a composition of community and modern elements.

In this respect, the conception of democracy has been bounded to the political rights of organization and participation in decision-making processes, beyond their electoral aspects which have been, however, also incorporated. This aspect of the forms of popular organization and social protest has been maintained during the twentieth century and been reactivated and extended towards its end and the beginning of the twenty-first century.

We need to emphasize that in this political cycle, mobilization and social protest have been strongly linked to the conquest of political rights: citizenship and the construction of the nation-state. Interest groups have also developed in this horizon.

Resistance to Neo-liberalism

A second cycle of mobilization and social protest emerged against the neo-liberal reforms in the continent. In this interpretative outline, one can think of neo-liberalism as a global strategy to decompose the primordial forms in favours of transnational capitals and of some states' sovereignty in particular. One of the central features of this strategy consists in weakening the forms of political construction of the national states in such a way that this favors the strategies of transnational accumulation. The development of modernity in Latin America has implied the buildup of nation-states, so as to articulate in a more consistent way the state and civil society, economy and social life. This has generated democratization in some countries and the articulation of some limits to the sovereignty of transnational powers.

This feature of modernity has become an obstacle for another of its facet, which has become contemporarily the predominant one, the one that consists of the tendency to a transnational concentration of wealth and resources.

There are, therefore, two sides of modernity. Neo-liberalism is a strategy to break down the articulation between modernity, nationalization, and democratization. Neo-liberalism implies a transnational privatization of the economy, bringing about the weakening of the primordial form in each country, including the United States and the European countries, as we are witnessing today. It also implies a reduction of some elements of citizenship, mainly those that connected with the redistribution of wealth and social rights. It also entails a redesign and a reduction of the spaces of representation and political participation, on the looking out for governability favorable to transnational control.

This type of strategy has generated two cycles of resistance and social protest. There was a first phase characterized by resistance to the implementation of the neo-liberal structures that has lasted for several years in many countries. It has been marked by periods of intense social conflict and street fighting. While in many countries neo-liberalism has generated some social consent, after some years, sometimes more than one decade, there begins another resistance wave to neo-liberal politics. This has been characterized by the protest against the disintegrating effects and forms of exclusion, inequality and poverty that it generates. On the other hand, there is resistance, which has perhaps been stronger, against the neo-liberal expansive wave that implies an advance mainly in the privatization of resources like water (since transport, trains, communication, and manufactures were privatized in the first installation cycle).

This second phase of resistance to neo-liberalism has been characterized by the articulation of several elements that are shared across countries. One of them relates to the idea of the reconstruction of the public, so as to stop the privatization of some collective goods as water and the defense of territories opened-up for intensive mining. The other component that is linked to the notion of the reconstruction of the public has to do with some elements of self-management. These forms of social protest and resistance to the neo-liberal pattern include some elements of alternatives that consist of experiences of collective self-management. This element appears, for example, in the factories taken over by workers and the management of social reproduction in the *piquetero* movement in Argentina (Svampa, 2003); in the experience of land occupation and reorganization of the economic and social life in the *Movimento dos Trabalhadores Sem Terra* in Brazil; as well as in the proposal of self-management of water that came out of the popular victory in the 'water war' in Cochabamba, Bolivia (Gutierrez, 2007).

The resistance to neo-liberalism has been carried out through a recreation of 'national-popular' agency in most of the countries of Latin America, although this is not its only component. The 'national-popular' is one of the features of modernity that has been articulated in the history of Latin American countries. It has been the type of 'historical block' that has been articulated to modernize some countries in the economic, social, and political sense. It has been the agency that has articulated a primordial form with more capacity for national feedback (Zavaleta, 1989).

The national-popular is also linked to the development of the public sphere and of public property in our countries; in this regard, it connects to institutions of collective goods as a result of the recognition of social rights, as well as a sphere of the public as the space of political life, articulation of public opinion and control over the government. Neo-liberalism implied a reduction of the public and that of collective goods. The forms of anti-neo-liberal mobilization have been linked to the rebuilding of the public in two senses so as to revert privatization and establish public spaces of deliberation about the direction of state and municipal companies that manage those resources.

The anti-privatization movements install a public space beyond the parties and the media, in which they begin to discuss the neo-liberal model and deliberate alternatives. In this cycle, we see again that feature of modernity that connects with the period of construction of the nation-state and the articulation of the public in national-popular ways. It faces another facet of modernity that relates to the growing transnationalization of the economy and of political decisions. There is a tense relationship between this dynamic bounded to modernity by the idea of autonomy, therefore of self-government and personal freedom, rights, citizenship, representation, democratization and redistribution, on the one hand, and that other dynamic which consists in capitalist development, property concentration, and strategies to maximize profit rates, on the other hand.

The anti-privatization movements that engendered the crisis of neo-liberal governments are movements that have been trying to articulate the primordial form, making articulations that respond more to inner forces, demands, necessities and projects than to the necessities of world capital accumulation. In fact, they have achieved some results in this respect. In several countries, the privatization wave has been broken, at least temporarily or in some areas. In others, they have led to redistributive policies, although these are secondary and remain oriented to maintaining the integrated population that was expelled out of labour markets by the neo-liberal dynamic of the world economy and its results in the local economies. They have produced government changes more than structural changes and have put some space and time limits, bringing about storms, to this neo-liberal side of modernity.

Indigenous Movements and Political Underground

A third form of articulation of protest and social mobilization has lately stemmed from the constitution and unfolding of indigenous movements, mainly in the Andean region, in Bolivia, Ecuador, and also in Chile, Peru and Colombia, as well as in meso-American territories. One of the features of the indigenous movements is that they question what many of them call internal colonialism, that is to say, the persistence of discrimination between the structures and cultural and political institutions of pre-colonial societies and the social and political forms of modernity that have maintained their supremacy and racist character after political independence.

The indigenous movements in all these countries have as a main feature the experience of a long and manifold process of unification: unification of several communities, territories and collectives that are part of the same culture as well as the unification of indigenous people of different cultures that live in the same territory. This has generated powerful indigenous unions, assemblies or confederations of indigenous people in these countries. These forms of unification in particular articulate two things: they have been one of the main forces that have been mobilized against neo-liberalism; but at the same time they have also questioned the older structures of neo-colonial modernity in their countries (Albó, 2002).

One of the main paths of neo-liberal development today consists in the expansion of intensive open-sky mining exploitation in indigenous territories. Because of the technology used and the intensity of exploitation, this kind of mining destroys those territories in very short periods of time. In about two years, it leaves territories without water and makes sick the affected populations. This is one element that engenders resistance in recent years.

This defense of indigenous territories is not the only motivation for political mobilization and for social indigenous protest. Also inequality and political exclusion have played a role. In this respect, huge indigenous mobilizations have also been geared to demand and promote state reforms oriented to an egalitarian inclusion and recognition of cultural diversity, to larger political participation in the national decisions and the recognition of territorial autonomies as indigenous autonomies. In this type of mobilization and social protest there is a combination of two aspects. On the one hand, there is the social movement resistance against the neo-liberal pattern. However, there is another facet that relates to the kind of organization and mobilization launched against neo-liberalism. Against the neo-liberal and neo-colonial structures, the movements use other sort of structures and social relationships, another kind of culture and other political forms that have survived throughout centuries of colonization and modern liberal and bourgeois rule.

In this sense, I suggest that we reckon that these types of movements combine a protest aspect internal to modernity with another element of *societal* movement, which is tantamount to saying that there are other societies that have been included in a colonial and neo-colonial way in the new states. These societies are moving inside not only to question neo-liberalism and the way it articulates a weak primordial form, but also the history of that former discrimination and hierarchical organization. What has given force to the anti-neo-liberal mobilizations has been this combination of national-popular movements with these *societal* movements based on indigenous community structures. They articulate a critique of the dominant side of contemporary modernity that is neo-liberalism with the critique of the constituent feature of modernity which is the colonial relationship between the conquered cultures and the ruling social order imposed on them.

The existence and persistence of organizational structures of social life and political authority that have been maintained in the everyday life of many cultures conceived as indigenous people in Latin America today have been recreated through several cycles of anti-colonial struggle. They have been reactivated and have enlarged their unification margins in the last decades. They can be thought according to the notion of political underground. In a parallel way to the structures of the nation-state or the representative republican state, they have been operating in another community group through spaces characterized by deliberative general assemblies and the selection of authorities, being articulated at a regional level. Political life develops in these spaces much more importantly than inside the structures of mediation, representation and participation organized by the state. These spaces of political life, authority and self-government have been unified in the last decades and, when they have generated cycles of mobilization against neo-liberal politicians, they have not only thrown the neo-liberal governments into crisis, but also the state structures as such, leading in some cases to constituent assemblies that have reformed these structures, at least partially, in the horizon of a *plurinational* state.

In this sense, we can see that there are non-modern forms of social and political life that have been articulated with some modern forms, as unions, parties and other civil society associations, to produce the crisis of modern structures and the neo-liberal trend. In the current protest cycle and social resistance in Latin America, mainly in countries where there is a presence of community structures, the critical political action has been made up of an articulation between community elements and some modern political forms, as much in civil society as in its mediations with the state. However, that *plurinational* state has remained basically a form of symbolic recognition of the cultural diversity that is not bound to a respect of the indigenous territories, as we clearly see in Bolivia and Ecuador, countries that follow the continental rule of deciding about the exploitation of resources in indigenous territories that imply its destruction and, therefore, the negation of the historical continuity of that cultural diversity.

Modernity has always experienced resistance forms, from its initial moments and constituent processes, since it implied the destruction and reorganization of former ways of social and political life, up to current times, in which a combination of community and modern political structures forms is part of the critical forces and the social resistance to the contemporary forms of modernity. Along with these communitarian forms there spread several modern forms of protest and social contestation.

References

Albó, X. (2002). *Pueblos indios en la polític.* La Paz: CIPCA.
Berman, M. (1988). *All that is solid melts into air.* New York: Penguin Books.
Cueva, A. (1977). *El desarrollo del capitalismo en América Latina.* Mexico: Siglo XXI.
Dussel, E. (1994). *1492 o el encubrimiento del otro.* La Paz: Plural.
González Casanova, P. (2006). *Sociología de la explotación.* Buenos Aires: CLACSO.
Gutierrez, R. (2007). *El ritmo del Pachakuti.* La Paz: Textos Rebeldes.
Quijano, A. (1989). *Modernidad, identidad y utopía en América Latina.* Lima: Y ediciones.
Marx, K. (1975). *El Capital.* Buenos Aires: Editorial Claridad.

Svampa, M. (2003). *Entre la ruta y el barrio. La experiencia de las organizaciones piqueteras*. Buenos Aires: Biblos.

Thomson, S. (2003). *We Alone will Rule: Native Andean Politics in the Age of Insurgency*, Madison: University of Wisconsin Press.

Zavaleta, R. (1982). Problemas de la determinación dependiente y la forma primordial. *América Latina: desarrollo y perspectivas democráticas*. Costa Rica: FLACSO.

Zavaleta, R. (1986). *Lo nacional-popular en Bolivia*. Mexico: Siglo XXI.

Zavaleta, R. (1989). *El estado en América Latina*. Cochabamba: Los Amigos del Libro.

Part III

Borders of Modernity and Frontiers of Exclusion: Rights, Citizenship and Contestation in Comparative Perspective

11

Half-Positions and Social Contestation: On the Dynamics of Exclusionary Integration

Craig Browne

Introduction

The contemporary phase of global modernity has extended social interconnections, especially beyond the national frame. However, new forms of exclusion, subordination and marginality have resulted from the processes that enable the extension of social relations. This paradoxical dynamic of system integration and social disintegration is one of the contemporary forms in which the capitalist system's contradictions are displaced onto other social institutions. The result, I argue, is fractures in the institutional means of social integration that developed during the preceding phases of modernity and conflicts that are conditioned by the contemporary consolidation of types of half-positions. These half-positions lie at the borders between the lifeworld of social actors, on the one hand, and the state and the market economy, on the other. Half-positions are prototypically those of workers without the full rights and entitlements of citizenship and citizens without the material resources and social recognition of wage labour. Half-positions are, in effect, the product of exclusionary integration, and this tendency of exclusionary integration is reinforced by the fact that race and ethnicity are often salient to the determination of those in half-positions. In this respect, Nancy Fraser (2009) is right to argue that a Critical Theory of globalization should explicate the justice claims over *who* is represented politically. Yet, my analysis shows that whilst Fraser's normative position is relevant to addressing certain dimensions of the subordination and injustice of half-positions, it does not encompass some significant features half-positions' modes of contestation.

The contestation that ensues from exclusionary integration of half-positions is related to two other significant forms of conflict in global modernity, but it also exhibits specific attributes that distinguish it from them. First, there is conflict between global capitalism and democracy, which overlays the dynamic of class conflict and that tends to generate reflexive modes of contestation, from the practices of the alter-globalization movement and anti-austerity protests to the mobilizations based on nationalist ideologies and the antinomian strands of major religions (Browne, 2002; Eisenstadt, 1999; Domingues, 2012). In my opinion, the conflict between globalization and democracy concerns the potential for collective self-determination and this is why this conflict often manifests itself in terms of competing agencies' attempts to shape and control the direction of modernity (Wagner, 2012). In fact, the conflicts associated with half-positions are in large measure a by-product of this conflict and they are a displaced version of its central dynamic. Nevertheless, the exclusionary nature of half-positions means that this category of individuals are more affected by the specific articulation of the conflict between democracy and globalization than they are capable of shaping its dynamic. This is one of the reasons why the contestation of half-positions needs to be understood in terms of distinctive experiences of reification and real abstractions (see Domingues, 2006).

Second, there is the conflict intrinsic to the relationship that institutions have to the social action that serves their reproduction. Institutions depend on the creativity of subjects and yet limit subjects' control over their own activity (Castoriadis, 1987; Boltanski & Chiapello, 2005). In other words, it is the conflict based on alienation. The half-positions of workers without citizenship and citizens without work are, to be sure, implicated in this conflict of compelled but thwarted participation. Yet, despite significant overlaps with the conflicts over alienation, the contestation of half-positions can be differentiated from it. The social integration necessary to participate is often what is precisely at stake in half-positions and a half-position entails some disassociation from mechanisms of social involvement, like the legally defined positions of either wage labour or citizenship. There are many analyses of vulnerability (Misztal, 2011), 'disafiliation' (Castel, 2003), 'precarity' (Standing, 2011), and 'marginality' (Wacquant, 2008) that draw attention to the emergence in capitalist nation-states of significant categories of individuals that are seemingly superfluous from the standpoint of the labour market and the neoliberal state (Bauman, 2004). The structural changes of the contemporary phase of global modernity are then generating a variety of antagonisms and injustices; however, the 2005 French Riots will be taken as a major exemplar of the conflicts emanating from half-positions. The rioters' acts of resistance, I argue, were conditioned by their exclusion from the dominant public sphere and the principal justice claim connected to their actions was that of retribution.

The consolidation of half-positions is particularly due to the character and limitations of the principal coordinating mechanisms of the third phase of modernity, especially the network mode of organization and the market. Jose Maurício Domingues argues that these forms of coordination have to varying degrees replaced the second phase of modernity's more state-organized coordination through principles of hierarchy and command, although modernity's third phase is actually a 'mixed articulation' of these different modes of coordination. The elements of earlier phases of modernity are not so much 'erased' in a process of succession as rearranged and realigned in a more layered and complex pattern (Domingues, 2012: 26). Half-positions reflect the disjunctions between these different forms of coordination, since the institutional inclusion as a citizen, may not, for example, be replicated at the level of wage labour. Similarly, the unemployed may simultaneously confront expectations of voluntary collaboration as a basis of social membership and other state agencies' authoritative commands, especially those of the police and the judiciary. Indeed, disjunctions between modes of coordination are relevant to the often indefinite objectives of the contestation deriving from half-positions, because the source of deprivation may be spatially distant global processes that are only indirectly encountered and the more directly experienced local context is conditioned by the interface with other institutions, like the family, the school system, the urban housing estate, welfare organizations, voluntary associations, police and informal social networks. Although half-positions have distinctive features, their consolidation crystallizes broad trends towards social disintegration. Robert Castel sought to define the social question's metamorphosis during the third phase of modernity in somewhat similar terms. Castel argued that the resurgence of market coordination was calling into question the capacity of society 'to exist as a collectivity linked by relations of interdependency' (Castel, 2003: XIX–XX).

Exclusionary Integration: Genealogies and Misalignment in the Third Modernity

The notion of half-positions presumes that the integration of individuals and groups in the capitalist societies depends on the combination of wage labour and citizenship. In fact, the insufficiency of one of these positions in the absence of the other was integral to T.H. Marshall's conception of social citizenship. Marshall (1950) described a conflict in capitalist societies between the 'warring principles' of 'market inequality and class divisions on the one side, and citizenship's egalitarian and universalistic principles on the other' (Somers, 2008: 82). Citizenship formed the basis of individuals' participation in public life and mitigated some of the effects of class inequalities. Significantly, Margaret Somers' historical genealogy of citizenship and Robert Castel's historical genealogy of wage labour each details how citizenship and wage labour have been institutionally elaborated in relation to each other (Castel, 2003; Somers, 2008). On the one hand, the social rights of citizenship represent a set of protections against the inequalities and vulnerabilities that are present in the market determination of wage labour. On the other hand, struggles over wage labour were critical to the extension of the social rights of citizenship. Wage labour provided a substantive means of participation and supplemented the formal equal liberty of citizenship. The circumstances of groups that were historically excluded from either citizenship or wage labour, particularly women and males without property, reveals the interconnection between these two channels of integration and the 'complex inequalities', to use Sylvia Walby's term, that ensues from the variation between them (Walby, 2009).

Somers' and Castel's respective historical genealogies of citizenship and wage labour are each significantly informed by Karl Polanyi's argument about the 'double movement' by society, which was conveyed by groups and movements against the disembedding of the market during the first phase of liberal modernity (Polanyi, 1957). It is worth noting that Polanyi considered that the system of protection that the European 'double movement' generated against the destructive dynamic of the disembedded and self-regulating market system was not attainable in colonial contexts, because colonies 'lacked the prerequisite, political government'. In Polanyi's opinion, the revolts against imperialism during this period were mainly attempts by the colonized populations 'to achieve the political status necessary to shelter themselves from the social dislocation caused by European trade policies' (Polanyi, 1957: 192). Polanyi argued that the market society of the first liberal phase of modernity was unsustainable. It was, as Castel (2003: 410) reiterates, 'only able to take hold in the first place because it was embedded in a social system where traditional patronage and "organic" forms of solidarity remained strong' and the related familial and communal protections initially 'blunted its potentially destabilizing effects'. Market society's protracted crisis culminated in the assertion of social regulation, but social protections had to be established on new bases due to the dissolution of previous social bonds. The capitalist expropriation of land and the commodification of labour had created a society dependent on wage labour and the movement of people from rural regions to industrial centres (Castel, 2003; Polanyi, 1957). The elaboration of the social rights of citizenship and the establishment of systems of regulation that qualified the market determination of wage labour's conditions were largely consolidated during the second phase of 'organized modernity', especially with the institution of the post-second world war democratic welfare state capitalism (see Wagner, 1994; Streeck, 2011).

Democratic capitalism represented a social model in which the welfare state alleviated inequalities to varying degrees in different national contexts on the basis of taxation revenues and provided the market with some degree of coordination. Critical Social Theory largely considered democratic welfare state capitalism a class compromise and argued that capitalism's contradictions were not resolved. Rather, the contradictions of capitalism were either transferred onto the state administration or manifested themselves in the displaced form of crises of social identity. Although Habermas' original conception of late-capitalism undoubtedly overestimated the extent to which the welfare state had irrevocably transformed the conditions of capitalist accumulation, his more recent analysis of *the postnational constellation* draws on Polanyi in order to highlight the persistent competing dynamics of the opening to markets and the closure of national protection against them (Habermas, 1976, 2001). In a sense, the denationalizing character of globalization is primarily the disembedding of the various forms of market-based exchange from the broad conditions of social integration. The third phase of modernity involves what Domingues (2012) describes as a more flexible and polarizing global dynamic of capitalist accumulation. It is a dynamic that reinforces the misalignment in the institutional channels of social integration; for instance, the third phase of modernity intensifies the differences in the temporalities and spatial extensions of capitalist markets and bureaucratic administration (see Sassen, 2008: 390–395). One of the consequences of the fracturing of the channels of integration is that individuals occupying half-positions encounter 'internal borders' that limit participation and membership (Somers, 2008; Bosniak, 2006; Balibar, 2004). In all cases, half-positions entail some *reduction in the ability to effectively access those forms of social protection* that had limited the subjective experience of structural transformations and social subordination. This is particularly important because the contestation of half-positions is shaped by experiences of how legitimate expectations of equal treatment are not upheld and the exclusion of those in half-positions from the dominant public sphere.

The exclusionary integration of half-positions discloses the fragility of the democratic regulation of capitalist inequalities through the social protections of citizenship. There have generally been significant exceptions to the normative universalism of citizenship. In most cases in the capitalist periphery, the elaboration of citizenship as a system of social protections remains at best prospective and even in the capitalist core there are important variations. These discrepancies in the institutional systems of social protection have had long-term consequences. It has already been noted how second modernity gave rise to improvements in the conditions of wage labour and citizenship, although these changes were the result of different, though related, features of modernity. The limiting of inequalities was generally a direct result of emancipatory social struggles, but the institutionalizing of fairer distributions of resources was often closely tied to a nation-state's response to economic crisis or the project of 'nation building'. The 'New Deal' in the United States of America, the so-called 'national settlement' that took place shortly after the federation of Australia at the beginning of the twentieth century, and the post-second world welfare state in the United Kingdom are instances of such developments. However, these progressive reforms incorporated aspects of exclusionary integration. Notably, the occupational categories of farm labourers and domestic servants were exempted from many of the New Deal's industrial regulations (Katznelson, 2005; Lieberman, 1998). This detrimentally affected the many African–Americans who were employed in these poorly renumerated areas of employment. In the Australian case, the limiting of inequality amongst male employees went together with discriminatory, racially based immigration policies and the denial of an equal status as citizens to the indigenous population (Lake, 2008; Beilharz, 2008).

The compromises that limited reformist initiatives were inconsistent with the universal principles that were mobilized to justify social citizenship and these historical instances of exclusionary integration continue to impinge on contemporary situations. Margaret Somers (2008) argues that exemptions from the New Deal labour regulations influenced the living conditions of the African–American population affected by the Hurricane Katrina emergency. In this way, the contemporary 'market fundamentalist' policies of limiting the social state intersect with the longer history of racial inequality. The dynamic of exclusionary integration in the third phase of modernity is predominantly a consequence of what I will term the globalization of the lifeworld. That is, the *globalization of lifeworld* refers to the contradictory tendencies resulting from the relative decoupling of processes of economic and political system integration from those of social integration. In short, the coordination of the disembedded market system can simultaneously have the opposite consequence of disorganizing the institutions of social integration, including the political institutions to which citizenship is affiliated. Yet, the decoupling of system integration from social integration is never total, and the renewal of the self-regulating market is an ideological project. Saskia Sassen is right to argue that 'global systems insert themselves in national domains where they once were non-existent', but that nation states have facilitated globalizing processes (Sassen, 2008: 227).

The developments in global system integration that have altered the parameters of the relationship between the state and the economy in capitalist societies are well known: the expansion in the wealth and power of financial markets, with the institutionalization of trade in national currencies following the breakdown of the Bretton–Woods system and the deregulation of finance, the growth in the number and size of multinational corporations in recent decades, with the corresponding increase in the proportion of economic activity that is intra-firm as well as the clustering of subsidiary business services, the internationalization of the division of labour and the development of supranational regimes of economic governance, with the influence to compel states to adjust social and economic policies (Held et al., 1999; Beck, 2005; Sassen, 2008). The growing autonomy of the capitalist economy is equally evidenced by the fact that capital's increased mobility compared to labour has coincided with a decline in many nation states of the proportion of state revenue that is derived from business taxation. There is another significant, though sometimes overlooked, implication of these new regimes of system integration. The strategic adaptation of nation states to the 'external' conditions of coordinated market competition increases the unevenness of the 'internal' economy. In short, as the notion of comparative advantage itself implies, most 'countries succeed in a few industrial sectors but not very well in most' (Hollingsworth & Boyer, 1998: 38). These divergences in industrial capacity regularly accentuate differences between regions and cities, as well as often coinciding with the socio-economic divisions in the labour and housing markets (Sassen, 2006).

The half-position of wage labour that lacks the full entitlement of citizenship applies to the situation of such categories as guest workers and illegal migrants. Of course, the connections that wage labour with reduced citizenship entitlements have to processes of global system integration is most evident in the creation of so-called 'free zones' that are exempt from many of the social protections of national labour regulations and national taxation obligations (Ong, 2006). Free economic zones are very concrete instances of the tendencies of diminishing the citizenship dimension of work and 'denationalizing' the economy. Yet, the erosion of the citizenship dimension of wage labour has occurred in core capitalist states and it is a broader tendency of 'flexible accumulation'. Boltanski and Chiapello (2005) describe this as the 'dismantling of the world of work' in the third phase of capitalism. It has included the dismantling of some of the social

protections of labour legislation on the grounds of deregulation and flexibility, the increase in the scale of part-time and precarious employment,
the use of sub-contracting and outsourcing, and new ways of segmenting
the workforce on the basis of qualification, gender, ethnicity and age, for
instance, 'seniority has become a factor less of security than insecurity'
(Boltanski & Chiapello 2005: 238). These processes have generally coincided with significant declines in the percentage of the workforce that are
members of trade unions.

Beside the regulation of the labour market and the social protections
that went together with citizenship, citizenship implies a certain valuing of
subjectivity. The latter distinguishes the citizen's experiencing the 'dismantling' of work conditions from that of those groups that are in a formal
sense in the *half-position* of workers without citizenship, particularly in
terms of the potential modes of contestation and, in Nancy Fraser's terms,
'representation' in the political sphere (Fraser, 2009). Indeed, recently in
Europe and North America the integration of non-citizens through wage
labour has been countered by the coercive state power that has been
directed towards non-citizens, particularly through enhanced 'security
controls', legislative changes and curtailing the informal means of participation in a community (Sassen, 2008; Bosniak, 2006; Balibar, 2004).
Étienne Balibar (2004: 123) provocatively considers that there are certain
parallels with South African apartheid in the recent coercion that European
states applied to 'the important group of workers who "reproduce" their
lives on one side of the border and "produce" on the other side, and thus
more precisely are *neither insiders nor outsiders*, or (for many of us) are
insiders officially considered outsiders'.

It can be argued then that a contradiction has emerged in global modernity between the normative justification of law based on appeals to cosmopolitan justice and human rights, on the one hand, and the simplification in
many Northern and Southern nation states of law into an instrument of
control in order to deal with social disorder and developments construed as
originating outside the boundaries of the nation, on the other hand
(Habermas, 2006; Comaroff & Comaroff, 2006). That is, law becomes for
those in half-positions a means of forced coordination, rather than an institution whose legitimacy is generated by public communication and the
participation of those affected. In this way, the state's coercive powers
increasingly mediate the disintegrative consequences of the globalization
of the lifeworld (Wacquant, 2008, 2012).

Similarly, the half-position of citizens that lack the full entitlements of
employment is closely related to the limits of welfare state intervention,
patterns of unemployment in contexts of 'deindustrialization', as well as

being related to increases in insecure forms of employment and the consolidated effects of segmented labour markets. The general underlying tendency in capitalist welfare states is that of the economy's inability to meet the former expectations of full employment and the strong segmentation of labour markets. One of the things that the the 2005 French riots highlights is a generational shift in this case of half-positions. Many of the rioters were in the half-position of being citizens without work, whereas their immigrant parents had occupied the contrasting half-position of workers without the rights of citizenship. In capitalist welfare states, half-positions' diminished circumstances are exacerbated by changes in the third phase of modernity's modes of coordination and the transference of former public entitlements into private functions that require individual, familial or communal network solutions, whether in the form of voluntary work or household expenditure (Bourdieu, 1999). The conditions of welfare recipients have likewise altered over the past decades in these nation states. Despite labour market failures, the introduction of 'workfare' and 're-commodification' extended the contractual principles of market exchange (Gray, 2004). Somers (2008: 8) argues that when the 'contractualizing' of citizenship intersects with entrenched inequalities, such as those of race, it can lead to situations that are similar to that which Hannah Arendt (1979) described as the losing of the 'right to have rights'.

Given these changes in the relationship between the different modalities of integration, the historical experience of colonization is in some respects a precursor to the pathologies of the globalization of the lifeworld. The conversion of social integration to the external conditions of system integration is a distinguishing feature of colonialism (Pels, 1997). The transnationalism of colonial systems produced fractured relations of social integration, especially given the systematically distorted relations of recognition between colonizers and colonized (Fanon, 1986). Although there are considerable variations in colonial formations, the imbalance between the metropolis and the periphery underpinned the exploitive relations of colonization. It determined the direction of the capitalist world system's commodity chains and established the preconditions for economic dependency. For the colonized, colonialism represented a system of partial involvement and unequal participation; the rights of citizenship were unevenly distributed. In colonial contexts, differences in social integration were used as a weight against the factual involvements of colonized populations at the level of system integration (Asad, 1991). It is possible to discern continuities with contemporary global integration in these colonial ruptures with equivalence and the equality of conditions. There can be little doubt that the disparity between economic circumstances underpins the integration of individuals as consumers in contemporary capitalist nation states.

The distribution of half-positions is uneven and it is the concentration of half-positions amongst marginalized populations that one finds further parallels with colonial relations of system integration and social disintegration. Half-positions are, in a sense, an inversion of the cosmopolitan potential of globalization, particularly, because they tend, though not exclusively, to coalesce around the ascribed categories of race and ethnicity. Yet, despite their contradictory nature and attendant potential to undermine the symbolic reproduction of the lifeworld, many half-positions are highly functional from the standpoint of system integration. The uncoupling of work from the rights of citizenship can be the very source of the value of the individual from the perspective of an employer and indirectly that of a consumer (Kearney, 1998: 128; Gray, 2004). Of course, this valuing then depends on sustaining marginality and the exclusion from citizenship. For this reason, the half-position is mapped directly onto subjectivity, rather than effectively mediated by the other channel of integration. Now, it is my argument that this dialectic of integration and disintegration *induces displaced reactions* to the experiences of reification and alienation. The binds that can develop for those occupying half-positions can result in frustrations that infuse episodes of violent contestation. Balibar likewise points to how the experience of 'internal exclusion' shaped the 2005 French riots and the rioters' destruction of the 'thing' 'from which they are contradictorily *excluded* as non-citizens', 'but of which they are themselves a part, that in a way is part of themselves and their identity' (Balibar, 2007: 51).

The displaced reactions to the globalization of the lifeworld are not limited to violent and disorderly modes of contestation; ideological confusions and distrust of social institutions are probably more common responses. In fact, this is one of the reasons why there are opposed types of social disintegration ensuing from increasing system integration. On the one hand, there are the subjective experiences *of* those occupying half-positions and its implications for social contestation will be explored in more detail. The antithetical relations to oneself and others that are generated by this exclusionary integration have already been highlighted. On the other hand, there are the anomic reactions *to* half-positions coalescing with race and ethnicity. These reactions can amount to an endorsement of social exclusion, as is evident in the types of resentment that are directed towards refugees and marginal groups (Hage, 2002). The reactions *against* those in half-positions sometimes reflects a divide between majority and minority cultures, with the former appealing to some association between the institution of the nation state and the idea of the nation as the foundation of social integration.

It is this conception of social integration that the denationalizing dynamic of globalization challenges and which can in turn lead to the socially regressive contestation that seeks to establish internal borders.

The recent xenophobic and racist reactions to minorities, immigrants and supranational institutions in many nation states can be viewed as simply the more visible and extreme versions of dominant classes or popular majorities' attempts to monopolize the influence over the institutional anchoring of social integration. That is, the dominant classes or popular majorities endeavour to exclude themselves from the *colonizing* aspects of the globalization of the lifeworld and to confine its effects to the minorities in half-positions, thereby reinforcing them. If this analysis is correct then it could explain the growth of so-called 'welfare chauvinism', that is, policies making it more difficult for migrants to access social rights and welfare benefits, whilst preserving them for nationals (Banting, 2000: 25; Huysmans, 2006). It is important to note that the social disintegration that coincides with the globalization of the lifeworld is not exclusive to the circumstances of migrants. Rather, it is relatively explicit in relation to immigrants because of citizenship's formal determination and migrants having been the negative object of displaced reactions to system integrating processes. Half-positions result from the uneven and polarizing developments in global, national and regional economies and the state's incapacity - or unwillingness - to prevent, in Bauman's (2011) terms, 'collateral damages'. The next section develops the claim that half-positions lead to forms of mobilization that differ from the more typical format of modern social and political movements. The 2005 French Riots were significant in terms of the scale of their unplanned coordination and the participants' reaction to the experiences of exclusionary integration (see Browne & Mar 2010).

Social Disintegration and Social Contestation: Reification, Racism and Retribution

There are several reasons why the 2005 riots in France illustrate the thesis that the current processes of system integration involve tendencies of social disintegration. The riots had considerable symbolic resonance and were often viewed as symptomatic of the social malaise of globalization (Balibar, 2007). The participants were largely the children of immigrants from former French colonies and exemplify the coalescing of half-positions. The riots were undoubtedly a form of symbolic action and laden with meaning, yet it is difficult to attribute a particular objective to them. In other words, the riots lacked the political elaboration of more traditional contentious politics, like those of the anti-racism movements and student protests (Lagrange & Oberti 2006; Wieviorka 2005; Lentin, 2004). In my opinion, the riot's imprecision of meaning is connected to experiences of reification and the displacement of contestation from the sources of inequalities to the institution of authoritative control and regulation. The perceived illegitimacy of intensive police intrusions formed the backdrop to the 2005 French riots, which were triggered by the death of two youths from an electrical surge whilst hiding in a power substation in the belief that the police were searching for them. The riots probably refract quite mediated and indirect experiences, given half-positions accumulate damages owing to weaker social protection (Offe, 1996: 33).

Underlying the riots were substantial and protracted structural problems of system integration. In particular, the segments of the French immigrant population have experienced sustained rates of high unemployment, itself a reflection of the decline in traditional manufacturing industries and the introduction of less labour-intensive methods of production. As a consequence, the archetypical half-position has undergone something of a generational change, from migrant labourers without the full rights of citizenship to French citizens without the material resources and social recognition of employment. Likewise, the riots appeared to signify the declining capacity of the French state to deal with problems of system integration. The state's policy options seemed to diminish as a consequence of fiscal problems that were simultaneously veiled by attributing demands for restraint to the European monetary union (Smith, 2004). Similarly, over the previous decade, the social policy of the French state shifted from active job creation through public and private industry sponsorship to the more market enhancing position of funding labour market training programmes (Palier, 2005; Levy, 2005, 1999). Despite the considerable resources that have been deployed, these programmes are limited in their capacity to transform the exclusion and lack of opportunity of the children of migrants from the outer suburban *cites* and *banlieues*. A diffused background of racism and the stigmatizing of the *banlieues'* inhabitants generated the sense of injustice that propelled the riots' retributive actions. In this context, racism often takes the precise form of systematically distorted communication. That is, the raising of validity claims concerning the rights of membership of French society for which there are neither the institutional conditions for their realization, nor the means for accessing them owing to the occupancy of half-positions (Habermas, 1970, 1984; Castel, 2006).

The devaluation of local place can likewise compound the damages of half-positions and reinforce the public discourses of the failures of integration. In the public imagination, the *banlieues* are associated with the past 'modernist' projects and the negative effects of bureaucratic planning (Castells, 1983; Wacquant, 2008). There are certain analogies with colonial disjunctions in these experiences of urban exclusion and the stigmatizing of the housing projects as materializing the periphery. The globalizing context may have altered the system problems that generate the colonization, in Habermas' terms, of lifeworlds by commodities and the state administration, yet this dynamic's salience to the 2005 riots is disclosed by the violence being principally enacted on private property in the form of automobiles and public property in the form of schools. Although these two types of property were undoubtedly defaced due to their accessibility, they resonate with half-positions' contradictory interchanges: automobiles signify the desired but exclusionary integration of consumerism and school is the institution that transmits cultural norms and values whilst generally allocating subordinate positions in the division of labour to the children of migrants.

There is no inevitable connection between half-positions and the enactment of violence. In fact, half-positions more generally lead to resignation and demoralization. The 'hidden injuries' of half-positions are connected to the 'in-between' situation of social integration that is conditional on consent or acquiescence to a position that is relatively subordinated and largely precludes the public expression of aspects of identity (Sennett & Cobb, 1973: 118; Cowlishaw, 2004). Hidden injuries are the *debilitating self-relations* that can develop from occupying half-positions and experiencing a constant denial of reciprocity in social interaction. On the one hand, this kind of disrespect may engender destructive forms of collective behaviour when conflicts that are normally veiled by everyday moral orders and the 'unarticulated condemnations' of social subordination are brought into the open by events which undermine the legitimacy of the coercive powers of the state (see Honneth 2007: 93). It is in precisely in these terms that the contestation of the 2005 French riots can be viewed and I will highlight two features that an investigation into the riots disclosed: retribution and creative disrespect (Browne & Mar 2010).

The 2005 French riots were a form of retribution for the perceived and experienced damages of material and symbolic denigration. Retribution is a kind of moral claim that is moulded by expectations that a full membership, whether as a citizen or paid employee, cannot be taken for granted. Furthermore, that even the tacit rules regulating the subordinated groups' relations to the institutional authority of the police have been transgressed and violated. This is not to deny that one could discern some order of claims for redistribution and recognition in the riots, but the action of retribution accentuates a lack of mutuality and it responds to the affective experience of humiliation. Retribution belongs to a moral economy that markedly differs from those of 'individual rights' and procedural claims to justice: it is a form of popular will and reflects limited means of redress. In particular, the primary aspect of retribution is to affirm the collective pride of the aggrieved group by challenging the expectations of the state concerning compliance with its authority. The riots did, however, involve actions of creative disrespect. That is, performative actions that give expression to a frustrated social agency in the absence of other means of effective access to the public sphere. These actions are creative in their making explicit the contestation over values and legitimacy.

Creative disrespect arises out of the attempt of a collective to reassert some form of self-control in relation to institutionalized subordination. For this reason, violent provocations and ritualized performances, like burning cars, taunting police and even exaggerating a racially stigmatized identity, are modes of self-assertion and ways of demarcating the limits to the intervention by authorities (see Cowlishaw, 2004). These actions may not be effective politics from a strategic point of view, but they are nevertheless modes of taking initiative outside the dominant public sphere and the official channels of representing grievances. Creative disrespect is a mode of communication by means other than those of discursive speech. Rather than a traditional dialogue, it can take the traumatic form of re-enacting some of the binds of half-position. Creative disrespect may involve making claims for dignity and respect in ways that are at the borders of legality and that may compound social exclusion, as in the case of riotous actions and modes of self-mutilation as a method of protest. The latter is not uncommon amongst highly traumatized groups and individuals (see Good et al., 2008).

Conclusion: The Globalization of the Lifeworld and its Variegated Displacements

The dynamic of exclusionary integration has been a constant feature of modernity; however, the manner of its articulation has acquired some new dimensions in modernity's third phase. In my opinion, the tendencies that result in the consolidation of the half-positions of workers without citizenship and citizens without work represent a major contemporary form of reification. The reifying experience of being subject to processes that appear independently of your actions and those institutions that supposedly provide some measure of social protection has generated displaced reactions and contemporary forms of disorderly contestation. The tendencies of disembedding and real abstraction that result in half-positions are not exclusive to developed nation states, although the connection to the deterioration of the basis of citizenship's social rights in the welfare state is distinctive to them and reflects differences in the normative expectations that have underpinned social integration. Despite the enormous disparities in material conditions, Partha Chatterjee (2004) highlights an analogous mode of exclusive integration in contemporary India. Chatterjee argues that the current phase of primitive accumulation involves a substantial and almost complete disembedding of the peasantry, yet there is not sufficient work available in the labour market for this dispossessed population. In his opinion, a portion of the dispossessed are now in the intermediate position of being part of 'political society', that is, subject to intense state regulation whilst 'not regarded by the state as proper citizens possessing rights and belonging to the properly constituted civil society' (Chatterjee, 2008: 58).

The analysis of the 2005 French riots served to highlight the disintegrative consequences of the globalization of the lifeworld and the types of social contestation that diverge from the more standard forms of social movement contention and their objectives. In the case of the 2005 riots, the pathological effects of half-positions was evident in the violent reaction to stigmatized personalities, the anomic relations to the institution of law that functions as a medium of forced coercion, and the cultural breakdown that is conditioned by the tension between a commitment to universalism and a restrictive interpretation of national identity in the public sphere. No doubt there is a specific intensity to the 2005 French riots, yet my allusions to parallel analyses suggest that conflicts over half-positions may become more pronounced in modernity's third phase. Indeed, structural adjustment regimes and austerity programs only seem to consolidate the misalignment in the institutional channels of integration. Finally, my analysis suggests that whilst much contemporary Critical Theory underestimates social complexity, the older assumption that the structural contradictions of capitalist modernity have not been resolved and that they manifest themselves in displaced forms remains relevant.

Acknowledgement

Craig Browne would like to thank Phillip Mar for research collaborations related to this chapter and Breno Bringel and José Maurício Domingues for suggestions and comments on an earlier version of the chapter.

References

Arendt, H. (1979). *The Origins of Totalitarianism*. New York: Harcourt Brace.
Asad, T. (1991). Afterword: From the History of Colonial Anthropology to the Anthropology of Western Hegemony. In G.W. Stocking, Jr. (Ed.), *Colonial Situations*. Wisconsin: The University of Wisconsin Press, pp. 314–324.
Balibar, É. (2004). *We, the People of Europe?* Princeton: Princeton University Press.

Balibar, É. (2007). Uprising in the *Banlieues*. *Constellations, 14*(1), 47–71.

Banting, K. (2000). Looking in Three Directions: Migration and the European Welfare State in Comparative Perspective. In M. Bommes and A. Geddes (Eds.), *Immigration and Welfare-Challenging the Borders of the Welfare State*. London: Routledge, pp. 12–33.

Bauman, Z. (2004). *Wasted Lives: Modernity and Its Outcasts*. Cambridge: Polity Press.

Bauman, Z. (2011). *Collateral Damage*. Cambridge: Polity Press.

Beck, U. (2005). *Power in the Global Age*. Cambridge: Polity Press.

Beilharz, P. (2008). Australian Settlements. *Thesis Eleven, 95*, 58–67.

Boltanski, L. and Chiapello, E. (2005). *The New Spirit of Capitalism*. London: Verso.

Bosniak, L. (2006). *The Citizen and the Alien*. Princeton: Princeton University Press.

Bourdieu, P. (1999). The Abdication of the State. In P. Bourdieu et al. (Eds.), *The Weight of the World*. Cambridge: Polity Press, pp. 181–188.

Browne, C. (2002). A New Nexus of Social Change? In B.E. Hanna, E.J. Woodley, E.L. Buys and J.A. Summerville (Eds.), *Social Change in the 21st Century Conference Proceedings*, Brisbane.

Browne, C. and Mar, P. (2010). Enacting Half-positions: Creative Disrespect in the 2005 French Riots. In C. Browne and J. McGill (Eds.), *Violence in France and Australia: Disorder in the Postcolonial Welfare State*. Sydney: The University of Sydney Press.

Castel, R. (2003). *From Manual Workers to Wage Labourers – Transformation of the Social Question*. New Brunswick: Transaction Publishers.

Castel, R. (2006). La Discrimination Négative, Le dé citoyenneté des jeunes de banlieue. *Annales 61*(4), 777–808.

Castells, M. (1983). *The City and the Grassroots*. Melbourne: Edward Arnold.

Castoriadis, C. (1987). *The Imaginary Institution of Society*. Polity Press: Cambridge.

Chatterjee, P. (2004). *The Politics of the Governed: Reflections on Political Society in Most of the World*. New York: Coloumbia University Press.

Chatterjee, P. (2008). Democracy and Economic Transformation in India. *Economic and Political Weekly. 43*(16), 53–62.

Comaroff, J.L. and Comaroff, J. (2006). Law and Disorder in the Postcolony: An Introduction. In J. Comaroff and J.L. Comaroff (Eds.), *Law and Disorder in the Postcolony*. Chicago: University of Chicago Press, pp. 1–56.

Cowlishaw, G. (2004). *Blackfellas, Whitefellas – The Hidden Injuries of Race*. London: Blackwell.

Domingues, J.M. (2006). *Modernity Reconstructed*. Cardiff: University of Wales Press.

Domingues, J.M. (2012). *Global Modernity, Development, and Contemporary Civilization*. London: Routledge.

Eisenstadt, S.N. (1999). *Fundamentalism, Sectarianism, and Revolution*. Cambridge University Press, Cambridge.

Fanon, F. (1986). *Black Skin, White Masks*. London: Pluto Press.

Fraser, N. (2009). *Scales of Justice*. New York: Columbia University Press.

Good, M.-J., Del Vecchio, Hyde, S.T., Pinto, S. and Good, B.J. (2008). *Postcolonial Disorders*. Berkeley: University of California Press.

Gray, A. (2004). *Unsocial Europe – Social Protection or Flexploitation?* London: Pluto Press.

Habermas, J. (1970). On Systematically Distorted Communication. *Inquiry, 13*(1–4), 205–218.

Habermas, J. (1976). *Legitimation Crisis*. London: Heinemann.

Habermas, J. (1984). *The Theory of Communicative Action: Reason and the Rationalisation of Society*, Vol. 1. Cambridge, MA: MIT Press.

Habermas, J. (1987). *The Theory of Communicative Action: Lifeworld and System* (Vol. 2). Cambridge: Polity Press.

Habermas, J. (2001). *The Postnational Constellation.* Cambridge: Polity Press.

Habermas, J. (2006). *The Divided West.* Cambridge: Polity Press.

Hage, G. (2002). *Against Paranoid Nationalism.* Pluto Press, Leichhardt.

Held, D., McGrew, A., Goldblatt, D. and Perraton, J. (1999). *Global Transformations.* Cambridge: Polity Press.

Hollingsworth, J.R. and Boyer, R. (1998). Coordination of Economic Actors and Social Systems of Production. In J.R. Hollingsworth and R. Boyer (Eds.), *Contemporary Capitalism.* Cambridge: Cambridge University Press, pp. 1–47.

Honneth, A. (2007). *Disrespect.* Cambridge: Polity Press.

Huysmans, J. (2006). *The Politics of Insecurity – Fear, Asylum and Migration in the European Union.* London: Routledge.

Katznelson, I. (2005). *When Affirmative Action was White.* New York: W. W. Norton.

Kearney, M. (1998). Transnationalism in California and Mexico at the end of Empire. In T. Wilson and H. Donnan (Eds.), *Border Identities: Nation and State at International Frontiers.* Cambridge: Cambridge University Press, pp. 117–141.

Lagrange, H. and Oberti, M. (Eds.) (2006). *Émeutes Urbaines et Protestations.* Paris: Presses de Sciences Po.

Lake, M. (2008). Equality and Exclusion: The Racial Constitution of Colonial Liberalism' *Thesis Eleven*, 95(1), 20–32.

Lentin, A. (2004). *Racism and Anti-Racism in Europe.* London: Pluto Press.

Levy, J. (1999). *Tocqueville's Revenge. State, Society, and Economy in Contemporary France.* Cambridge, MA: Harvard University Press.

Levy, J. (2005). Redeploying the State: Liberalization and Social Policy in France' In W. Streeck and K. Thelen (Eds.), *Beyond Continuity – Institutional Change in Advanced Political Economies.* Oxford: Oxford University Press, pp. 103–126.

Lieberman, R. (1998). *Shifting the Color Line: Race and the American Welfare State.* Cambridge, MA: Harvard University Press.

Marshall, T.M. (1950). *Citizenship and Social Class.* Cambridge: Cambridge University Press.

Misztal, B. (2011). *The Challenges of Vulnerability: In Search of Strategies for a Less Vulnerable Social Life.* Houndsmill: Palgrave Macmillan.

Offe, C. (1996). *Modernity and the State: East, West.* Cambridge: Polity Press.

Ong, A. (2006). *Neoliberalism as Exception.* Durham and London: Duke University Press.

Palier, B. (2005). Ambiguous Agreement, Cumulative Change: French Social Policy in the 1990s. In W. Streeck and K. Thelen (Eds.), *Beyond Continuity – Institutional Change in Advanced Political Economies.* Oxford: Oxford University Press, pp. 127–145.

Pels, P. (1997). The Anthropology of Colonialism: Culture, History, and the Emergence of Western Governmentality. *Annual Review of Anthropology, 26*, 163–183.

Polanyi, K. (1957). *The Great Transformation.* Boston: Beacon Press.

Sassen, S. (2006). *Cities in a World Economy*, 3rd ed. Princeton: Princeton University Press.

Sassen, S. (2008). *Territory, Authority, Rights.* Princeton: Princeton University Press.

Sennett, R. and Cobb, J. (1973). *The Hidden Injuries of Class.* New York: Vintage.

Smith, T.B. (2004). *France in Crisis.* Cambridge: Cambridge University Press.

Somers, M. (2008). *Genealogies of Citizenship.* Cambridge: Cambridge University Press.

Standing, G. (2011). *The Precariat – The New Dangerous Class.* London: Bloomsbury.

Streeck, W. (2011). The Crises of Democratic Capitalism' *New Left Review 71*(Sept–Oct), 5–29.

Wacquant, L. (2008). *Urban Outcasts.* Cambridge: Polity Press.

Wacquant, L. (2012). The Wedding of Workfare and Prisonfare in the 21st Century. *Journal of Poverty, 16*(3), 236–249.

Wagner, P. (1994). *Sociology of Modernity*. London: Routledge.

Wagner, P. (2008). *Modernity as Experience and Interpretation*. Cambridge: Polity Press.

Wagner, P. (2012). *Modernity – Understanding the Present*. Polity Press: Cambridge.

Walby, S. (2009). *Globalization and Inequalities: Complexity and Contested Modernities*. London: Sage Publications.

Wieviorka, M. (2005) *Violence in France*, Social Science Research Council, www. riotsfrance.ssrc.org/Wieviorka/

12

Abyssal Lines and Their Contestation in the Construction of Modern Europe: A De-Colonial Perspective of the Spanish Case

Heriberto Cairo and Keina Espiñeira

Introduction

If we read any leading exponent of modern social science, we may get the impression that states are above all a territorial phenomenon and that their borders are as natural as the fact that they have capitals. Furthermore, one would think that the differences between territories went no further than the fact that they occupy different geographical positions, and that borders are universal, being similar in nature within the modern multi-state system. All states would be equal under international law and their borders would also be equal. However, the problem is that the facts repeatedly show the word 'border' is being used to refer to widely differing cases. It might be the line separating Luxembourg and Belgium, or those separating Israel and Lebanon, North and South Korea, the United States and Mexico or Spain and Morocco.

Nevertheless, we should not make the mistake of thinking that each border is a unique case. Borders are individual but not unique. Each one has its own history, geography and record of friendly or tense relations, but they can be classified using various cleavages which have become commonly accepted and can be seen in classic studies of borders: natural/artificial, endogenous/exogenous, arbitrary/conventional, etc. Most of these divisions are to some extent 'false dilemmas' (Foucher, 1991). For example, both the lines that trace a natural feature and those drawn on a map, to be subsequently transferred to the landscape, are artificial in the sense that they are the result of an agreement between two states. In this paper, we are going to examine the cleavages separating both intra-European borders and colonial borders. Firstly, we hope to show that the usual treatment of borders ignores the inception of the modern colonial world system and fails to distinguish between two types of logic, two legal models, two policies for determining and marking borders, which can be seen with great precision in the scenario chosen for this analysis. Secondly, we try to analyse the challenges to modern state borders, and particularly to colonial borders. We will use the case of the Spanish borders to illustrate our arguments, and we will try to use a de-colonial approach.

Modernity and its Darker Side: De-Colonial Thinking and Abyssal Lines

De-colonial thinking has been developed by a group of Latin American scholars (linked in several ways to the 'modernity-coloniality group').[1] It is a 'particular kind of critical theory' (Mignolo, 2007a: 155) that follows the path of sociologist Anibal Quijano and philosopher Enrique Dussel. Arturo Escobar (2007: 144) summarizes well the main features of the conceptualization of modernity/coloniality used by the group: (a) the origins of modernity are in a colonial project: the Conquest of America by the Europeans in the sixteenth century; (b) colonialism is constitutive of the capitalist world system and modernity; (c) consequently, a world perspective has to be adopted to explain modernity; (d) physical and cultural domination of extra-European peoples is a necessary dimension of modernity; and (e) Eurocentric universal categories structure the hegemonic form of knowledge in the modern/colonial world system.

Therefore, de-colonial thinking offers an opportunity to look at the *coloniality* of the modern world-system, 'the darker side of modernity', according to Mignolo (2008). Coloniality does not refer only to the past, but to the present day arrangement of the *difference* between European – Western – peoples and the rest of the world. There is a *spatial colonial difference* that 'worked through the concept of barbarians, an idea taken from the Greek language and historical experience, but modified in the sixteenth century to refer to those who were located in an inferior space' (Mignolo, 2007b: 470–471), and a *temporal colonial difference* that 'became apparent toward the end of the eighteenth century in the idea of *primitives*' (Mignolo, 2007b: 470). Both merged and formed a *traditional* world in the exteriority of modernity, subjugated by the imperiality referred to by Slater (2010).

Agnew asserts that the 'modern geopolitical imagination' (2003: 15) emerged during the European Renaissance and implied the capacity to see the world as a whole, usually divided in binary geographies. It was Eurocentrism that created epistemic frontiers that set the modern binary geographies by the creation of the imperial difference (with the old Ottoman, Chinese or Russian empires) or the colonial difference (with

Indians and Blacks in America and Africa): 'It was from and in Europe that the classification of the world emerged and not in and from Asia, Africa or America – borders were created therein but of different kinds' (Mignolo & Tlostanova, 2006: 206).

Imperial difference and colonial difference are present nowadays at the border between the United States of America and Mexico (Kramsch, 2002) and the external borders of the European Union (EU), which are the manifestation of a new form of global apartheid (Van Houtum, 2010).

The global apartheid is well understood in the work of Boaventura de Sousa Santos about the *abyssal lines* that divide social reality into two realms: 'the realm of 'this side of the line' and the realm of 'the other side of the line'' (2007: 3). The *amity lines* between European powers in the sixteenth century were the first *abyssal lines* that marked the deep division between the European system of states and the rest of the world.

But abyssal lines are still present today in one form or another. The separation is so far-reaching that what happens 'on the other side of the line' vanishes; it is as if it did not exist. And what characterizes abyssal thinking most clearly is the impossibility of the co-presence of the two worlds divided by abyssal lines.

Bordering Processes in Spain

The Spanish case illustrates very well the contrasts between the construction of borders between equals and the construction of abyssal lines. We are going to consider the bordering processes of two different periods: first, when the borders were delimited and demarcated, which in Spain – like generally in Europe – occurred in the nineteenth century, enabling states to consolidate their structure; and, second, when the internal borders of the EU were softened and its external borders hardened in the last three decades.

The Precise Delimitation and Demarcation of Boundaries in the Nineteenth Century

We are going to briefly analyse the treaties which defined the limits of the Kingdom of Spain. These were signed in a very short space of time, although they involved negotiations with three very different powers. The Treaty of Peace with Morocco, better known as the Treaty of Wad-Ras, was signed in 1860, the series of border treaties between France and Spain were signed between 1856 and 1868 and the Treaty on Borders with Portugal signed in 1864.

The Bayonne agreements, which traced the exact position of the line separating France and Spain at different sections, met an explicit desire to solve local problems in the border areas of both countries. The need to fix the border exactly, and above all to establish it on the ground, was seen as necessary to maintain peace locally. There appears to be no question about the Pyrenees being the frontier between the two states. Although they might not be seen as the best frontier by Basques or Catalans, both states are responding, at least formally, to the demands of their citizens near the border.

Neither was the 1864 border treaty between Spain and Portugal simply an agreement to fix a border which had been agreed a long time earlier. The objective was to put an end to a situation at the border considered to be unacceptable by the two governments.

In short, two types of reason are given: one related to the disturbance of everyday peace at the border and the other connected with the incongruity of certain situations. Although the archives referring to the treaty contain letters from the inhabitants of the area complaining about events (incursions, robberies, altercations, etc.) which 'disturb the peace' at the border, it is no less the case that the states involved had a clear interest in defining precisely what we could call the 'opaque' areas of the border. That is, the treaties came about more from a desire to establish state sovereignty than to put an end to the harmful effects of certain situations on the communities mentioned in the treaty, which lived 'under the shadow of ancient feudal traditions'.

Long before the treaties were signed there had been a desire to ensure respect for the laws of states, confirming their sovereignty and guaranteeing peace. This was the 'territorial pact' referred to by Michel Foucault: 'The State could say: 'I am going to grant you land' or 'I guarantee that you will be able to live in peace inside your borders'. This was the territorial pact, and guaranteeing borders was the main function of the State' (1977: 3). Peace is an essential part of this pact and in the case of Spain and Portugal it culminated in the 1864 treaty. Subsequently this aspect was to be replaced by a concern with security.

However, the peaceful demarcation of the Spanish–Portuguese and Spanish–French borders, by civilized diplomats with the assistance of military experts, is in stark contrast to the exceptionally violent methods used in the same period to secure (and advance to a certain degree) Spain's borders in the *presidios* of Ceuta and Melilla. Alleging attacks on the Spanish army in North Africa, especially in Ceuta, the Madrid government sent forces to deal with the situation. Hostilities lasted from November 1859 to March 1860, when the Moroccan army was decisively defeated.

A little over a month after the end of the war, the Treaty of Wad-Ras was signed in Tétouan, under which Spain extended the territory of Ceuta and consolidated the extension of Melilla (conceded in a previous treaty signed in Tétouan on 24 August 1859). It was also to receive in perpetuity the tiny territory of Santa Cruz de Mar Pequeña to establish a fishery (this later became the colony of Ifni). Morocco was obliged to permit a limited presence of Christian missionaries, to allow Spanish diplomatic representatives to take up residence wherever they chose and to pay a war indemnity, Tangier remaining under Spanish occupation until this was paid.

This is clearly not a treaty between equals and copies others imposed on non-European powers, such as those signed between the European nations and for example, China or Japan. The international law applied to civilized European states had no meaning in the colonial context. Although force was used in the relations between civilized states, it was used differently against the uncivilized, barbaric 'other' world, where it could be applied without restrictions, given the nature of that world.

Both types of treaty were intended to put an end to situations considered unacceptable but they were based on radically different methods. In the cases of the border between Spain and Portugal and the border in the Pyrenees, a detailed study of the terrain had been carried out to appreciate the cases of the two states involved, and after protracted diplomatic negotiations, agreements were reached which were intended to be equitable. In the case of Tétouan, however, one side imposed on the other the territorial concessions it considered necessary to establish 'protected' borders in the interests of its 'security'.

The Foucaultian 'territorial pact' called for guaranteed borders, not only to ensure peace across them but also to 'normalize' peace throughout the territory. The extent to which this was achieved is hard to determine but it is clear that the sovereignty with which the pact was associated became increasingly fictitious. Borders made by Europeans were transformed, diluted and reconfirmed in the same places and in others a great distance away. In sum, borders between European countries were generally delimited in the nineteenth century 'to consolidate peace and harmony between neighbouring peoples', while borders with the uncivilized 'other' answered to the need 'to guarantee the protection and safety' of their own people.

Re-Bordering Spain (and Europe): The Schengen Agreement Opens and Closes Borders at the Same Time

The democratic convergence of the two countries in the Iberian Peninsula since the last quarter of the twentieth century has meant that the border between Spain and Portugal is permeable, it is no longer an obstacle and can even stimulate a new type of cooperation: cross-border cooperation has become part of a new Iberian role in the European Community. In other words, the border between Spain and Portugal, like the border between Spain and France, has ceased to be a wall dividing states and imaginary communities with an exclusive identity, and become a dynamic, cooperative frontier zone which makes the border a driving force for the societies on either side of it. Since Spain and Portugal became members of the EU, certain types of cross-border contacts and relations have been intensified, especially economic and trading links, although distances are maintained in symbolic and cultural areas. These distances are an obstacle to greater interaction, which would be beneficial and help to bring about greater economic development and higher standards of welfare for the districts along the border.

In contrast to the historical disputes, we now have the issue of cross-border cooperation. There is a renewed discourse regarding borders, which in Europe can be linked to the process of integration: cross-border cooperation is a genuinely European invention, whose development is now inevitable (Kramsch, 2003). Since the 1970s, attempts have been made to establish links between border areas in different states. In 1976, the Moselle-Rhine cross-border institution was set up. The European Outline Convention Framework on Transfrontier Co-operation between Territorial Communities or Authorities, launched by the Council of Europe, was signed in 1980, establishing for the first time the legal framework for cross-border cooperation and a common definition for member countries. The second article defines cross-border cooperation as 'any concerted action designed to reinforce and foster neighbourly relations between territorial communities or authorities within the jurisdiction of two or more Contracting Parties and the conclusion of any agreement and arrangement necessary for this purpose'. Since then numerous cross-border Euroregions have been set up.

We thus find ourselves in a new situation: the borders between Spain and France and between Spain and Portugal are no longer on the periphery; they occupy a more central position, which will allow them to progress and develop. The area's aims incorporate modernity and tradition, as in the case of promoting rural and ecological tourism, which is seen by many as an authentic panacea for the economic growth of these previously marginal areas. The communication channels across these borders are multiplying, as is the number of visits and exchanges of different kind between the two sides.

The Schengen Agreement implied another step in this process of de-bordering. It provided the legal architecture for the 'demolition' of internal EU borders. The Treaty was signed by the Benelux countries,

France and Germany, in Luxembourg in 1985. It originally included Germany, France, Italy, Spain, Austria, Portugal, Greece, Belgium, the Netherlands and Luxembourg. The implementation of the Agreement started in 1995, and subsequently, most of the EU states have been incorporated into the Schengen Area (except for Bulgaria, Cyprus, Ireland, Romania and the United Kingdom).

However, the Treaty also implies the tightening of the EU external borders and the changes that have taken place to the south of Spain, around Ceuta and Melilla, are of another kind (Ferrer-Gallardo, 2008). At the beginning of the 1990s, the borders of these areas were completely porous, allowing the development of 'atypical trade' (the local name for smuggling). There were hundreds of paths running between Spain and Morocco and little attention was paid to controlling the passage of people and goods. However, after the signing of the Schengen Agreements (1991), vigilance at the borders was tightened and shortly afterwards fences were built around the cities.

In the process of abolishing the internal borders with Portugal and France, the outer perimeter acquired new geopolitical dimensions. Being part of the common external border of Schengen-land meant its relocation as south border of Europe and the assumption of new roles and functions in the spatial ordering of human mobility.

In the mid-1990s, as the Maghreb started to consolidate itself as a transit region, Morocco became one of the main throughways for sub-Saharan migrants to pass into Europe (see Alioua, 2008; Collyer, 2007; Collyer & De Haas, 2012; Driessen, 1996; De Haas, 2008). The implementation of the System of Integrated External Surveillance (SIVE)[2] and the launch of the European Agency for the Management of Operational Cooperation at the External Borders of the EU (Frontex)[3] brought significant changes to the routes taken by African migrants heading to the EU. At the land borders of Ceuta and Melilla, this increased the migratory pressure. During the autumn of 2005, hundreds of migrants crossed the fences that enclosed the cities. Border patrol guards on both sides of the border repressed the attempts to enter and as a consequence, 14 migrants were killed and many more wounded. Since then, as well as the new fortification of the fences, efforts were extended through different forms of bilateral (Spain-Morocco) and multilateral cooperation agreements as part of the EU Neighbourhood Policy and the refinement of the EU strategy of externalizing border control (see Casas et al., 2011; Cobarrubias et al., 2013; Pinyol, 2012).

Surveillance and securitization techniques were extended along the Spanish–Moroccan border in order to monitor and control clandestine entrances and border-crossings. In this context, the fortification of the land perimeter in Ceuta and Melilla became a tangible and symbolic example of the 'fortress of Europe'. Whilst the double fence was rising with EU financial assistance, migrant settlements on the surrounding hills between the Spanish enclaves and Morocco proliferated – in Belyunes (Ceuta) or Rostrogordo and Gurugú (Melilla). Migrant protests and riots demanding the recognition of human rights grew in the context of continuous and periodic campaigns of raids into the settlements, and the detentions and deportations carried out by security forces on both sides of the border (see Gold, 1999, 2000; Planet, 1998; Mutlu & Leite, 2012; Soddu, 2006).

Contestation to Borders

The delimitation of definite borders with Portugal and France in the nineteenth century or the current securitization of borders with Morocco have been processes accomplished not without contestation. Their characteristics are completely different, but like any other power relation, they have been subjected to resistance.

As we have seen, local populations were the main objective of the bordering processes in the first phase of modernity – nineteenth and early twentieth century, according to Domingues' (2011) definition – therefore, we would expect to find mainly local opposition. While in the third phase of modernity (Domingues, 2011) borders are more heterogeneous, some seem to have vanished, and others have been widened and deepened in order to manage complex flows of people beyond the neighbouring countries. In both of these cases, the network has been the organization principle as far as opposition to b/ordering processes is concerned. Let us show this by looking at it at these two specific periods of bordering processes.

Local Opposition in the Nineteenth Century

During the previous elaboration of the treaties of the Pyrenees and of Lisbon, and in their aftermath, there were resistances to the provisions set out. They have been related to the way of demarcating local borders, that, for instance in the Spanish–Portuguese case, was materialized in three stages (see Cairo & Godinho, 2013): First, the members of the Borders Commission collected all the information available about the border at specific places. Second, the representatives of the states, joined by local and regional agents visited the conflictive places. And third, the final decisions were taken at the level of ministries, incorporating the previous information or not.

While there were too many biases in this process, the main problem was the final decision, which was sometimes taken irrespective of the interests and sentiments of the local populations. Knocking down the boundary markers or moving them was relatively common for a long time in some of these places. Individual decisions by locals about their chosen nationality, contradictory to the jurisdiction where the population was allocated, was another path of resistance to the central state's agreements.

At the Spanish–Moroccan border, the events were much harsher. The relative peace achieved after the Treaty of Tetouan was broken as early as 1890, followed by three years of clashes around Melilla between the Spanish army and local Riffian armed groups, *cabilas*. A long colonial war, the Riff War, began in 1909, even before the establishment of French and Spanish Protectorates in Morocco in 1912. In 1921, an independent Republic of Riff was declared in the mountainous areas of North Morocco under the leadership of Mohamed ben Abd-el-Krim el Jatabi (see Woolman, 1971). Its main goal was to drive out the Europeans from the region, and to construct a modern state. The Republic lasted until 1927, when the Spanish and French troops defeated the Riffian.

In conclusion, the local population in Morocco resisted the border imposed by the Spanish government and tried to expel them from North Africa. The failure of the Rifiian movement in the 1920's gave way to a period of relative calm, but it did not imply the disappearance of opposition.

Transnational Contestation in the Current Phase of Modernity

Since the Schengen agreement, in recent years, the opposition to borders has focussed on abyssal lines. National and transnational protests have been related to the event of global migrations, passing from the global South to the countries around the centre of the world system. Contestation to borders acquires in this way a double face: it denounces the hardening of some borders and rejects the tough controls to migration. But contestation acquires also a constructive dimension, trying to imagine and build an 'Other territory'.

Transnational Protests Against the EU Border Regime and the Spanish Foreigners Act

The 1990s were the years of the first joint transnational protests against the EU border regime. Making claims about freedom of movement and the defence of migrant and refugees' rights, a growing number of initiatives to strengthen solidarity emerged, connecting different struggles and anti-racist movements beyond the EU borders. In 1997, social organizations from Europe and Africa organized the Noborder Network.[4] Under this coordination, the 'No-Border Camps' campaign started in 1999. The first camp was carried out during the Tampere European Council (Finland, 15–16 October 1999). There were agreements reached on the basis for a common EU asylum system, a common policy on legal immigration and the guidelines of the fight against illegal immigration, visa policies, surveillance systems, detention centres and readmission agreements.

No-Border Camps are conceived as 'temporary autonomous zones,' which function as political devices. Nomad camps are established at the 'borders' of Europe, from north to south and from east to west, to visualize the extension of the migration-border regime whilst carrying out protest actions – connected with antiglobalization movements such as the World Social Forum or the European Social Forum. With the aim of building, during these days, a space to exchange ideas and experiences, especially in support of the self-organization process of migrants from a political perspective, the structure of No-Border camps operates along these lines, fostering open spaces of discussion, networks, common projects and training workshops.

In Spain, the first *Ley de Extranjería* (Foreigner Law) was adopted in 1985. Fifteen years later, after the regularization process of 1991 and all those changes resulting from the coming into force of the Schengen Convention, the reform of the law was approved. Law 8/2000 intended to respond to the new perceived challenges of migration and border control, re-adjusting the Spanish regulations to the EU standards. In the months prior to its coming into force, protests intensified, especially those led by the *Sin Papeles*, undocumented immigrants. After some racist incidents in the agricultural village El Ejido, in February 2000, a huge and historical struggle for the regularization of all migrants and against the *Ley de Extranjería* took place all over Spain. In Huelva, Almería, Sevilla, the Canary Islands, Ceuta, Melilla, Barcelona and Madrid – just to name a few – migrants got organised, occupied churches, universities and public buildings and started hunger strikes. Under the slogan *Ningún Ser Humano es Ilegal* (No human being is illegal), a civil disobedience campaign was articulated, emerging to assume an active role against the Immigration Act.

The *Sin Papeles* movement and the struggles against the different Immigration Acts constructed a political space that did not exist before. Differing from the assistentialist perspective, this political space expressed an opposition to global capitalism and its geopolitical configuration in a radical way, a protest against the border regime, against deportations and a fight for the freedom of the people to decide where to live or work. This dynamic movement led some years later to a consolidation of support networks which would be able to mobilize and articulate denunciation campaigns in a short period of time.

In 2008, prior to the adoption of the European Directive on common standards and procedures for the return of illegally staying third-country nationals (Directive 2008/115/EC), the campaign *Contra la Directiva de la Vergüenza* (Against Directive of Shame) was launched. Informative acts and demonstrations took place across Spain (and Europe) denouncing the new rules of the return policy and the generalization of confinement as a control practice applicable to all third-country nationals who do not or no longer fulfil the conditions for entry, stay or residence.

Immediately after this policy came into force, the number of deportations increased in Spain, giving rise to the extension of police identification raids in public spaces and in everyday life: public transport stations, schools, hospitals, places of entertainment, call centres, shops, even in embassies, consulates or regularization institutions. Social responses against identification raids and checks are another illustrative example of the consolidated support networks. In the city of Madrid, various initiatives emerged in order to coordinate an organized and collective response.[5] The *Brigadas Vecinales de Observación de Derechos Humanos* (Human Rights Neighbourhood Monitoring Brigades)[6] carry out periodic incursions into places subject to frequent raids so as to inform, observe and assist with the identification and possible detention of illegal immigrants. The initiative *Alerta!* (Alert!) has the goal of alerting, by way of Internet devices in real-time, about important events that happen in the neighbourhood and require attention, solidarity and citizen action. In addition, there have been various campaigns collecting signatures to submit complaints to state institutions, such as the campaign *Porque la vida no es una cárcel. Paremos los controles* (Because life is not a prison. Stop controls). This was signed by 130 social organizations and a complaint then submitted to the Spanish Ministry of Home Affairs against identity raids and detentions.[7] Or the campaign *Quéjate ante los controles racistas* (Protest against racial controls), which denounces the racist nature of police controls based on selective identification in function of physical characteristics.

Also in 2009, a further reform of the Ley de Extranjería gave rise to another widely supported campaign. The Manifesto *La ley de extranjería nos hace desiguales. ¡Parémosla!*[8] (The Foreigner law makes us unequal. Let's stop it!) denounces the punitive nature of the new law (LO 2/2009), and more specifically challenges the criminalization of solidarity. Along the same lines, the campaign *Salvemos la hospitalidad*[9] (Save hospitality) has been carried out whereby non-government organisations (NGOs), religious congregations and citizens have claimed the right of hospitality and solidarity.

Opposition to the Fences and the Confinement of Immigrants

The number of migrants arriving in *pateras – small* boats – to the shores of Spain increased throughout the decade 1990–2000. The implementation of SIVE and Frontex operations in the Strait of Gibraltar, as we have seen, had a significant impact on increasing migration pressure on the land borders of Ceuta and Melilla. Since the bloody repression of jumps of the fences in 2005, the protests aroused addressed this double dimension of control, the fortification and militarization of the border-perimeter and the progressive externalization of control to neighbouring states (van Houtum & Boedeltje, 2009). During the following months, several caravans travelled to Ceuta and Melilla to protest against the 'Fence of Death'. For the people inside, this struggle entailed creating an alliance with those who try to cross the borders, in defense of their right to exist.

From Morocco several organizations called for a Euro-African Non-Governmental Conference to analyse the impact of EU policies on African populations, especially those concerning fundamental freedoms. It was held in El Harhoura (Rabat) during the summer of 2006. The goal was to provide alternative routes to the border closure policies, repression and the externalization of migration control. As a result the *Euro-African Manifesto. Migration, human rights and freedom of movement* was adopted, which currently has 135 signatory organizations and is the founding text of the Euro-African Network[10]. The Euro-African conference was a further step in the process of building solidarity and carrying out joint projects between activists from Africa and Europe.

In the course of recent years, the landscape of border fortification has expanded beyond the borders of Ceuta and Melilla. In its annual mapping, Migreurop[11] has shown the spreading of the retention/detention 'camps' throughout the geography of the EU and neighbouring states. A 'camp' in the sense that is understood by Migreurop, may eventually be a process and not a physical space. The 'Europe of the camps' is configured by a set of confinement devices that exist as forced breakpoints along the migratory journeys once inside the EU.

In Spain, the first actions calling for the closing of migrant detention centres emerged in the late 1990s and grew over the next decade, as the practice of confinement acquired greater centrality in immigration control policies. In 2007, the campaign *Cerremos nuestros Guantánamos* (Let's close our Guantánamos) was launched. Demonstrations, hunger strikes, vigils and the erection of camps took place in several cities, identifying and naming migrant detention centres as 'the European Guantanamos': spaces of exception, legal limbos, blind and silenced mechanisms of the temporalisation of presence through confinement.

The functioning of these centres is opaque, as confirmed by NGO reports that denounce the obstacles to its accessibility, the poor conditions of the inmates and the continuing cases of rights violations (APDHA, 2008; Ferrocarril Clandestino, 2009; Migreurop, 2011; Pueblos Unidos, 2012). *Migrant Detention Centres in Europe: Open the doors! We have the right to know!*[12] is a campaign carried out in different places of Europe to demand the access of NGOs and journalists. With this aim, the campaign *Open Access Now!* takes the form of visits to the centres to test the reality of access and gather information about detention practices around the EU.

Disobey the Border to Construct a 'Territory Other'

The contestation has not only been to denounce, but it has also tried to create counter-spaces. During the early 2000s, the Strait of Gibraltar became an emerging area of cross-border resistance and protest. Self-organizing temporary spaces were set up between Andalusia and northern Morocco, connecting Tarifa-Tánger, Larache-Cádiz, Ceuta-Tetuán or Melilla-Nador. In 2001, the No-Border Camp took place for the first time in the region, in the town of Tarifa. After the movement of occupations of buildings and seclusions of immigrants, anti-racist and anti-borders groups working at a local level were consolidated in different places. The border camp highlighted the question of how to continue and how to connect the different struggles with a transnational and transborder dimension.

Two years later, in the midst of the global campaign against the Irak War, Indymedia Estrecho was founded. It was certainly a catalysing moment. Around mediactivism multiple nodes were activated, the militant action research was assumed as a key tool in the exploration of the intersections between knowledge production and social change. Among the founding groups, the idea of building a new transborder territory connecting the two shores of the Strait was developed, based on decentralization, multi-presence and new technical resources.

Fadaiat means 'transit spaces' in Arabic. It is the name taken by a political, technological and artistic laboratory sited on both sides of the Strait. Cartographies elaborated within the Fadaiat/Observatory project pointed out the role of Information and Communication Technologies (ICTs) in the building of antagonist transborder networks. ICTs allow 'the generation of a new kind of public space by creatively hybridising traditional spaces with new virtual spaces' (Fadaiat, 2006a: 173). *Madiaq Territory: New Geographies (2003–2007)* emerges as a project mapping the geopolitical space of the Strait of Gibraltar. It came to map the mechanisms of militarization and the southern extension of the border linked to productive-economic flows, at the same time mapping the processes defying the border/order system, and highlighting transborder workers, social movements and multiple communication flows. The map is seen as a *trace*, as a coding system, a visualization of the collective memory. Therefore, the map, as a way to understand spatial relationships and to create correspondences between power, control and resistances, is a form of organization and social network action.[13]

The objectives of the Project are clear: 'We are building a multiple territory, both geographic and infographic, social and technological, that extends infinitely in four directions: toward the South and toward the North; toward the depths of carnal bodies and toward the immaterial nonsphere that grows in the fertile land of words without owners' (Fadaiat – Observatorio Tecnológico del Estrecho, 2006b: 175).

Madiaq's Cartographies visualize the Strait as a highly dynamic border space that cannot be represented through static lines; rather, border(s) are seen as mobile, fluid, porous and ambivalent. There are different time/spaces in which they are strengthened or smoothed. Organizational forms are constantly moving, tracking and interconnecting circuits of mobility and control.

Conclusion

Borders are one of the features constitutive of modern states. Since the nineteenth century their precise demarcation has been one of the objectives of the central governments of states. However, we should not think that all borders are equal: independently of other differences, we have seen that there have been two kinds of inceptions of the border, one between European or civilized neighbours, and another with uncivilized people, the abyssal lines we have analysed.

The border round Ceuta and Melilla is a colonial phenomenon, marking the dividing line between friends and enemies. The EU law establishes the suppression of borders between European countries (at least, those in the EU) and yet it insists on the border separating it from the outside world, branding undesirable foreigners as criminals and laying down orders for their repatriation (Kramsch & Brambilla, 2007; van Houtum & Pijpers, 2007). The community of European Christian peoples is still opposed to the rest of the world, as in Schmitt's (1979) analysis of the seventeenth and nineteenth centuries.

From the amity lines of the sixteenth century to the nineteenth century treaty of Wad-Ras, or today's Integrated External Border Surveillance System and the fences around Ceuta and Melilla, we are dealing with the logic of the imperial difference which underlies the modern colonial world system. They are not exactly the same type of line but they imply the same geopolitical position regarding the *nomos* of the earth: the stabilization of what is inside and outside. They are the abyssal lines referred to by Santos (2007).

On the other hand, the border between Spain and Portugal or Spain and France was, is and will possibly continue to be a boundary between neighbours, suitable for maintaining peace locally and nationally. The obsession with establishing a precise demarcation of the border, and thus of sovereignty, which we find in the 1864 treaty has been combined with the desire for cross-border cooperation and the construction of various connecting infrastructures (bridges, motorways, power lines, etc.) that we have seen since the Schengen Agreement.

Contestation to the imposition of borders has always taken place, but it has been very different in kind and degree. In the nineteenth and early twentieth centuries, the opposition to the borders in Spain was mainly local, either at the Spanish–Portuguese, Spanish–French or Spanish–Moroccan border, but completely different in scope. In the Peninsula there was individual and mainly symbolic resistance to central decisions about local borders, but in North Africa there was collective and armed action against what the border meant, the presence of Europeans in what local people considered their homeland.

The contestation to borders in the current phase of global modernity acquires much more different profiles. It occurs mainly in relation to the abyssal borders, in our case the Spanish–Moroccan border. It is not only local, but also binational and even transnational. New political devices are explored, such as in the No Border Camps initiative, and even new reasoning about the territory and how its cartography is developed, as in the project *Madiaq*.

All this means that there have been important changes in modernity bordering and its contestation, both in the European societies and in the periphery. National states were not the end of history and supranational entities like the EU are not the definite solution for all the problems. The *old mole* is still working.

Acknowledgements

The research in this article was supported through funds from the Spanish Ministry of Economy and Competitiveness, Award CSO2012-34677, Project 'Cooperacion transfronteriza y (des)fronterizacion: actores y discursos geopoliticos transnacionales en la frontera hispano-portuguesa'.

Notes

1   A brief history could be found in Mignolo (2008).
2   The SIVE technology uses a series of radar sensors, video cameras, thermal and infrared rays that provide real-time information about movements and crossings in the

Strait. It began in 2002, initially in Cádiz and Fuerteventura, and from 2004 in the whole of the Canary Islands and Andalusia.

3   The European Border Agency (Frontex) was established on October 2004. In May 2005, it started to work with a few pilot projects. Today it is permanently involved in militarized sea and land operations on the external border.

4   www.noborder.org (accessed on 2 July 2013). Other actions were implemented such as the 'Deportations Alliance' against the air companies that participate in deportations, or the 'Campaign to Combat Global Migration Management', against the International Office of Migrations.

5   On 15 February 2009 was leaked to the media an internal circular of the Police Station of Villa Vallecas (Madrid) with detailed instructions on the number of immigrants to detain per week—35 persons—, and the nationalities prioritized—Moroccans—See: Europa Press 15/02/09 www.europapress.es/madrid/noticia-documento-interno-ordena-policias-madrid-detener-cupo-semanal-extranjeros-papeles-20090215130202.html?rel The Spanish newspaper *El Mundo* reported that at least dozen police stations in Madrid had imposed detention quotas. Source: www.elmundo.es/papel/2009/03/10/espana/2609974. html (accessed on 17 June 2011).

6   www.brigadasvecinales.org (accessed on 12 July 2013).

7   www.ferrocarrilclandestino.net/spip.php?rubrique20 (accessed on 12 July 2013).

8   Published in June 2009, source: www.ferrocarrilclandestino.net/spip.php?article133 (accessed on 10 June 2009)

9   Manifiesto available at: www.pueblosunidos.org/cpu/index.php?option=com_content&task=view&id=58&Itemid=94 (accessed on 1 April 2012)

10   www.manifeste-euroafricain.org/spip.php?article15 (accessed on 12 July 2012)

11   Migreurop emerged in 2002 as a network of activists and researchers with the purpose of informing about the multiplication of migrant retention/detention camps, because they understand that visualizing and highlighting these spaces of control through actions and campaigns is critical to launch a public debate on the extension of borders and migration policies within the EU, and the role of confinement and expulsion. They have published an atlas of critical geography of migrations in Europe (Migreurop, 2009).

12   www.openaccessnow.eu (accessed on 10 July 2013).

13   In December 2004, Madiaq Cartography was published on paper with a circulation of about 15,000 copies. The second phase took place between 2006 and 2007 with the aim of keeping updated the content and developing a more complex and interactive mapping system.

References

Asociación Pro Derechos Humanos de Andalucía (APDHA) (2008). *Centros de retención e internamiento en España*. Retrieved from www.apdha.org/index.php?option=com_content&task=view&id=548&Itemid=45

Agnew, J. (2003). *Geopolitics: Re-visioning World Politics*. Routledge, London.

Alioua, M. (2008). La migration transnationale – logique individuelle dans l'espace national: l'exemple des transmigrants subsahariens a l'epreuve de l'externalisation de la gestion des flux migratoires au Maroc. *Social Science Information, 47*(4), 697–713.

Cairo, H. and Godinho, P. (2013). El Tratado de Lisboa de 1864: la demarcación de la frontera y las identificaciones nacionales. *Historia y Política, 30*, 23–54.

Casas, M., Cobarrubias, S. and Pickles, J. (2011). Stretching Borders Beyond Sovereign Territories? Mapping EU and Spain's Border Externalization Policies. *Geopolítica(s). Revista de estudios sobre espacio y poder, 2*(1), 71–90.

Cobarrubias, S., Casas-Cortes, M. and Pickles, J. (2013). Re-bordering the neighbourhood: Europe's emerging geographies of non-accession integration. *European Urban and Regional Studies*, *20*(1), 37–57.

Collyer, M. (2007). In-Between Places: Trans-Saharan transit migrants in Morocco and the Fragmented Journey to Europe. *Antipode*, *39*(4), 668–690.

Collyer, M. and De Haas, H. (2012). Developing dynamic categorisations of 'transit migration'. *Population, Space and Place*, *18*(4), 468–481.

De Haas, H. (2008). *Irregular Migration from West Africa to the Maghreb and the European Union: An Overview of Recent Trends*. Geneva: International Organization of Migration.

Domingues, J.M. (2011). Beyond the Centre: The Third Phase of Modernity in a Globally Compared Perspective. *European Journal of Social Theory*, *14*(4), 517–535.

Driessen, H. (1996). The 'New Immigration' and the Transformation of the European-African Frontier. In T. Wilson and H. Donnan (Eds.). *Border Identities. Nation and State at International Frontiers*. Cambridge: Cambridge University Press, pp. 96–116.

Escobar, A. (2007). Worlds and Knowledges Otherwise: The Latin American Modernity/Coloniality Research Program. *Cultural Studies*, *21*(2–3), 179–210.

Fadaiat - Observatorio Tecnológico del Estrecho (2006a). *Fadaiat: libertad de movimiento-libertad de conocimiento* Barcelona. Avaliable at: http://straddle3.net/constructors/projects/51.es.php (accessed on 09/07/2013).

Fadaiat - Observatorio Tecnológico del Estrecho (2006b). Madiaq Territory. New Geographies. In B. Ursula and H. Brian (Eds.), *The Maghreb Connection: Movements of Life across North Africa*. Barcelona: Actar, pp. 175–181.

Ferrer-Gallardo, X. (2008). The Spanish-Moroccan Border Complex: Processes of Geopolitical, Functional and Symbolic Rebordering. *Political Geography*, *27*(3), 301–321.

Ferrocarril Clandestino (2009). *Voces desde y contra el CIE de Aluche*. Retrieved from www.ferrocarrilclandestino.net/spip.php?article140

Foucault, M. (1977). Michel Foucault: la sécurité et l'État (entretien avec R. Lefort) *Tribune socialiste*, *24–30*(November), 3–4.

Foucher, M. (1991). *Fronts et frontières. Un tour du monde géopolitique*. Fayard, Paris.

Gold, P. (1999). Immigration into the European Union via the Spanish enclaves of Ceuta and Melilla: A Reflection of Regional Economic Disparites. *Mediterranean Politics*, *4*(3), 23–36.

Gold, P. (2000). *Europe or Africa? A Contemporary Study of the Spanish North African Enclaves of Ceuta and Melilla*. Liverpool: Liverpool University Press.

Kramsch, O.T. (2002). Crossing the Topographies of Modernity in the U.S.-Mexico Borderlands: Towards an Ethnography of 'Out of Place' Ideas. *Frontera Norte*, *14*(28), 7–19.

Kramsch, O.T. (2003). *Postcolonial Ghosts in the Machine of European Transboundary Regionalism*. Governance and Places Working Paper Series 2003/03, Nijmegen School of Management, Nijmegen.

Kramsch, O.T. and Brambilla, C. (2007). Transboundary Europe through a West African Looking Glass: Cross Border Integration, 'Colonial Difference' and the Chance for 'Border Thinking'. *Comparativ/Zeitschrift für Globalgeschichte und vergleichende Gesellschaft*, *17*(4), 95–115.

Mignolo, W. (2007a). Introduction. Coloniality of Power and De-colonial Thinking. *Cultural Studies*, *21*(2–3), 155–167.

Mignolo, W. (2007b). Delinking. The Rhetoric of Modernity, the Logic of Coloniality and the Grammar of De-coloniality. *Cultural Studies*, *21*(2–3), 449–514.

Mignolo, W. (2008). La opción des-colonial: desprendimiento y apertura. Un manifiesto y un caso. In H. Cairo and W. Mignolo (Eds.), *Las vertientes americanas del pensamiento y el proyecto des-colonial* (Trama editorial/GECAL, Madrid), pp. 175–208.

Mignolo, W. and Tlostanova, M.V. (2006). Theorizing from the Borders: Shifting to Geo- and Body-Politics of Knowledge. *European Journal of Social Theory*, 9(2), 205–221.

Migreurop (2009). *Atlas des Migrants en Europe. Géographie Critique des Politiques Migratoires*. Paris: Armand Colin.

Migreurop (2011). *CIE, Derechos Vulnerados. Informe sobre los Centros de Internamiento de Extranjeros en España*. Retrieved from www.migreurop.org/article2055.html? lang=fr

Mutlu, C.E. and Leite, C. (2012). Dark Side of the Rock: Borders, Exceptionalism, and the Precarious Case of Ceuta and Melilla. *Eurasia Border Review*, 3(2), 21–39.

Pinyol, G. (2012). ¿Una oportunidad perdida? La construcción de un escenario euroafricano de migraciones y su impacto en las fronteras exteriores de la Unión Europea. In R. Zapata-Barrero and X. Ferrer-Gallardo (Eds.), *Fronteras en movimiento: migraciones hacia la UE en el contexto mediterráneo*. Barcelona: Edicions Bellaterra, pp. 255–280.

Planet, A. (1998). *Melilla y Ceuta: espacios frontera hispano-marroquíes*. Melilla, Ciudades Autónomas de Melilla y Ceuta: UNED Melilla.

Pueblos Unidos (2012). *Atrapados tras las rejas. Informe 2012 sobre los Centros de Internamiento de Extranjeros en España*. Retrieved from www.pueblosunidos.org/cpu/ formacion/InformeCIE2012.PDF (accessed on 10 July 2013).

Santos, B. de S. (2007). Para além do Pensamento Abissal: Das linhas globais a uma ecologia de saberes. *Revista Crítica de Ciências Sociais*, 78, 3–46. [English translation (2007). Beyond Abyssal Thinking: From Global Lines to Ecologies of Knowledges. *Review, XXX*(1), 45–89].

Schmitt, C. (1979). *El Nomos de la Tierra en el derecho de gentes del "Jus publicum europeaum"*. Centro de Estudios Constitucionales, Madrid. [translation of *Der Nomos der Erde im Völkerrecht des Jus Publicum Europeaum*. Berlin: Duncker & Humblot, 1974]

Slater, D. (2010). The imperial present and the geopolitics of power. *Geopolítica(s). Revista de estudios sobre espacio y poder*, 1(2), 191–205.

Soddu, P. (2006). Ceuta y Melilla: gestión fronteriza, derechos humanos y seguridad. *Anuario del Mediterráneo 2006* (Fundación CIDOB/Institut Europeu de la Mediterrània, Barcelona) www.iemed.org/anuari/2006/earticles/eSoddu.pdf (accessed on 12/06/2009).

van Houtum, H. (2010). Human Blacklisting: The Global Apartheid of the EU's External Border Regime. *Environment and Planning D: Society and Space*, 28(6), 957–976.

van Houtum, H. and Boedeltje, F. (2009). Europe's Shame: Death at the Borders of the EU. *Antipode*, 41(2), 226–230.

van Houtum, H. and Pijpers, R. (2007). The European Union as a Gated Community: The Two-Faced Border and Immigration Regime of the EU. *Antipode*, 39(2), 291–309.

Woolman, D.S. (1971). *Abd el Krim y la Guerra del Rif*. Barcelona: Oikos-Tau.

13

From International Legality to Local Struggle: How and Why Human Rights Matter to Social Movements in Argentinean Democracy

Gabriela Delamata

Assessing Local Productivity of the Human Rights Language

The origin of the invocation of human rights in Latin America must be sought in the transitions to democracy of the 1970s and during the 1980s. In that framework, but within a regional political context where transitions from dictatorships to democracies were processes negotiated between the military and political parties and led to the passing of amnesty laws,[1] Argentina represented a case of exceptional dynamism of the language of human rights, which paved the way for the legal investigation of the dictatorship crimes, one of the first measures announced by the democratic administration, towards the end of 1983.[2] More specifically, the Argentine transition is unthinkable without the role played by the lawyers of the human rights movement in the importation of that notion, which framed state repression according to the international commitment to punish human rights violations.

The comparatively early immersion of the human rights international legality into the Argentine juridical and political practice had a series of significant consequences in social action. In particular, it forged an innovative human rights movement, which developed new legal tactics when the country also had its amnesty law in 1987, until it was declared unconstitutional by the Supreme Court as it violated international treaties of human rights (Sikkink, 2011). But, beyond the particular case of this movement, juridical internationalism also affected the future dynamics of social mobilization. Specifically, the law of human rights and the new generations of lawyers trained in that pattern (Vecchioli, 2009) supplied the social movements with a true instituting dimension. From a longitudinal perspective, the activation of the law field to respond to the collective claims of society is a key factor of the configuration of different cycles of social mobilization: proactive – promotion of social change/challenge of existing rules – during the 1980s; defensive (sectorial) in good part of the 1990s; and proactive, from 2003 on.

This chapter argues that the process of transnational diffusion of human rights standards, created by the international community after World War II (Pinto, 2004), and its reception/activation in Argentina, is a core figure of the 'assemblage' between global modernity and social contestation in the local ground. The exercise that will be proposed next minces through that relationship in the temporal dimension of the democratization process. This perspective underlines the historical productivity of the invocation of human rights in Argentina, which went from internally articulating claims for justice during the dictatorship, on to acquiring constitutional status in the 1990s, to finally attaining new potential in the development of contemporary social movements. The choice of a temporal perspective is also appropriate to tackle the processes of importation/translation/appropriation (mediations) of legal resources that along the years have strengthened this human rights based approach in social and political action.[3]

In the last decade there has been growing protagonism of legal struggles into the repertoires of action of social movements. By resorting to the speech of rights, collective actors have been able to endow themselves with a power to act and transform they lacked at the beginning of the protest. While the legal studies testify to a widespread expansion of the legal strategies in the social field, the sociology of social movements seldom considers the legal processes that make part of ongoing episodes of social mobilization. The omission is more evident, or consequent, in the literature on territorial movements (environmentalist and popular), that stress their demand for autonomy (Svampa, 2008), understood as a preference for self-organization outside the state as a way to cope with different social issues.[4] In spite of the above, this stress on autonomy takes different nuances. On the one hand, there exists a greater recognition of the increasing weight of institutional petitions into the repertoire of action of environmentalist movements, in particular (Svampa et al., 2009; Svampa & Sola Álvarez, 2010). On the other hand, autonomy is exacerbated, meaning exodus and community recreation, by approaches that evaluate current social policies supplied by the State, in terms of 'governmentality' (Zibechi, 2011). From this perspective, which rests on arguments from Foucault and Chatterjee, all state-centered strategy by the targeted population would entail a neutralization of the autonomy of popular movements.

With its great differences, the first approach fails to explain the present reorientation of the grassroots environmental organizations' repertoire of action towards the creation of legal regulations, whereas the second one is blind to the mobilization of the urban poor around the axis of equality and rights. Lawyers and judges are central actors, activists, in these processes. We call judicial activism, in a broad sense, the practices that lawyers and organizations deploy in relationship to various social causes, through legal argumentation and legal action, trying to influence the decision making process and public policy.[5] Although it is true that state transformation or social change brought on by many legal struggles are far from being comprehensive or complete, we propose an approach which (re)assess the instituting properties of the law field in the social arena, better interrogates on its potentiality and its reach, and also sheds light on some other possibilities of legal activism, which may turn out to be on occasions less effective in bringing about institutional change than in strengthening the popular movement. Some concrete processes that exemplify these variants will be explored in some detail further on, when we tackle last decade socio-legal struggles.

The chapter is structured as follows. In the next section, we present a summary reconstruction of the principal milestones in rights mobilization and activism from the democratic transition to the national constitutional reform, which took place in 1994. As a result of this exposition, it will be possible to identify two cycles of mobilization into that phase as related to the participation of the human rights language in contentious politics. In the second part, we focus on the 'post-constitutional' (reform) rights mobilizations, trace their main features and illustrate this period, synchronically, by briefly analyzing three cases of contemporary socio-legal mobilization. In the final section, as a conclusion, we take up the discussion on international legality and social movements in Argentine democracy.

From the Rise of the Human Rights Movement to the Constitutional Reform

In this section, we follow a course that begins with the developing configuration of the human rights movement, stops at the feminist women movement – another movement that encourages the process of internationalization of local law started in 1983 – and analyzes the effects, on the field of collective action, of the innovations introduced into the Constitution through its reform.

In their classical book about transnational networks, Margaret Keck and Kathryn Sikkink explain the performance of the Argentine human rights movement during the military dictatorship by means of the boomerang effect, in which the actors who faced repression played in two levels: looking for allies in the international arena and exerting pressure from outside on the government to carry out national political changes (Keck & Sikkink, 1998). The boomerang effect speaks of the configuration of the human rights movement also in its symbolic and performative dimensions, through the framing of crimes so far innominated (enforced disappearances) into notions and recommendations of the international legality (Böhmer, 2013: 174–175). In the local field, the human rights movement encompassed both the 'organizations of the family members' and those organizations devoted to the legal defense against social and political persecution, which at that time changed their axis of intervention. With lawyers in exile, these organizations revealed to international institutions and NGOs the situation the country was living, and made public in Argentina the reports elaborated by those agencies. The Inter-American Commission on Human Rights (ICHR) visit to Argentina in 1979 represented the most relevant instance, as in its official statement, locally known in 1980, the ICHR consolidated the complaint of a systematic plan of repression, and recommended, as well, the prosecution of those found responsible. The language used by these international agencies, alien to the local political activists, reconverted, in the new interpretative framework, the movement's organizations, and geared public debate in the value of human rights and the possibility to claim those rights (Filippini, 2011; Novaro, 2011).

The knotting of the Argentine transition to the international treaties of human rights started to become effective in the first years of democratic administration, when various instruments were simultaneously ratified, bringing about a multiplication of the rights available in the Argentine juridical system. In the socio-political field, this kind of institutional development would be particularly encouraged and seized by the women's movement conceived in democracy. The movement played a significant role in the transnational sphere and importing international principles to promote changes in the state was an axis of its local political agenda. Based on the new notion of equality, non-discrimination and non-violence, important reforms in domestic law saw the light in those years, which provided the same legal bases around civil and political issues for women and men.[6] By that time, the women's movement also started framing 'reproduction and sexuality' into the axis of human rights – opposing the cataloguing of those issues as objects of population policies. Around those grammars, women called for the intervention in the debate for the constitutional reform in 1994 and in the legislative debate in the 1990s (via 'reproductive health') until current campaigns (legal abortion). Finally, the women's movement strengthened a pattern of activism (social or collective) strongly oriented to public incidence, based on an organizational layout with robust presence of technical bodies, and in alliance with parliamentary actors and the judiciary (Petracchi & Pecheny, 2007).

Into the 1990s, President Menem's eagerness for re-election got the support of the main opposition party, the Unión Cívica Radical, to reform the

Constitution. By this means, several issues that were beyond the nucleus of the reform found a way into the Constitution. The Constitution reformed in 1994 incorporated, with constitutional status, various international treaties of human rights, and created some other rights directly. This initiative captured demands of the human rights movement, of the women's movement and also demands of non-government organizations (NGOs) devoted to the protection and defense of rights, some of which of professional kind (environmental rights, consumers rights, etc). The reform also brought about innovations in the rules of access to justice, through the inclusion of collective protection, a tool which allows the victim, the NGOs and the ombudsman to start legal action in case of violation of collective and diffuse rights.

That said, in the field of collective actions, the main effect of the reform was an expansion of those NGOs committed to public interest law, of high professional level and technical competence, which broadened their agenda to include the protection of economic, social and cultural human rights (CELS, 2008). In the latter half of the 1990s, these and other platforms, such as law clinics created in many universities, started 'trying out' the new procedural instruments provided by the reform in different judicial cases (Böhmer, 2013: 180–182).

Otherwise, the impact of the reform in the field of social protest was null or non significant. At that time, Argentina showed large demonstrations by the organizations of the people directly affected by unemployment (Delamata, 2004). Given their assembly mechanisms of decision making and methods of public claiming, such as road pickets, those organizations were innovative. But regarding the space of negotiation set up with the state, they were defensive, by targeting basic material needs of their members, and conservative, by expanding current 'social plans' that were provided by the government as a means of mitigating poverty. At this point, the initiative to redirect the movement's struggle into the alternative choice of a 'social income guaranteed to all citizens' proposed by one of the organizations was not accepted by the majority (Schuster, 2005: 61–62), nor did the social rights incorporated into the Constitution, by means of the international treaties, or the new notions of equality recognized by the reform (Abramovich, 2009: 4–5), acquire mobilizing status in the movement for consequently revising the current public policy.

Contemporary Socio-Legal Struggles

In contrast to the collective contestation of social consequences of market-oriented policies implemented during the 1990s, the emerging social conflicts accuse the effect of the constitutional reform. New social movements, similar to those taking place in other countries of the region, regarding issues at stake, appropriate the Constitution and convert public claims into legal petitions.

The interaction of social movements with the legal frame in the post-constitutional phase is clearly different from the process of importation and internationalization of legal standards, which has been characteristic of the repertoire of action of social movements since the early 1980s. In that period, social movements *invented* previously non-existent rights through transnational activism. After the reconfiguration of the legal frame in 1994, social movements *appropriate* constitutionally recognized rights, in an interaction with the legal body which can be named 'alien', inasmuch as they did not practically participate in its creation. This experience may entail a critical and distrusting approach to law or it may denote lack of knowledge of the new recognized rights. In any case, rights need to be translated in order to acquire social existence (Merlinsky, 2013). The translation of constitutional rights into frames and tools of action may encompass from an active participation of the social movement in the (re) interpretation of the law to a supremacy of the juridical technique in the making of the argumentative process. As displayed by our examples of socio-legal mobilization next, there exist practices of collective 'actualization' of law, 'learning of rights' through advocacy networks, and also, main resource to the expert interpretation of law, as a strategic goal of the social movement.

Lastly, the use of law to translate collective claims also implies a new positioning of the constitutional and normative order in relationship with the appearance of new social and public problems. Around certain issues (environment, housing and 'personal' rights included), young legal communities –i.e., specialists in matters of recent constitutionalization – have been begetting 'segments' or 'subfields' of the law of human rights, with their own systems of norms, which represent powerful niches for juridical and social activism. Thus, a fluid interaction between the juridical field, in some instances and jurisdictions, and the social ground, which facilitates the appropriation of rights by mobilized actors, has to be considered.

In what follows, we present three cases of contemporary socio-legal mobilization that span a wide range of social actors and involve different practices of law appropriation. The whole set shows a joint commitment of social movements and groups along with legal activists in the enlargement of institutional 'spaces *for* the autonomy' (Zapata Barrero, 1996) – legal rights – of the individual and collective actors and demands.

Grassroots Environmental Organizations as Law Creators

One of the cases that better illustrates the dynamic of the environmental field in Argentina – which has been evolving from local conflicts, which are also recent, to the legalization and incipient institutionalization of various environmental issues – is the process of normative building boosted by citizen assemblies that oppose open-pit mining.[7] This movement, possibly the longest standing and largest in territorial scope,[8] (also) grew by means of direct action to resist new mining projects and appealing to citizen consultation to decide on them. In a second stage, when grassroots organizations already counted on some allies in the provincial legislatures,[9] they reoriented their actions towards parliamentary incidence and participated in instances of legislative deliberation. As a result of this transition, between 2003 and 2011, nine provinces prohibited mining with toxic substances on their territories – with seven standing laws today – 12 being affected (out of a total of 23) by the allocation of mining projects.[10]

The concept, used by Melé (2011) of 'local actualization of law'[11], allows us to capture the activity of the citizen assemblies, their technicians and lawyers in the appropriation of environmental law. On the one hand, they took advantage from legal scales and resorted to federal environmental legislation (Constitution and general law), to create robust protection in the provincial grounds (prohibitions). On the other hand, localization of law engaged the social actors in the interpretation (actualization) of the constitutional notion of environment. In the instances of parliamentary incidence, the environmentalist assemblies challenged the classical understanding of 'sustainable development' set in the first line of the constitutional definition, by emphasizing certain values, such as ecological, patrimonial and cultural ones, to weigh environment and development within a standard of 'strong sustainability' (Gudynas, 2010).[12]

Finally, the attaining of legal regulations through the provincial legislatures allowed the assemblies to guard wide territories from mining exploitation well beyond the local ambits. The change in repertoire and the benefits of legal petition relegated the requests for citizen consultation to decide, a procedure which was among the first demands of the movement.

Community Advocacy and New Repertoires of Popular Action

Our second example of socio-legal mobilization takes place in the city of Buenos Aires, precisely in its most under-privileged neighborhoods, the *villas* (shanty towns). Since they came into being, during the second quarter of the twentieth century, these shanty towns have been interacting with the state, in particular the local one, around habitat issues and demands. At the beginning of 2000, the combination of dwindling economic resources which were provided by the state and population growth in the shanty towns caused the political networks that intermediated between the institutions of government and the representatives of the neighbors to fray. This situation began to manifest through a series of disperse protests against the city authorities, demanding some goods and services. Almost immediately, these social claims moved to the local courts, bringing about a process of judicialization of shanty town' issues, which has no precedent. Apart from making the government carry out works in various shanty towns, the process of judicialization introduced the neighbors into the language of the rights related to their urban residence and brought about a strengthening of the popular movement. In a research work developed together with Alejandro Sehtman and María Victoria Ricciardi (2014), we analyzed the factors that explain the process and its effects. Quoting that paper, it can be stated that the strong and committed activity of local courts, since they were created in 2000, in the protection of social rights, and of habitat and housing in particular, is central to understand the beginning and dynamic of the process of judicialization. Their effects, instead, are more related to a particular feature of the judicial intervention in the shanty towns. Under that strategic institutional line, the set of actors that gave impulse to the causes on shanty towns – rights NGOs, judges and representatives of the Public Ministry of the Judiciary – understood that the purpose of assuring access to justice and recognition of rights to the inhabitants of those popular neighborhoods necessarily had to include, as a part of their activity, the 'raising of awareness of rights'. In technical terms, a displacement came about from the public interest litigation model to the advocacy of the community type (more geared to the empowerment of the subjects) (Acosta et al., 2013: 300). It is not surprising, consequently, that shanty towns neighbors then declared that they 'learned the rights written in the Constitution' and they now know how to use them.

The rulings issued in the judicial cases did not achieve a structural change in the habitat conditions of the neighbors, however, the whole process of judicialization contributed to creating the opportunities for ultimately attaining that goal. Firstly, it led to an expansion of the rights-based petitions into the repertoire of actions of the shanty towns inhabitants. Subsequently, judicial intervention encouraged the formation of mobilization structures among activists from different shanty towns, gathered together around the judicial and legislative actors, who were the most dynamic ones during the process of judicialization. These networks look forward to the urbanization of the neighborhoods or, in the terms of the Constitution of the City of Buenos Aires, the 'social and urban integration' of the shanty towns.

Legal Activism and Egalitarian Marriage

The protagonists of the third case are the Lesbian, Gay, Bisexual and Trans (LGBT) movement, judicial actors and judicial activists. In 2002, the LGBT movement had attained the sanction of the Civil Union Law in the city of Buenos Aires, an institute which recognizes some social rights to same-sex couples but without bringing to debate their legal equalization with heterosexual couples (Hiller, 2010). Some years later, the organizations headed a new campaign in order to broaden legal recognition directly oriented to the institutions. On July 15, 2010, the Senate of the Nation passed the bill that opened the matrimonial regime of the Civil Code to any couple, regardless of their sexual identity, gender or sexual orientation of its members, Argentina thus becoming the first Latin-American country to recognize the right of marriage to gays and lesbians. As Mariano Fernández Valle states, the measure was both the consequence of LGBT activism – which, with little mobilization in the public space, had achieved the support of several social, academic and political sectors in the last years – and the result of the triumph of 'the arguments of personal autonomy and of equality/non-discrimination/non-violence supported by constitutional and international standards' (Fernández Valle, 2010: 179, 181).

Various analysts agree that the strategies of judicial mobilization and expert legislative incidence developed by the movement were decisive to give direction to the parliamentary debate that ended up with the passing of the *egalitarian marriage* law. Both strategies positioned the constitutional *mandate* in a place of hierarchy, and this displaced, in particular, the proposal to plebiscite the initiative, motioned by some legislators opposed to the legal equalization, with the object to 'democratize' the decisions and thus settle the conflict around the matrimonial reform (Hiller, 2010).

Both the judiciary, in several rulings, almost all of which rooted in the city of Buenos Aires, as later the constitutional lawyers who pronounced themselves in a favorable position to the opening of the marriage regime in the legislative instance, established that the legal equalization is obligatory in the Argentine constitutional rule of law state. Constitutional experts indicated that the right to get married regardless of sexual orientation is of constitutional status according to treaties of human rights incorporated to the Constitution and the jurisprudence of the Supreme Court. They also argued that matrimonial restriction due to sexual orientation contradicts the requirement of *equal treatment for all the life plans autonomously decided*, in correspondence with a non-textual interpretation of clauses of the national Constitution (see Clérico, 2010).

The results of the voting in both national Legislative Chambers reflected a wide transversality of vote, with divided voting among the majority forces (Carrasco, 2011). This array showed that expert discourse could anticipate for law makers an interpretation of the law and, thus, outweigh, partisan identities as a main source of political determinations.

International Legality and Social Movements

What has been developed in the above sections allows us to detect types of invoking rights social movements. While the human rights movement, the women's movement and also the LGBT movement share a marked normative internationalism in their configuration and claiming strategies, environmentalist movements or the struggles for housing resort to, 'appropriate' constitutional (constitutionalized) human rights in the deployment of their demands, since the changes produced in the organizational fabric and/or the mobilization structures of the movements. These differences are rooted in the historical progression of the socio-legal dynamic of Argentine democracy. However, it is necessary to settle which other features present in contemporary struggles testify to the belonging to a same pattern, initiated through the importation of human rights standards by the movement of the same name in the early 1980s. To answer this question, we go back first to the particularities of the constitutional reform in order to later establish common features around that pattern.

We argue in this work that the onward and systematic importation of human rights standards to the internal law system, with its peak on the constitutional reform of 1994, provided the framework in which social movements were founding their demands, with a watershed in the reform itself. As it was mentioned before, the Argentine constitutional reform received the influx of the human rights movement in particular and welcomed its demands above all. By means of the international conventions of human rights, the reformers included in the constitution – with a criterion of welfare and equality – plenty of 'unsatisfied lacks and needs that affect the development of the potentialities of the persons and the peoples' (cf. Ávila Santamaría, 2011). This incorporation of interests *objectively* defined took place together with a relatively minor participation of subjective interests in the reform, namely, of a (more) direct participation of particular demands of social movements in the Constituent – as was the case in Brazil, Venezuela, Bolivia and Ecuador.[13] This characteristic of the constitutional process of reform makes it possible to understand, not only in a basic temporal dimension but also as experience of the law, that emergent social movements since 1994 appropriate 'human rights (as) introduced by the reform'.

This said, then, in which deeper way is the pattern of human rights alive in the contemporary socio-legal struggles? In the first place, we may state, through a specific awareness of the rights. This awareness indicates that the persons and the groups are the holders of the rights and thus their creators. As Catalina Smulovitz points out, the pattern of the human rights during the transition to democracy EXCLUDE COMMA, placed the state in the role of protecting the rights and 'those who petition for their protection', in the place of creators of law (Smulovitz, 2008b: 57–58). This relationship inverted completely the descendant equation of creation and allocation of rights 'State-corporations-citizens', proper of the populist democratic tradition that lived through three quarter parts of the twentieth century in Argentina. In the second place, that pattern is even present in the way rights are procedurally created. Actors call the state to 'apply the rights', narrowing through legal argumentation the space for political determinations in the decision making process, or demanding rights by judicial means, when these are not obtained through the political agencies. This modality of intervention runs from the juridical transnationalism of the 1980s to the legal struggles of the present. In particular, this is about a way of defining and enforcing rights that permanently displaces from the repertoire of action of social movements the recourse to direct or participatory democracy, so vivid in strategies of the movements deployed in the above mentioned countries and also in Uruguay (cf. Alvarez, 1993; Avritzer, 2009; Pérez Flores et al., 2010; Lissidini, 2012).

'Global neoconstitutionalism' is an extended phenomenon in Latin America, through the incorporation in the Constitutions of generous declarations of rights and mechanisms of constitutional control since the 1980s (Rodríguez Garavito, 2008). Judicial activism is also expanded (Sieder et al., 2011) and current social struggles incorporate legal 'counter-hegemonic' strategies (Santos & Rodríguez Garavito, 2007). The singularity of the Argentine case may be found, then, in the (comparatively early) social immersion, namely, symbolic, performative, strategic and not purely institutional, of main substantive and procedural features of international legality and the development of portentous activist juridical networks in interlocution with social dynamics.

Notes

1   Amnesty laws were passed in Brazil (1979) – shortly after the beginning of the political opening initiated by the military government – Uruguay (1986) – two years after the pact of transition in which the army received guarantees non-persecution. In the case of Chile (1990) it was the Supreme Court which ratified the military self-amnesty of 1978, a few months after the return of democracy.

2   In 1984, a law passed by the national Congress repealed the self-amnesty which the military had rapidly passed before the elections of October 1983, and in 1985 the trial to the military juntas was conducted.

3   It may be necessary to clarify that we do not understand 'global juridical modernity' under any civilizing perspective, but, as this work intends to show, in terms of reshaping the arena of social struggle.

4   In this text, Maristella Svampa presents four principal dimensions of the social movements in contemporary Latin America: territoriality, direct action, diffusion of

assembly models and the claim of autonomy, 'also understood as a strategic matter, which recalls "self-determination" (to be endowed with one's own law) as much as a more utopian horizon, namely, the creation of "alternative worlds'" (2008: pp. 77–79; my translation).

5   The definition spans the advocacy of public interest, 'which seeks the modification of "the public", the institutions, the law', through 'recognition of rights and the access to institutions of segregated communities' (Acosta et al., 2013: 300), as much as judicial activism in particular, understood as the involvement of courts or the judiciary actors in public or social causes and in the control of public policies (Abramovich & Pautassi, 2009: 1). Both forms of activism may include an interest in citizen participation and mobilization inside and outside the institutional spaces (Pisarello, in Acosta et al., 2013: 301).

6   During the second half of the 1980s three laws were passed: the Law of Joint Custody, Absolute Divorce and the Law of Protection against Family Violence. In 1991, the Quota Law was passed, establishing that 30 per cent of the positions in party lists destined to representation posts should be filled by women.

7   On this dynamic of the environmental field, see Merlinsky (2010, 2013), Delamata (2009, 2013), Christel (2012).

8   The movement is integrated by a hundred local grassroots organizations located along the Cordillera and pre-Cordillera region which have been enlarging the mobilization during the last decades, alerted by the expansion of the industry.

9   The Argentine state contains three territorial levels of government: the national or federal state, the provinces or provincial states and the municipalities.

10   These legal prohibitions can be considered a record if we bear in mind that as far as we know, there exist similar regulations in just a few countries of Europe, Central America and some states in the United States of America. The anti-mega mining movement also was the principal social force of support to the treatment of the national law of Glaciers Protection, which guard those drinking water sources, passed in 2010.

11   The author points out that 'at the coe of local instantes of participation or debate, the interchanges around the modalities of actualization of law, constitute times of formula-tion, definition, of juridical qualification of the local situation' (Melé, 2011: 5–6; my trans-lation).

12   The 'classical' definition of sustainable development seizes the 'ecological mod-ernization' approach, which establishes a peaceful relationship between economic growth and the environment. The 'strong sustainability' trend underlines the existence of limits of the ecosystems and incorporates ecological values to the environment and development, beyond those which are purely economic (Gudynas, 2010: pp. 46–50).

13   This relationship/distinction between objective and subjective interests comes from considering that, as pointed out by Ramiro Ávila Santamaría, 'the catalogue of rights [in a Constitution] responds to two realities: 1. the recognition of deep social problems that have to do with unsatisfied lacks and needs that affect the development of the potentialities of the persons and the peoples; 2. the struggles and demands of organizations and move-ments of the society' (Ávila Santamaría, 2011: 62; my translation).

References

Abramovich, V. (2009). El rol de la justicia en la articulación de políticas y derechos socia-les. In V. Abramovich and L. Pautassi (Eds.), *La revisión judicial de las políticas socia-les. Estudio de casos.* Buenos Aires: Ediciones el Puerto, pp. 1–89.

Abramovich, V. and Pautassi, L. (Eds.). (2009). *La revisión judicial de las políticas socia-les. Estudio de casos.* Buenos Aires: Ediciones el Puerto.

Acosta, M., Bercovich, L. and Chelillo, M. (2013). Modelos para armar: una posible tipología de la relación Abogacía de Interés Público - comunidades segregadas. In L. Bercovich and G. Maurino (Eds.), *Los derechos sociales en la Gran Buenos Aires.* Buenos Aires: Eudeba, pp. 291–309.

Alvarez, S.E. (1993). *Deepening* Democracy: Popular Networks, constitutional Reform and Radical Urban Regimes in contemporary Brazil. In R. Fisher and J. Kling (Eds.), *Mobilizing the Community, Local Politics in the Era of Global City.* Newbury Park: SAGE Publications, pp. 191–219.

Ávila Santamaría, R. (2011). *El neconstitucionalismo transformador. El estado y el derecho en la Constitución de 2008.* Quito: Ediciones Abya-Yala and Universidad Andina Simón Bolivar.

Avritzer, L. (2009). *Participatory Institutions in Democratic Brazil.* Baltimore, MD: The John Hopkins University Press.

Böhmer, M. (2013). La lógica político-institucional del Poder Judicial en la Argentina. In C. Acuña (Ed.), *¿Cuánto importan las instituciones? Gobierno, Estado y actores en la política argentina.* Buenos Aires: Siglo Veintiuno Editores and Fundación OSDE, pp. 157–208.

Carrasco, M. (2011). El matrimonio igualitario en el parlamento argentino. Antecedentes parlamentarios. Los proyectos que se convirtieron en ley. El tratamiento en ambas Cámaras y las votaciones. In N. Solari and C. Von Opiela (Eds.), *Matrimonio entre personas del mismo sexo. Ley 26.618. Antecedentes, implicancias. Efectos.* Buenos Aires: La Ley, pp. 163–189.

CELS. (2008). *Litigio estratégico y derechos humanos.* Buenos Aires: Siglo Veintiuno and CELS.

Christel, L. (2012). Incidencia de las resistencias sociales en las legislaciones mineras provinciales. Los casos de Córdoba y Catamarca (2003–2008). (Master's Thesis). Universidad Nacional de San Martín, Buenos Aires.

Clérico, L. (2010). EL matrimonio igualitario y los principios constitucionales estructurantes de igualdad y/o autonomía. In M. Pecheny et al. (Eds.), *Matrimonio igualitario. Perspectivas sociales, políticas y jurídicas.* Buenos Aires: Eudeba, pp. 145–170.

Delamata, G. (2004). The Organizations of Unemployed Workers in Greater Buenos Aires: Giving New Meanings to Popular Sectors' Practices. *Working Paper* 8. Berkeley: Center for Latin American Studies, University of California.

Delamata, G. (2009). ¿La ciudadanía poblana? El movimiento asambleario de Gualeguaychú y la construcción y el reclamo de un derecho colectivo. In G. Delamata (Ed.). *Movilizaciones sociales: ¿nuevas ciudadanías? Reclamos, derechos, Estado en Argentina, Bolivia y Brasil.* Buenos Aires: Biblos, pp. 237–275.

Delamata, G. (2013). Actualizando el derecho al ambiente. Movilización social, activismo legal y derecho constitucional al ambiente de sustentabilidad fuerte en el sector extractivista megaminero. *Revista de Sociología de la UBA: Entramados y Perspectivas, 3*(3), 55–90.

Delamata, G., Sehtman, A. and Ricciardi, M.V. (2014). Más allá de los estrados…Activismo judicial y repertorios de acción villera en la Ciudad de Buenos Aires. In L. Pautassi (Ed.), *Acceso a la justicia en contextos de marginación social. La región metropolitana de Buenos Aires bajo análisis.* Buenos Aires: Biblos, pp. 397–444.

Fernández Valle, M. (2010). Después del <matrimonio igualitario>. In M. Pecheny et al. (Eds.), *Matrimonio igualitario. Perspectivas sociales, políticas y jurídicas.* Buenos Aires: Eudeba, pp. 179–204.

Filippini, L. (2011). La persecución penal en la búsqueda de justicia. In CELS/ICTJ. *Hacer justicia. Nuevos debates sobre el juzgamiento de crímenes de lesa humanidad en Argentina.* Buenos Aires: Siglo XXI, pp. 19–47.

Gudynas, E. (2010). Desarrollo sostenible: una guía básica de conceptos y tendencias hacia otra economía. *Otra Economía*, *4*(6), 43–66.

Hiller, R. (2010). Matrimonio igualitario y espacio público en Argentina. In M. Pecheny et al. (Eds.). *Matrimonio igualitario. Perspectivas sociales, políticas y jurídicas.* Buenos Aires: Eudeba, pp. 85–130.

Keck, M. and Sikkink, K. (1998). *Activists beyond borders. Advocacy networks in international politics.* Ithaca: Cornell University Press.

Lissidini, A. (2012). Democracia directa en Uruguay y en Venezuela: Nuevas voces, antiguos procesos. Paper presented at the Seminario General de Investigación, Escuela de Política y Gobierno, Universidad Nacional de San Martín, Buenos Aires.

Melé, P. (2011). Actualisation locale du droit. Paper presented at the *Séminaire Géographie et droit, géographie du droit,* Carcasonne, UMR PRODIG, CERSA, 28/29-10-2011. Retrieved June 27, 2014, from http://droit.univ-tours.fr/m-mele-patrice-1116.kjsp?RF=DROIT

Merlinsky, G. (2010). La acción colectiva ambiental en Argentina: ¿nuevas ciudadanías? Prepared for the *Environment and Citizenship in Latin America Workshop*, Simon Fraser Institute.

Merlinsky, G. (2013). *Política, derechos y justicia ambiental. El conflicto del Riachuelo.* Buenos Aires: Fondo de Cultura Económica.

Novaro, M. (2011). La visita de la CIDH. In *Cables secretos. Operaciones políticas en la Argentina de los setenta.* Buenos Aires: Edhasa, pp. 117–157.

Pérez Flores, F., Mendonça Cunha Filho, C. and Coelho, A. (2010). Participación ampliada y reforma del estado. Mecanismos constitucionales de democracia participativa en Bolivia, Ecuador y Venezuela. OSAL Año XI N° 27.

Petracci, M. and Pecheny, M. (2007). Argentina: contexto político y social de la política de salud y derechos sexuales y reproductivos. In M. Petracci and M. Pecheny (Eds.), *Argentina. Derechos humanos y sexualidad.* Buenos Aires: CEDES, pp.13–27.

Pinto, M. (2008). *El derecho internacional. Vigencia y desafíos en un escenario globalizado.* Buenos Aires: Fondo de Cultura Económica.

Rodríguez Garavito, C. (2009). *La globalización del estado de derecho. El neoconstitucionalismo, el neoliberalismo y la transformación institucional de América Latina.* Bogotá: Universidad de Los Andes.

Smulovitz, C. (2008a). La política por otros medios. Judicialización y movilización legal en la Argentina. *Desarrollo Económico*, *48*(189–190), 287–305.

Smulovitz, C. (2008b). Organizaciones que invocan derechos. Sociedad civil y representación en la Argentina. *Postdata*, 13: 51–79.

Santos, B.S. and Rodríguez Garavito, C. (Eds.). (2007). *El derecho y la globalización desde abajo. Hacia una legalidad cosmopolita.* Barcelona: Anthropos.

Schuster, F. (2005). Las protestas sociales y el estudio de la acción colectiva. In F. Schuster et al. (Eds.), *Tomar la palabra. Estudios sobre protesta social y acción colectiva en la Argentina contemporánea.* Buenos Aires: Prometeo Libros, pp. 43–83.

Sieder, R., Schjolden, L. and Angel, A. (Eds.). (2011). *La judicialización de la política en América Latina.* México: Universidad Externado de Colombia.

Sikkink, K. (2011). La dimensión trasnacional de la judicialización de la política en América Latina. In R. Sieder, L. Schjolden and A. Aangell (Eds.), *La judicialización de la política en América Latina.* México: Universidad Externado de Colombia, pp. 283–314.

Svampa, M. and Pereyra, S. (2003). *Entre la ruta y el barrio. La experiencia de las organizaciones piqueteras.* Buenos Aires: Biblos.

Svampa, M. (2008). Movimientos sociales y nuevo escenario regional. Las inflexiones del paradigma liberal en América Latina. In M. Svampa (Ed.), *Cambio de época. Movimientos sociales y poder político.* Buenos Aires: Veintiuno and CLACSO, pp. 75–92.

Svampa, M., Sola Álvarez, M. and Bottaro, L. (2009). Los movimientos contra la minería metalífera a cielo abierto: escenarios y conflictos. Entre el <efecto Esquel> y el <efecto La Alumbrera>. In M. Svampa and M.A. Antonelli (Eds.), *Minería Transnacional, narrativas del desarrollo y resistencias socials.* Buenos Aires: Biblos, pp. 123–180.

Svampa, M. and Sola Álvarez, M. (2010). Modelo minero, resistencias sociales y estilos de desarrollo: los marcos de la discusión en la Argentina. *Ecuador Debate, 79,* 105–126.

Vecchioli, V. (2009). Expertise jurídica y capital militante: reconversiones de recursos escolares, morales y políticos entre los abogados de derechos humanos en la Argentina. *Pro-Posiçoes, 20, 2*(59), 41–57.

Zapata Barrero, R. (1996). Ciudadanía y Estados de Bienestar o *De la ingravidez de lo sólido en un mundo que se <desnewtoniza> social y políticamente. Sistema, 130,* 75–96.

Zibechi, R. (2011). *Política y miseria. La relación entre el modelo extractivo, los planes sociales y los gobiernos progresistas.* Buenos Aires: Lavaca.

14

Social Contestation, Citizenship and Modernity in Democratic South Africa

Marcelle C. Dawson

Introduction

Democracy is arguably a quintessential feature of modernity. As Giddens (1993: 289) suggested, some theorists would go so far as to argue that '[c]ompetitive capitalism allied to liberal democracy is the culmination of historical development, a social order that reconciles economic efficiency with a mass democratic representation.' Indeed this is what South Africa strove towards in the reconstruction of the state and nation after the fall of the apartheid regime. The 'new' South Africa is one in which every adult has the right to vote, but bread-and-butter issues, like access to basic services, housing and healthcare remain firmly on the agenda of marginalized communities.

South Africa's political economy is characterized by a *dominant* party, capitalist democracy. While some view the creation of wealth among a group of people who, under apartheid, were largely excluded from economic advancement as the ideal way to ensure that wealth will filter down to those who were excluded from opportunities to advance their socio-economic status, the myth of the 'trickle-down effect' was very soon dispelled by the reality of increasing socio-economic inequality between black people. Moreover, the dearth of political representation to the left of the ruling African National Congress, combined with a more open, democratic context and a disaffected electorate, created a set of circumstances conducive to the emergence of a group of vibrant and diverse community movements in the late 1990s and early 2000s.

While anti-apartheid resistance was aimed at ushering in a democratic era, the various social contestations that continue to unfold in post-apartheid South Africa struggle to give democracy meaning by expanding the rights of citizens beyond the rights and freedoms of liberal democracy. But can democracy within the constraints of capitalism ease social inequality? Drawing on empirical investigations in South Africa as well as insights into popular mobilization elsewhere on the African continent, this chapter addresses the interconnected issues of social contestation, citizenship and modernity. It argues that citizenship in contemporary South African context is flimsy, owing largely to the liberal, capitalist underpinnings of its relatively young democracy. The discussion highlights the need for citizenship education for an anti-capitalist society as a progressive step towards the attainment of social equality.

Modernity, Development and Liberation In South(Ern) Africa: A Reflection on Current Debates

This chapter assumes, as a starting point, that the world is currently moving through a third phase of modernity; a phase that Giddens (1990, 1993) calls 'late' or 'radical' modernity, which is characterized by 'a steep growth in the complexity of social life' (Domingues, 2011: 518). The development path followed by South Africa in this period has, of course, been affected profoundly by the preceding era of apartheid, or what some referred to as 'colonialism of a special type', referring to 'the co-existence and articulation of a colonial relation between black and white people and a developed capitalist economy within the confines of a single national state' (Wolpe, 1988: 29). Colonial relations were manufactured by the apartheid state through a series of laws including the Prohibition of Mixed Marriages Act (1949), Immorality Act (1950), Population Registration Act (1950), Separate Amenities Act (1953) and the Bantu Education Act (1953), among others. With regard to the physical structuring of urban areas, the most significant legal tool that was used to entrench the race-specific residential patterns already in existence was the Group Areas Act of 1950. This piece of legislation ensured that the racist regime had access to cheap, exploitable labour that was readily available to do the dirty work of capitalism and build a modern state. Two decades after, the end of apartheid race is by no means dormant as a socio-political fault-line. However, class inequality – no longer pervasive only between black and white, but more starkly apparent among black South Africans – is one of the most salient features of South African society. Socio-economic disparity is perhaps, as Giddens (1993: 292) put it, one of the 'social injustices' that is inherent to late modernity; a condition that inevitably invites mass mobilization. More than two decades later, Giddens' assertions about modernity remain as relevant as ever.

To contextualize the South African case, it is perhaps necessary to reflect, just briefly, on the status quo in developing nations. Popular resistance against apartheid ushered in a democratic state in which every South African adult has the right to vote. Having achieved democracy only in

1994, South Africa was somewhat of a latecomer, compared to its peripheral counterparts like Brazil and India. Nonetheless, in the contemporary period, these and other developing nations have shown some interesting parallels. Between 2000 and 2008, Brazil, China, India and South Africa experienced remarkable GDP growth, although statistics from South Africa and Brazil suggest that their growth was 'more erratic and less impressive' (Arnal & Förster, 2010: 15). Despite gains in productivity, increased rates of labour force participation (until 2008) and access to new financial markets, high levels of inequality continue to mar the modern configurations in these countries, with the exception, perhaps, of India. Using the Gini-coefficient as a measure of income inequality, where 1 indicates complete inequality and 0 represents complete equality, statistics suggest that South Africa, with its Gini-coefficient of 0.63 in 2012, is one of the most unequal countries in the world. China's 2012 figures stand at 0.43, while India is less unequal at 0.33 (Human Development Report, 2013: 153–154). Brazil's level of inequality is relatively high (0.55), but has decreased since 2001 as a result of higher educational attainment and the implementation of a range of social programmes, largely owing to popular pressure (Néri, 2010). Nonetheless, the phenomenon of the working poor is not uncommon in these countries. For instance, despite its relatively low levels of income inequality, some authors describe the working conditions in India as modern day slavery (de Regil, 2010). Other authors suggest that India's employment growth has been concentrated in the informal sector and that these workers as well as those in flexible formal employment lack social protection, employment security and benefits (Mazundar, 2010: 157). Despite China's impressive economic growth, income distribution is widening (Ravallion & Chen, 2007; Fang et al., 2010). In South Africa, the yawning wage gap coupled with astoundingly high unemployment figures gnaw at the democratic gains obtained in 1994. Official statistics suggest that unemployment in South Africa stood at 24.7 per cent in the third quarter of 2013 (Statistics South Africa, 2013). These figures set it apart from its peripheral counterparts where unemployment is more comparable to the OECD average of 7.8 per cent in the same period (OECD StatExtracts). These conditions of inequality and poor working conditions certainly make the ground more fertile for popular resistance. Certainly, South Africa has witnessed an increase in the number of community uprisings in the last decade, with some scholars referring to this phenomenon as a 'rebellion of the poor' (Alexander, 2010).

The discussion now returns to its focus on South Africa. It considers some relevant debates on liberation, modernity and development, thereby providing a useful transition into the core of this chapter, which centres on the nature of social contestation in contemporary South Africa. Liberation from apartheid was depicted in both popular and academic texts as South Africa's 'miracle transition' despite overwhelming evidence to the contrary (Bottaro & Stanley, 2011; Clark & Worger, 2013) More honest reflections revealed several flaws in South Africa's 'rainbow nation', which cast doubts on the romanticized narratives about the country's transition to democracy (For more critical reviews of South Africa's post-apartheid transition, see McKinley, 1997, 2001; Bond, 2000a, 2000b; Guelke, 2005). For instance, the commodification of basic services, ushered in by the Growth, Employment and Redistribution policy in 1996, had the effect of deepening existing socio-economic inequalities. While other economic strategies like the government's Broad Based Black Economic Empowerment facilitated the emergence of a burgeoning black middle class as well as a small black elite, the post-1994 context for the majority of black South Africans was not substantively different from their experience of apartheid, particularly as far as their socio-economic position was concerned.

To get to grips with the relationship between modernity and social con-testation in South Africa, I turn to the work of writers who, very early on, began to see through the rhetoric of the African National Congress (ANC) when it came into power in 1994. The following discussion sheds light on the tensions arising from the ANC's increasingly fervent drive to follow global economic trends and replicate certain aspects of global modernity within a context where the majority of South Africa's population was (and still is) reeling from the effects of an abhorrent system of racial and capital exploitation. Amidst a palpable sense of hope and genuine belief in the 'better life for all' that liberation would bring, authors such as Martin Murray (1994) cautioned that the ANC was sowing seeds that would lay the founda-tion for the establishment of a black capitalist class while leaving the old structures of class privilege virtually untouched. Similarly, others pointed out that the ANC would begin to 'ignore increasingly disenfranchised move-ments deemed "populist", whose redistributive demands it cannot satisfy, and will drift towards economic liberals nested in business and conserva-tives located in the state, whose powers it cannot defeat' (McDonald, 1996: 232). The increasing distance between the ANC and its constituency, and the numerous compromises that the ANC made in the interests of further modernizing the South African economy are explored at length in contribu-tions by authors such as Bond (2000a, 2000b), Marais (2001), McKinley (1997, 2001) and Saul (2001) and these oft-cited debates do not require repetition here. The crux of their various arguments is that it was not long after the end of apartheid that the promises of liberation began to ring hollow.

The seeds of the disparity between what was promised and what was actually 'delivered' under democracy were sewn much earlier during the struggle against apartheid. Here, I consider one of the possible historical reasons for present day disaffection on the left. The South African Communist Party (SACP), which has been in an alliance with the ANC since the 1950s, had adopted a Stalin-inspired two-stage theory of revolution. This strategy formed the basis of early challenges to colonialism as a special type and espoused that a National Democratic Revolution should precede a socialist one. In the words of Joe Slovo, General Secretary of the SACP from 1984 to 1991:

> Our struggle is seen as 'bourgeois-democratic' in character so that the immediate agenda should not go beyond the objective of a kind of 'de-raced' capitalism. According to this view there will be time enough after apartheid is destroyed to then turn our attention to the struggle for socialism. Hence there should be little talk of our ultimate socialist objectives. The working class should not insist on the inclusion of radical social measures as part of the immediate agenda because that would risk frightening away potential allies against apartheid (Slovo, 1988).

This strategy was ideologically confused and it lacked an intersectional approach to fighting oppression. In theory, its supporters recognized that both democratic and socialist transformation were necessary. In practice, however, the drive towards democratic change was prioritized and divorced from efforts to place the means of production in the hands of the workers, and the struggle was therefore intrinsically limited. Commenting on the inadequacy and farcical nature of this strategy, seasoned activist Trevor Ngwane (2006) observed that '[t]he SACP used to tell us that there would be two stages. Now that we are in stage one, they are starting to tell us that there will be many many stages in stage one.'

In a document referred to as 'The Green Book', Slovo is quoted as saying that 'the ANC is not a party, and its direct or open commitment to socialist ideology may undermine its basic character as a broad national movement' (ANC, 1979). In its current role as the ruling party, the ANC has clearly not wanted to lose its appeal as a broad church. Neither the ruling party, nor the SACP have attempted to drive the second stage of the revolution. The third alliance partner, namely the South African Congress of Trade Unions, has arguably come closest to articulating a socialist agenda, and has been at the forefront of the vociferous industrial action in the post-apartheid period, but – lacking independence from the ANC – COSATU has failed to play a decisive role in resolving workers' demands.

Assessing the ANC's role in the shift to the post-apartheid period, Howarth (1998: 203) claimed that the party guided South Africa through a 'democratic *transition*' in which 'negotiating elites [oversaw] the installation of formal liberal-democratic procedures', while what was sorely lacking was 'democratic *transformation*', which he conceived of as a 'longer-term process of restructuring the underlying social relationships of a given society' (emphasis added). Echoing these sentiments, Bond (2000b) encapsulated this argument in his notion of 'elite transition', which he used to suggest that the shift from apartheid to democracy was (and continues to be) steered by a small band of power-mongers in such a way that the capitalist class is consolidated. Yet, the ANC managed to retain its legitimacy and placate its constituency, to a certain extent, partly through skilful and persistent reminders of what it stood for as a 'liberation party', which veiled some of its failures as the 'ruling party', but also partly through its expansion of the social protection system since 1994. Reminiscent of the welfare models that characterized the second phase of modernity in industrialized nations, South Africa's social policy system has arguably been exemplary in demonstrating that 'technical interventions aimed at reducing poverty and providing some protection against destitution' (Marais, 2011: 238) can also have 'profound implications for the distribution of state resources and for patterns of integration and social exclusion' (Devereux, 2010: 4).

South Africa's efforts to placate capital, while simultaneously attempting to assuage the majority of voters by responding directly to their material demands arguably represent an example of what Domingues (2011: 519) calls 'modernizing moves', the nature of which depends on a country's 'own civilizational background but also on how they answer to the Western institutions and imaginary, as well as colonial experiences.' Greenstein (2009) conceived of the character of South Africa's 'modernizing moves' since the end of apartheid as an 'alternative modernity'. This term is used to describe a particular kind of development discourse that 'reflects the ongoing vitality of the promises of development' but that has two distinct but parallel trajectories, namely 'catching up with the global modern North' on the one hand, 'while retaining local cultural distinction' on the other (Greenstein, 2009: 72). Greenstein's discourse analysis of a series of public addresses by former president, Thabo Mbeki, reveals that while South Africa's globalizing tendencies have resulted in tangible outcomes, particularly in respect of the economy, attempts to infuse policy and practice with a local flavour by relying on indigenous knowledge and skills are nothing short of rhetorical, especially as far as ANC/party discourse is concerned (Greenstein, 2009: 82). However, because this rhetoric has been shown to carry weight, in some circles at least, the impression that we are left with is that South Africa is following in the footsteps of its Western counterparts, fuelled by the belief that 'there is no alternative', but claiming all the while that its policies – no matter how closely aligned with the West's neoliberal agenda – are indeed 'the product of South African local deliberations and decisions, reflecting African continental considerations as well' (Greenstein, 2009: 83). In other words, South Africa's 'modernizing moves' neither completely reject global modernity, nor embrace its prescriptions outright. But is there really anything 'alternative' about this expression of modernity? Greenstein's depiction is somewhat unconvincing. Is it not simply another aspect of the plurality of modernity; a variant – and quite a common one at that – already apparent in the global south?

Across much of Africa, out of the ashes of colonialism, rose not a liberated nation, but rather one throttled by the grip 'neo-colonialism' on one hand and by the oppressive rule of dictators on the other. While not wanting to undermine the liberation struggles that were driven by nationalist movements, it is fair to argue that it was indeed the leaders of these very movements who, in the period of neo-colonialism, 'suture[d] the local economy into the rhythm and dictates of the metropolitan masters' (Desai, 2013: 74). African Studies luminary, John Saul, details, very cogently, the metamorphosis of modernization projects on the African continent, whose tale is simultaneously inspiring and woeful. Taking stock of liberation struggles in Africa from the mid to late twentieth century, Arrighi and Saul (1973), influenced by the likes of Frantz Fanon and Amilcar Cabral, warned of the counter-revolutionary tendencies of the emerging bureaucratic elite and the limited potential of nationalist movements to promote development. For these and other critical authors, Africa would stagnate and even regress under conditions where its 'modernizing moves' were inextricably linked to international capital and where a local elite, rather than the masses, became the beneficiaries of economic development. For Saul, the successful defeat of white domination was only half the battle won and 'the next liberation struggle', which is the title of his 2005 book, would need to entail a fight against rampant capitalism if Africa was determined to free itself from the clutches of the West. In an insightful, albeit somewhat repetitive, four volume series (but also in a range of earlier works, for example Saul 1993, 2001a, 2001b), Saul painstakingly analyses how southern Africa came to face a period of second liberation and how it could potentially succeed in its quest (see Saul 2006, 2008, 2011, 2014). He captures the continent's third phase of modernity vividly:

> What ... we now had in place of the nationally-premissed, western-sited, "Empires" that Africa had come to know all too well was indeed something new. For it was, first and foremost, an "Empire of Capital" itself, one that, through increasingly mobile capitalist enterprises, through supranational agencies ... now works actively to enforce the demands of global capital for profit and also to guarantee the (relative) stability of the overall system. As for Africa, what we now saw, under this novel imperial regimen, was a *recolonization* of the continent. (Saul, 2014: 6, emphasis added)

Saul acknowledges the work of Fanon (1963), which was premonitory for South Africa in many ways, but deliberately substitutes Fanon's 'neo-colonialism' with 'recolonization', arguing that 'this latter form of imperialism is being enacted by *capital* itself rather than primarily – as in the past – by some specific national (western) centre of empire or another' (Saul, 2014: 7, original emphasis See also Saul 1993, 2011).

Looking within and beyond South Africa's borders, we can begin to see how 'modernizing moves' on the continent do not represent an 'alternative modernity' as much as a typical trajectory of social change where ruling elites bow and scrape to capital's demands, concede just enough to silence some of their detractors, quell (often violently) the most dissenting voices, and so retain a stranglehold on the state, all the while exacerbating the worst excesses of (neo)colonialism (and apartheid in South Africa's case).

The ensuing discussion reflects on original research from South Africa, but also shares the insights of others on popular struggles elsewhere in Africa. While South Africa is indeed different from its neighbours in many respects, and while it would be disingenuous to treat sub-Sahara as homogenous, examining South Africa in the context of its regional counterparts helps to show that, despite the differences, many of its people are in the same dire predicament as the most marginalized people in other African countries. Moreover, the patterns of social contestation across the continent are driven by similar conditions. Missing this point promotes South African exceptionalism and it also masks the grave and glaring socio-economic inequality that gnaws at the fabric of South African society and fuels much of the popular politics in the country. For most, South Africa is not Africa's success story. Like other parts of Africa, and indeed elsewhere in the world where unbridled capitalism flourishes, 'evils and dangers' are unleashed, which 'impinge on general consciousness more directly than before, and they are very often a direct stimulus to social mobilization and revolt' (Giddens, 1993: 292). It is worth noting that Giddens (1993: 292) also made room for apathy as a response to the 'fractured world of late modernity', but across Africa, indifference is certainly not the chosen path.

Shaping and Shaped by Popular Resistance: 'Modernizing Moves' in Southern Africa

While Saul is understandably critical of the restricted meaning that liberation has come to have in southern Africa, hence *Liberation Lite* (Saul, 2011), he is – equally justifiably – sanguine about the potential of popular struggles to resist recolonization. He is not alone in his optimism. Scholars like Peter Dwyer, David Seddon and Leo Zeilig, among others, continue to contribute to a growing body of critical, yet high-spirited, research on past and present popular resistance on the African continent. It is beyond the scope of this chapter to discuss the Marikana massacre of 2012, but it is worth noting the suggestion by some scholars that this horrific event has altered the terrain of social contestation in contemporary South Africa (In this regard see Alexander et al., 2012; Satgar, 2012; Saul & Bond, 2014).

For Dwyer and Zeilig, social contestation lies 'at the heart of Africa's politics'. They cite the shutting down of talks at the World Trade Organization (or the 'Battle of Seattle' as it became known) in late 1999 as one of the key impetuses that harvested and harnessed anti-capitalist energies. For these authors this event represented 'a courageous attempt to generate political alternatives, even if these efforts have not been successful' (Dwyer & Zeilig, 2012: 15). Certainly this event and its underlying ideology attracted a new crop of activists to the post-apartheid movements that emerged in South Africa from the late 1990s onwards. However, for many of South Africa's social movements, there were more discernible triggers and reference points far closer to home: grave disappointment in what political liberation had achieved, a labour movement that had tied its mast to the ruling party and limited choice on the electoral front, to mention a few. The movements also had a wealth of experience in the form of seasoned anti-apartheid activists, disaffected with the ruling ANC, who were able to coordinate marginalized voices. Concerns have been raised that the demands articulated by some movement leaders were disconnected from and not representative of the 'ordinary supporters' who threw their weight behind the emerging movements. For example, the Anti-Privatization Forum emerged officially in 2000 as an umbrella organization comprising a range of community affiliates, political groupings and individual supporters. From its inception it espoused a socialist ideology, but leaders came from diverse socialist traditions and, although 'socialism' may have been proclaimed as the destination, they did not necessarily agree on the route that was required to get there Cottle (2004). Its shortcomings and ultimate demise notwithstanding, the APF was the key *socialist* social movement to have made its mark during post-apartheid South Africa's first decade of dissent (2000–2010).[1]

One of the several terrains on which the APF contested government policy and practice was service delivery. In order to understand more concretely the connection between global modernity and social contestation, the discussion considers community resistance against water commodification in South Africa. The debate is couched in a critical interrogation of citizenship as a quintessential feature of the modern condition. Here, I will reflect on and advance some of my earlier work in which I argued that popular resistance against the commodification of water challenged capitalism by implicitly rejecting citizenship under the conditions of liberal democracy and demanding a radical reconceptualization of its practical contents (Dawson, 2010). More than a decade ago, Hendricks (2003: 21) made the insightful observation that citizenship in post-apartheid South Africa reinforces class inequality by making it 'acceptable and possible under capitalism'. Extensive empirical investigations into community protests against water commodification from the early 2000s onwards bore out Hendricks' assertions, thus challenging the assumptions by Marshall (1963: 87) that the project of citizenship is centred on bringing about social equality and by Crompton (2008: 139) that 'social citizenship . . . enabl[es] . . . the . . . "losers" to participate in society, hence its role in class abatement'. These arguments may have found support in established Western democracies, but evidence from South Africa suggests that as long as a capitalist framework continues to inform social, political and economic transformation, citizenship will lack any meaning and depth for the majority of South African citizens. In this respect, I concur with Kabeer (2005: 23), who cautioned against 'vertical' views of citizenship, which dwell on 'the relationship between the state and the individual'. Instead Kabeer endorsed 'horizontal' understandings of citizenship, which stress the importance of the 'relationships *between* citizens' (emphasis in original) and thus encourage us to think of citizenship as involving collective action and solidarity (see also Kabeer, 2005: 7). Resource (and other) struggles that give birth to rights must therefore vehemently oppose individualism and actively resist the individualizing tendencies of market forces, which stealthily creep into every aspect of our daily lives, regulating even the provision of basic services.

In response to inadequate access to basic resources by the majority of the black population, the ANC-led government introduced a system of pre-payment into resource distribution. To recover the costs of making basic resources available, South Africans who had newly been granted citizenship in 1994 and who previously lacked access to basic services, were expected to agree to having a prepaid device installed in their homes and to pay upfront for the services that they used, much in the same way as one would use a 'pay-as-you-go' mobile phone and top it up when necessary. Proponents of prepaid meters held the view these devices would extend service provision and bring the population up to speed with modern technology. However, from a social contestation viewpoint, this cost-recovery strategy represented a hindrance in that it individualized struggle and undermined the ability to act collectively.

My own research on the impact of the installation of water prepaid meters in Soweto, Johannesburg (Dawson, 2008) corroborated the findings of a similar study by Ebrahim Harvey, who argued that prepaid meters are used as a form of 'remote control' (Harvey, 2005: 121), in the sense that local councillors no longer needed physically to take a reading on water meters or keep track of bills and arrears. Moreover, prepaid meters meant that councillors no longer had to be involved personally in cutting off water supplies. Instead, these responsibilities were transferred to the poor. If residents could not afford to recharge the meter, they found themselves in a situation where they effectively cut *themselves* off from the water supply (McInnes, 2003: 4; Harvey, 2005: 121).

In light of the consequences of commodified service delivery in post-apartheid South Africa, one could argue that the modern project of building an inclusive nation-state was imbued 'with a discourse of "responsible citizenship" [meaning] that national reconstruction was only possible if each individual citizen realized that while liberation had provided them with rights, it had also imposed duties on them' (Von Schnitzler, 2008: 907). In other words, alongside the rights that citizenship afforded, there was a 'fiscal responsibility' to the state (Von Schnitzler, 2008: 907). From the state's point of view, it had successfully defused a potentially destabilizing political problem in the shantytowns, using a small, highly modern, technological device, which essentially turned citizens into consumers (Von Schnitzler, 2008: 911).

In sum, it can be argued that the lack of access to resources experienced under apartheid fuelled a form of contestation that was characterized, in part, by the 'right to have rights' (Arendt, 1986). One of the first 'modernizing moves' after the end of apartheid was thus to build a non-racial democracy with inclusive citizenship rights. Under the post-apartheid dispensation, in an attempt to modernize the system of resources distribution, the state imposed the installation of prepaid meters in the homes of those who previously had been denied this right. Thus, those citizens who had newly joined resource grids had to pay upfront for a certain allowance of basic services, meanwhile others continued liberally to enjoy as much of the resource as they needed in return for the monthly payment of utility bills. Hence, the government's attempt to extend service provision to all its citizens merely entrenched race, class and geographic disparities in the sense that one group of citizens – mostly black, poor and living in the shantytowns – had to purchase in advance as much of the resource as they could afford, while another group – mostly suburban and middle class – could pay retrospectively for the resources that they had already enjoyed. Commodified resource distribution was met with heightened levels of social contestation that had, at its core, an anti-privatization stance. Moreover, while the struggle against apartheid was largely about obtaining rights, the nature of social contestation in the post-apartheid period is partly about thrashing out the meaning and content of those rights.

Considering the high levels of inequality in countries like South Africa and Brazil, it is unsurprising that debates on citizenship in these counties are similar in many respects. Earle's study of social movements and citizenship in Brazil revealed that the possession of passports and birth certificates is less central to discussions about citizenship rights than might be the case in the United Kingdom for example (Earle, 2008: 3). Instead, considerations of inclusion and exclusion tend to centre on access to basic resources. In Earle's words, '[w]here a person lacks access to these services, they are often regarded as having "limited citizenship", even if formally they have Brazilian nationality and the paperwork to prove it' (2008: 2). These sentiments echo across South Africa where, despite the formal accoutrements of citizenship that facilitate inclusion in the nation, the 'cost of belonging' (Dawson, 2010) is so exorbitant for some people that formal citizenship is practically meaningless. For these people, citizenship without social rights lacks substance. Following scholars like T. H. Marshall, Earle (2008: 2) argued that '[t]he provision of social rights, the *substance* of citizenship, can … have an important psychological impact upon perceptions of status, membership of society and, as a consequence, upon a sense of dignity'. However, as the earlier discussion pointed out, the extension of social rights under capitalism will not lead to equality, because the capitalist system depends on inequality for its very existence. Thus, the acquisition of full citizenship is not merely a function of granting access to basic services and other social rights. While the extension of substantive citizenship is indeed an advance on formal citizenship, it is not a sufficient condition for social equality. In the final section of this chapter, I briefly consider citizenship education as a means to alter the ways in which citizens engage with the state.

Citizenship Education for Equality: Some Concluding Thoughts

[W]hile the power of corporations and capitalism by and large … remains at the societal level formidable and emancipation cannot be complete if they are not radically tackled, the state is a site of power – and struggle – that remains exceedingly important in contemporary modernity (Domingues, 2013: 95).

The assertion above invites us to reconsider the relationship between state and citizen. In the South African context, much of the social contestation in the post-apartheid period has focused on making demands on the state to distribute more resources in a more equitable manner. Mobilization efforts have rarely been driven towards ensuring that 'the state [is] re-colonized by society, in order to make it more representative of the people's will, of the popular coalitions that may change the face of contemporary modernity away from neoliberalism, fragmentation, administration of poverty' (Domingues, 2013: 96). Making demands on the state without challenging its legitimacy hampers the potential of social contestation to fundamentally change the 'rules' of citizenship.

A more equitable society would entail people-centred, citizen-led governance, where citizens are not merely docile beneficiaries of government policy whose sense of belonging is derived primarily from the ability to vote in elections. The development of an active and critically engaged citizenry cannot only be fostered at the level of ideas, or within the confines of the academy or limited political circles. As we know, education at the primary level is a critical agent of socialization. The 'hidden curriculum' (Willis, 1997) in most modern education systems teaches children how to be good citizens for capitalism. As McCowan (2009: 4) noted, '[i]t is as common for citizenship education to be justified on the basis of the maintenance of order and control in society, and of legitimization of current political institutions, as on the development of empowered political agents.' In South Africa citizenship education is taught through the subject of 'Life Orientation' (LO), which entails lessons on 'civics, guidance, physical education (PE) and religious education' (Fleetwood, 2012: 3). A breakdown of the content of LO suggests that it does not foster political agency:

> In LO, learners are to be taught about their democracy, their Constitutional rights and responsibilities, and the value of accepting and appreciating the different cultures and religions in the country, all of which aims to contribute towards strengthening South Africa's democracy and building a united nation. (Fleetwood, 2012:3)

For Mathebula (2010: 11), an ardent critic of the compulsory citizenship education programmes in South African schools, '[t]hese value-based education documents promote obedience, if not unquestioning loyalty, to the South African government'. McCowan's work (2009) is instructive here. He argued that it is critical to work out what the ideal citizen or society is before developing and implementing the curriculum. Starting midway through the process – by revising the curriculum for example – without due consideration of the desired outcome, will likely give rise to a range of unintended consequences. Moreover, if conceptions about the ideal society and citizen are state-centric and driven by political elites (who are, in many cases, also business elites), rather than by the people, outcomes can only but be limited and unequal. If we wish to depart from liberal (and limited) democracy, an ideal curriculum should ideally reflect anti-capitalist principles. Once this is in place, mobilization efforts can be driven – by an active citizenry – into thrashing out the means by which to achieve this end.

Notes

1   It should be noted that there were other movements that had been established prior to 2000, such as the Treatment Action Campaign (1998) and the Concerned Citizens Forum (1999), but it was really in the 2000s that the efforts of these movements crystalized into a distinctive period of social contestation in South African politics that was different from, yet linked to anti-apartheid resistance.

References

African National Congress (1979). The *Green Book: Report of the Politico-Military Strategy Commission to the ANC National Executive Committee*. Last accessed at www. marxists.org/subject/africa/anc/1979/green-book.htm on 28 October 2013.

Alexander, P. (2010). Rebellion of the Poor: South Africa's Service Delivery Protests – A Preliminary Analysis. *Review of African Political Economy*, *37*(123), 25–40.

Alexander, P., Lekgowa, T., Mmope, B., Sinwell, L. and Xeswi, B. (2012). *Marikana: A View from the Mountain and a Case to Answer*. Johannesburg: Jacana Media.

Arendt, H. (1986). *The Origins of Totalitarianism*. New York: Andre Deutsch.

Arnal, E. and Förster, M. (2010). Growth, Employment and Inequality in Brazil, China, India and South Africa: An overview. In OECD, *Tackling Inequalities in Brazil, China, India and South Africa: The Role of Labour Market and Social Policies*. OECD Publishing.

Arrighi, G. and Saul, J.S. (1973). *Essays on the Political Economy of Africa*. New York: Monthly Review Press.

Bond, P. (2000a). *Cities of Gold, Townships of Coal: Essays on South Africa's New Urban Crisis*. New Jersey, Eritrea: Africa World Press.

Bond, P. (2000b). *Elite Transition: Globalisation and the Rise of Economic Fundamentalism in South Africa*. London and Pietermaritzburg: Pluto and University of Natal Press.

Bottaro, J. and Stanley, J. (2011). *History for the IB Diploma: Democratic States*. Cambridge: Cambridge University Press.

Clark, N.L. and Worger, W.H. (2013 [2004]). *South Africa: The Rise and Fall of Apartheid*. Oxford: Routledge.

Cottle, E. (2004). Ideology and Social Movements. *Development Update*, *5*(2), 95–128.

Crompton, R. (2008). *Class and Stratification*. 3rd ed. Cambridge: Polity.

Dawson, M.C. (2008). *Social Movements in Contemporary South Africa: The Anti Privatisation Forum and Struggles Around Access to Water in Johannesburg*. DPhil Thesis, University of Oxford.

Dawson, M.C. (2010). The Cost of Belonging: Exploring Class and Citizenship in Soweto's Water War. *Citizenship Studies*, *14*(4), 381–394.

de Regil, A.J. (2010). India's Living-Wage Gap: Another Modern Slave Work Ethos. TLWNSI Issue Brief, *The Jus Semper Global Alliance*, August.

Desai, A. (2013). South Africa: Between the Second Transition and a Second Term – A Second Sharpeville. *Capitalism Nature Socialism*, *24*(1), 73–83.

Devereux, S. (2010). Building Social Protection Systems in Southern Africa. Paper prepared in the framework of the European Report on Development. Last accessed at http://erd.eui.eu/media/BackgroundPapers/Devereaux%20-%20BUILDING%20SOCIAL%20 PROTECTION%20SYSTEMS.pdf on 14 June 2013.

Domingues, J.M. (2011). Beyond the Centre: The Third phase of Modernity in a Globally Compared Perspective. *European Journal of Social Theory, 14*(4), 517–535.

Domingues, J.M. (2013). Democracy, Freedom and Domination: A Theoretical Discussion with Special Reference to Brazil via India. *Shifting Frontiers of Citizenship: The Latin American Experience.* Leiden: Brill.

Dwyer, P. and Zeilig, L. (2012). *African Struggles Today: Social Movements since Independence.* London: Haymarket Books.

Earle, L. (2008). Social Movements and Citizenship: Some Challenges for INGOs. *Policy Briefing Paper* 20, Intrac.

Fang, C., Yang, D. and Meiyan, W. (2010). Fast Growth, but Widening Income Distribution in China. In OECD, *Tackling Inequalities in Brazil, China, India and South Africa: The Role of Labour Market and Social Policies.* OECD Publishing.

Fanon, F. (1963). *The Wretched of the Earth.* (Translated into English by Constance Farrington). New York: Grove Press.

Fleetwood, T. (2012). *Post-apartheid Education and Building 'Unity in Diversity': Voices of South African Youth.* PhD Thesis, Durham University.

Giddens, A. (1990). *The Consequences of Modernity.* Stanford, CA: Stanford University Press.

Giddens, A. (1993). Modernity, History, Democracy. *Theory and Society, 22*(2), 289–292.

Greenstein, R. (2009). Alternative Modernity: Development Discourse in Post-Apartheid South Africa. *International Social Science Journal, 60*(195), 69–84.

Guelke, A. (2005). *Rethinking the Rise of Apartheid: South Africa and World Politics.* Houndmills, Basingstoke: Palgrave Macmillan.

Harvey, E. (2005). Managing the Poor by Remote Control: Johannesburg's Experiments with Prepaid Water Meters. In D.A. McDonald and G. Ruiters (Eds.), *The Age of Commodity: Water Privatisation in Southern Africa.* London: Earthscan.

Hendricks, F. (2003). Class and Citizenship in Contemporary South Africa. *Society in Transition, 34*(1), 1–12.

Howarth, D. (1998). Paradigms Gained? A Critique of Theories and Explanations of Democratic Transitions in South Africa. In D. Howarth and A. Norval (Eds.), *South Africa in Transition: New Theoretical Perspectives.* New York: St. Martin's Press.

Human Development Report (2013). *The Rise of the South: Human Progress in a Diverse World.* UNDP.

Kabeer, N. (2005). The Search for Inclusive Citizenship: Meanings and Expressions in an Interconnected World. In N. Kabeer (Ed.), *Inclusive Citizenship: Meanings and Expressions.* London and New York: Zed Books, pp. 1–27.

Marais, H. (2001). *South Africa: Limits to Change - The Political Economy of Transition.* London, New York: Zed Books; Cape Town: University of Cape Town Press.

Marais, H. (2011). *South Africa Pushed to the Limit: The Political Economy of Change.* London: Zed Books.

Marshall, T.H. (1963). *Sociology at the Crossroads and Other Essays.* London: Heinemann.

Mathebula (2010). *Citizenship Education in South Africa: A Critique of Post-Apartheid Citizenship Education Policy.* PhD Thesis, Wits University.

Mazundar, D. (2010). Decreasing Poverty and Increasing Inequality in India. In OECD, *Tackling Inequalities in Brazil, China, India and South Africa: The Role of Labour Market and Social Policies.* OECD Publishing.

McCowan, T. (2009). *Rethinking Citizenship Education: a Curriculum for Participatory Democracy.* London: Continuum.

McDonald, M. (1996). Power Politics in the New South Africa. *Journal of Southern African Studies, 22*(2), 221–233.

McInnes, P. (2003). Rights, Recognition and Community Mobilisation to Gain Access to Basic Municipal Services in Soweto. *Social Inequality Today*, Conference Proceedings. Macquarie: Macquarie University.

McKinley, D. (1997). *The ANC and the Liberation Struggle: A Critical Political Biography*. London: Pluto Press.

McKinley, D. (2001). Democracy, Power and Patronage: Debate and Opposition within the African National Congress and the Tripartite Alliance Since 1994. In R. Southall (Ed.). *Opposition and Democracy in South Africa*. London: Frank Cass.

Murray. M.J. (1994). *Revolution Deferred: The Painful Birth of Post-Apartheid South Africa*. London: Verso.

Néri, M.C. (2010). The Decade of Falling Income Inequality and Formal Employment Generation in Brazil. In OECD, *Tackling Inequalities in Brazil, China, India and South Africa: The Role of Labour Market and Social Policies*. OECD Publishing.

Ngwane, T. (2006). *Distorted Theory, Distorted Revolution: The Theory of Two Stages of Revolution and the NDR is a Myth. Debate and Discussion, Anti-Privatisation Forum*. Last accessed at http://apf.org.za/spip.php?article133 on 28 October 2013.

OECD. StatExtracts. N.d. Short-Term Labour Statistics: Unemployment Rates by Age and Gender. Last accessed at http://stats.oecd.org/Index.aspx?DatasetCode=STLABOUR on 17 January 2014.

Ravallion, M. and Chen, S. (2007). China's (Uneven) Progress Against Poverty. *Journal of Development Economics*, *82*(1), 1–42.

Satgar, V. (2012). Beyond Marikana: The Post-Apartheid South African State. *Africa Spectrum*, *47*(2–3), 33–62.

Saul, J.S. (1993). *Recolonization and Resistance: Southern Africa in the 1990s*. Asmara, Eritrea: Africa World Press.

Saul, J.S. (2001a). Cry for the Beloved Country: The Post-Apartheid Denouement. *Monthly Review*, *52*(8), 1–51.

Saul, J.S. (2001b). *Millennial Africa: Capitalism, Socialism, and Democracy*. Asmara, Eritrea: Africa World Press.

Saul, J.S. (2006). *Development after Globalisation Theory and Practice for the Embattled South in a New Imperial Age*. London: Zed Books.

Saul, J.S. (2008). *Decolonization and Empire: Contesting the Rhetoric and Practice of Resubordination in Southern Africa and Beyond*. Gurgaon, Haryana: Three Essays Collective.

Saul, J.S. (2011). *Liberation Lite: The Roots of Recolonization in Southern Africa*. Gurgaon, Haryana: Three Essays Collective.

Saul, J.S. (2014). *A Flawed Freedom: Rethinking Southern African Liberation*. London: Pluto Press.

Saul, J.S. and Bond, P. (2014). *South Africa - The Present as History: From Mrs Ples to Mandela and Marikana*. Johannesburg: Jacana Media.

Slovo, J. (1988). The South African Working Class and the National Democratic Revolution. *Umsebenzi Discussion Pamphlet Published by the South African Communist Party*. Last accessed at www.sacp.org.za/docs/history/ndr.html on 28 October 2013.

Statistics South Africa. (2013). *Quarterly Labour Force Survey, Quarter 3*. Pretoria: StatsSA.

Von Schnitzler, A. (2008). Citizenship Prepaid: Water, Calculability, and Techno-politics in South Africa. *Journal of Southern African Studies*, *34*(4), 899–917.

Willis, P. (1977). *Learning to Labour*. London: Saxon House.

Wolpe, H. (1988). *Race, Class and the Apartheid State (Apartheid & Society)*. Cape Town: James Currey.

Index